CW01676662

Front cover:
Back row L-R: David, William, John, Charles, Henry
Front row L-R: Jim, Charles (sen), Annie, Annie (sen), Rose, Patrick, 1914/1915
Included top left, Jennie
Included top right, Mary

THE MAGILLS OF THE MEETINGHOUSE

CAIRNCASTLE

PAUL MAGILL

FOREWORD BY FELIX McKILLOP

CONTENTS

Foreword vii

Introduction ix

1 Charlie and Annie 1-17

2 The Family at Home 18-35

3 Charlie in World War 1 36-42

4 Emigration to USA and Canada 43-65

5 Emigration to Australia 66-71

6 Seven Sons, Seven Policemen 72-85

"The Fighting Magills"

7 Davy - Heavyweight and Light-heavyweight Champion of Ireland. 86-133

8 Pat and John 134-142

9 Jim - Ireland's only triple ABA Champion 143-172

10 In Search of a Family Tree 173-190

FOREWORD

Some of my earliest memories were hearing of the boxing exploits of the Magill brothers of the Meetinghouse, Cairncastle many years earlier. For some years during the early 20th century the Magill brothers fulfilled ambitions and reached new horizons which the rest of us can only dream of. Here were local men making large waves far outside the parameters of their small rural community. Respected and admired their endeavours fired this child's imagination. I yearned to find out more. This publication will satisfy that desire.

This is a story of determination, courage, self belief, and a willingness to succeed - it is also tinged with deep personal tragedy. Twelve Magill children - 5 girls and 7 sons - were born (one died, aged 2 years) and raised on a small holding of just over an acre. Their father Charles made best use of what little land they had and enhanced a meagre income by carting goods and repairing roads within the local council area. It was clear that a large family on such a small holding was not sustainable and as each child came to maturity moving away from home was the only viable option. The seven sons joined the local police force. Some remained in their chosen career, while others sought better opportunities in far away lands.

No one is better placed than Paul Magill, historian, and son of one of the seven brothers, to compile a history of the family. Paul has lovingly and painstakingly researched the various routes which his family followed and his research has taken him far from their Cairncastle home, to England, Australia, Egypt and the USA. This book is a journey taken by members of an ordinary rural family who scaled extraordinary heights during an economically depressed era in the early years of the 20th century. The route is well mapped out with photographs and other illustrative material and the story is set within the context of a wider political and social backdrop. Enjoy a precious insight into a very special family.

Felix McKillop

ACKNOWLEDGEMENTS

In addition to all those family members who have contributed their memories, photographs and help, I wish to acknowledge the support I have been given from so many others. I would like to thank the following: Felix McKillop who inspired me to write this history and has been my mentor throughout, providing historical and technical help at every stage of the writing process; his local history publications, especially "Townlands, People and Traditions" 2006, have been the basis for much of our genealogical knowledge; Fred Heatley for preserving the memory of the boxing careers of Davy and Jim Magill; my friend Rev. John McLaughlin for introducing me to the world of genealogy in the Internet Age. I am indebted to Mrs. Jean Armstrong for her constant support and rich sources of family reminiscences. Thanks to Dan McKillion, Jim Maxwell, Sally Kane and to Stewart and Beth Morton for their fund of local knowledge; to Adrian Wilson, Miles Templeton, Moira Scarcliffe and to Andrew Jenkins for their assistance; to Hugh Robinson for information on St. Patrick's, C of I graveyard; to Dr. Brian Turner for his research on surnames in the Glens of Antrim; to the staff of Larne and Ballymena libraries; to the photograph restorers of Rootschat; to the staff of PRONI and GRONI; to PSNI Museum; to the staff of the Somme Heritage Centre; to the Museum of the Royal Irish Fusiliers; to Museum Victoria's Immigration Discovery Centre; to the Ellis Island Foundation; to the National Archives of Canada.

A special thank you to Mary-Attracta Connolly in Australia for her research and assistance and to Phillip Tardif in Australia for access to his web-site on the North Irish Horse Regiment in World War One and for giving permission to quote from his grandfather's diary; to Denis O'Hara, to Jimmy Black of Newforge and to Jimmy Harkin for help and access to information on Jim Magill. Thanks are due to my wife Marie for her patience and support, and to Sheila and Jim Magill for proof-reading the final copy.

INTRODUCTION

Back row L-R: David, William, John, Charles, Henry
Front row L-R: Jim, Charles (sen), Annie, Annie (sen), Rose, Patrick, 1914/1915

We all have our old family photographs with faces faded and names long forgotten. As a child I remember being fascinated by the large portrait of my father's family, "the Magills of the Meetinghouse," in which everyone posed with the customary seriousness the occasion demanded. Victorian and Edwardian sitters, I subsequently learnt, were required to appear formal and unsmiling, as smiles and laughter conveyed an impression of levity and frivolity. The picture looked down from the living room wall in what was then the home in Cairncastle of the youngest three in the photo, my uncle Jim and aunts Rose and Annie and her husband John and family. I knew some of those in the photograph, but many others were complete strangers to me, my grandfather having died before I was born and my grandmother when I was three.

There were nine of the eleven children of the family in the picture, the two eldest daughters, Jane and Mary, having already gone to America. One uncle followed them to New York, another went to Australia and a third was lost at sea in World War Two. I heard that the family dog, posing so well for the cameraman, had a pipe in its mouth. I learnt that the photograph had probably been taken some time in 1915, just after the outbreak of World War One; it was a time when photographers were busy all over the country, capturing images of families before their loved ones went off to war. But who were the others in the picture and what were their stories?

There are some whose place in history is already recorded. The horse shoe on exhibit in the Ellis Island Exhibition on Immigration to the United States, poignantly labelled *"Father's gift to emigrant son before leaving Cairncastle, Charles Magill,"* is a unique record of Charlie's arrival in the United States. The boxing careers of Davy and Jim were recorded in detail in countless newspapers but are remembered today by an increasingly passing generation. However others like Pat were mystery men to me. I had visited the National Maritime Museum in Melbourne in 2005, unaware that my own uncle, Pat, had endured the same immigrant experience. I had been to the battle fields of the Western Front at Ypres in Belgium, not realizing that my uncle Charlie had spent his young years here in the nightmare of World War One. There was a lot to learn about these uncles and aunts in the photograph.

This book started off life as an attempt to discover my family tree, but I soon wanted to get beyond the lists of births, deaths and marriages of genealogy in order to know more about the lives and experiences of my ancestors. It wasn't long before I learned that life for 'ordinary people' can often be extraordinary. The discovery of a family scrapbook on the boxing career of one of the family, Davy, made me realize that here was a story that had to be told. In the following pages, I have focused on this one family in particular. It was a family whose story began in 1889 when Charlie Magill married Annie Connolly and did not end until the death of their youngest child Annie, at the age of 95, in 2006.

We are often told that it is a good thing 'to remember where we came from'; it keeps us grounded and gives us a sense of belonging, but over generations families drift apart and vital information is lost. How often in my search did I hear from relatives when I enquired about their parents and grandparents "*I wish I had asked those things when they were here."* More than one told me of the difficulties of getting information as "*that generation was reticent and guarded about revealing personal details of their lives."* In addition, *"many of us were either too young or too busy with our own lives to think much about it."* Most of us grew up in a world in which grandparents were long dead and we did not know much of our distant relations, separated by time and continents. But thanks to all of those relatives whether in Ireland, the USA, Canada or Australia, I have now written a record of the family. I have not been able to thank you all individually for your contributions but you will recognise your input.

1 Charlie and Annie

The Family Home, 1937

The year 1889 was a year of momentous events. It was the first centenary of the outbreak of the French Revolution; to mark the occasion the Eiffel Tower first opened to the public. Two years earlier, Queen Victoria had celebrated her Golden Jubilee after 50 years on the throne and a quarter of the map of the world was still shaded in the red of the British Empire. On the 30th January, 1889, Crown Prince Rudolf, son of Archduke Ferdinand and heir to the Habsburg Empire, entered a suicide pact with his seventeen year old mistress, at Mayerling, outside Vienna. In Austria, in the town of Branau, Adolf Hitler was born.

For those who looked through the pages of the Larne Reporter that last week in January, they could read of "General Gordon's Last Hour - An Eye-Witness Account" or of "Preparations for Queen Victoria's visit to Biarritz." Nearer home was the news of "The Gweedore Evictions" and tragedies of colliery explosions and ship-wrecks. In Ireland, the political world was thrown into turmoil when the Parnell-O'Shea Divorce Scandal first hit the headlines. But life for the ordinary people went on. While one marriage was breaking up, another was just beginning.

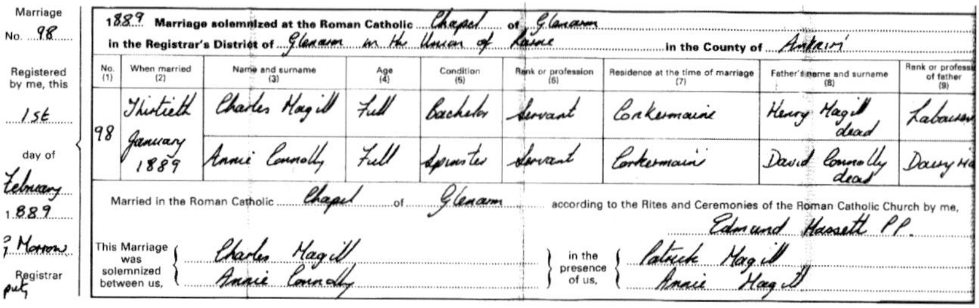

Marriage No. 98

Registered by me, this 1st day of February 1889 J. Morrow Registrar

1889 Marriage solemnized at the Roman Catholic Chapel of Glenarm in the Registrar's District of Glenarm in the Union of Larne in the County of Antrim

No. (1)	When married (2)	Name and surname (3)	Age (4)	Condition (5)	Rank or profession (6)	Residence at the time of marriage (7)	Father's name and surname (8)	Rank or profession of father (9)
98	Thirtieth January 1889	Charles Magill	Full	Bachelor	Servant	Corkermaine	Henry Magill dead	Labourer
		Annie Connolly	Full	Spinster	Servant	Corkermain	David Connolly dead	Dairyman

Married in the Roman Catholic Chapel of Glenarm according to the Rites and Ceremonies of the Roman Catholic Church by me, Edmund Hassett P.P.

This Marriage was solemnized between us, Charles Magill, Annie Connolly; in the presence of us, Patrick Magill, Annie Magill

Marriage certificate 30 January, 1889

It was on Wednesday, 30th January 1889, the same day as the Mayerling tragedy took place, that Charlie Magill and Annie Connolly wed. It was an ordinary enough beginning to married life for Charlie of the Meetinghouse and Annie Connolly of Aughagash, when they married in the Church of the Immaculate Conception, Glenarm. The weather that day was unremarkable for the time of year. There was no snow and the forecast promised it would be "unsettled with showers." No doubt, as was the custom, they both had to walk the five or six miles to the church in Glenarm. There were no newspaper accounts with descriptions of the bride and her finery as exist for the fashionable weddings of the gentry of the time and the little information that we have comes from the entry in the Registrar's Book. It tells us that the marriage was conducted by Father Edmund Hassett, the parish priest of Glenarm. The newly weds were both described as of *'full'* age; in fact while Charlie was 24, Annie was only 19 and hadn't yet reached the *'full'* age of 21, but it was not unusual for the figures to be massaged. In the 19th century, girls could legally marry at the age of 12 and boys at 14, providing they had parental consent. Both were designated as *'servants'* on their marriage certificate. This was the case with most of those in the countryside who did not have independent means i.e., "gentlemen," or those who were farmers or tradesmen; they are listed as servants or labourers in 19th century occupation lists. As was customary, the entry only gives us the names and occupations of the fathers, *'Henry Magill, labourer'* and *'David Connolly, dairyman,'* both of whom it tells us were deceased at the time and it names the witnesses as *'Patrick* and *Annie Magill.'* The marriage was to last for the next 52 years and during that time they were to bring up a family of 12 children, one of whom, Anne, was to die as a child.

It is not known when they first met but it's likely they had known each other from childhood, as they lived only a few miles from each other. The young couple had been born just over a decade after the catastrophe of "The Great Famine" (1845-1849) which their parents' generation had lived through. We know little about Charlie's early years. While we are unsure if his mother, Rosy, was still alive at the time, Charlie's father Henry, had died just a year before on 5 January 1888. It was probably his father's death which made it possible for Charlie to acquire the family house in the "Meetinghouse" and embark on marriage. He had two sisters, Elizabeth and Mary, but Mary too had died in

St. Patrick's, Church of Ireland, Cairncastle

1881, at the age of 14 from 'Phthisis,' a form of Tuberculosis which was prevalent at the time. The other thing we know about him, was that he had been a noted oarsman in his day and his successes were related in "The Larne Reporter" on August 6, 1887, when he was 23. In what must have been a major event in the locality at the time, he carried off several prizes in the "Ballygally Jubilee Regatta"; in 1887 Victoria had been on the throne for 50 years. The report claimed that along with the visiting gentry, there were thousands of spectators present, hundreds of whom had taken up their positions in front of the Coastguard Station (later the Post Office), to witness the spectacle. His crew won the big event of the day, the Jubilee Challenge Cup, rowing 'Paddy-go-Easy' to triumph over the Belfast boat which came in second. It was on another less happy occasion, in a rowing race in Belfast Harbour, that Charlie and his crew were on the receiving end of the shipyard men's rivets, that came to be known as 'Belfast confetti.'

Charlie's young wife Annie Connolly came originally from Aughagash, near Feystown. Her parents, David and Catherine Connolly, like many in those days, had left the countryside and gone to the rapidly growing city of Belfast. There they lived at 17 Foreman Street, in the Old Lodge Road area wherein the Belfast street directory he is described as employed as a labourer and later as a dairyman. A story handed down through Annie's daughters, tells of a connection between her parents and the wealthy Lyons' family of Lissue House, Lisburn. While historians warn us that word-of-mouth stories passed down over the years should be taken with a pinch of salt, they cannot be discounted totally as they may often contain a core of truth. According to the tradition, Annie used to relate to her children how as a child she would ride around the grounds of the Lyons' estate on a pony. Lady Lyons had given an amber glass bread plate as a wedding gift to Annie's mother and this same plate travelled to the United States in 1907 in Aunt Jennie's steamer trunk; it eventually ended up on display in the Ellis Island Immigrant Museum in New York. However, the origins of the "Lyons story," like so many others, have been lost in the mists of history. It was a family tradition that was often related by aunt Rose here and crossed the Atlantic with aunt Jennie. We can never be certain but what is known is that Annie was only five years old when her father, at the age of 45, died from heart

Cairncastle c 1900

disease in 1875 in Belfast. Catherine Connolly, her mother, returned to Feystown as a young widow of 37 with Annie and her younger brother, Willie. It was there that Annie grew up and attended the local school at Feystown, but by the time of her marriage, she was living in Corkermain.

Times had improved since the years of her parents during the Great Famine, when the newly built workhouse in Larne (later to become the Moyle Hospital), was packed to overflowing. The nearby villages of Glenarm and Carnlough provided for the most needy of the surrounding area, from their own soup kitchens. Their parents' generation had lived through it all. Lady Londonderry's Land Agent, John Lanktree, wrote to her in England as early as March 1846:

"*The Potato Plague is beginning to be acutely felt here. In the Drumcrow district* (the townland adjoining, Annie's home at Aughagash) *of this Estate the greater number of the tenants have not had a potato to eat for some weeks ....*" Later in December 1848 he noted that: "*others* (emigrants) *chiefly from Drumcrow - after landing in America were seized with fever - which raged there in an unprecedented manner and perished.*"

Whether or not they realized it, the experience of hardship during the Famine years, must have influenced Annie and Charlie's generation.

The Shaw family crest, Ballygally Castle

Life for the majority of people in this part of County Antrim, on the Antrim Coast remained frugal, through to the close of the nineteenth century. As elsewhere in Ireland, most of the males found employment as labourers on the land of richer farmers or in building work and the females worked as domestic servants. Many made their living, renting small farms and as in the case of Charlie, working on the building of the extensive walls and supporting batteries which followed the Coast Road's 26 miles north from Larne. The building of the Antrim Coast Road, from Larne to Cushendun, had begun in the 1830's and had been the biggest civil engineering project ever undertaken in Ireland. An uncle of Charlie, on his mother Rose's side, had been a local road contractor and this became the trade of Charlie too.

In the 17th century, Sir Randal MacDonnell, Earl of Antrim, had made grants of land throughout north and east Antrim which were taken up by Scots in increasing numbers.
One such grant was made on 21 Feb 1621:

"John Shaw.... *Six score acres at Carnfunnock and four score acres at the northern part of Corkermain* (the townland where the Magills of the Meeting-house lived) *at a yearly rent of £13.13.4."*

Another read:
"1 February 1634 to John Shaw elder of Ballygally of all that 18 score acres of land in Ballygally, Tarnmoney, Nogher, Carncashlen (Carncastle) *at a yearly rent of £24."*

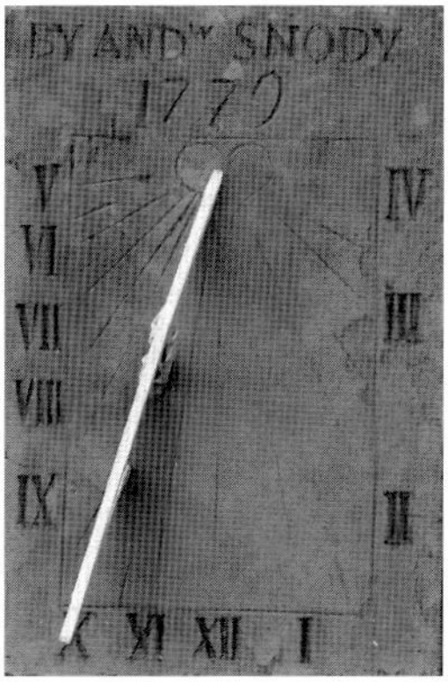

While the castle at Ballygally had been built in 1625 in Scottish Baronial style for the landlord and his wife, James Shaw and Isabella Brisbane, other settlers who came across from Scotland with Shaw, were given lands in the surrounding countryside. Their names McKee, Crawford, etc., listed in the Hearth Money Rolls of 1669 are still the common family names in the area. The nucleus of their settlement was a mile inland from the castle at today's Cairncastle around the 'Meetinghouse.' Many of the familiar features of today can be traced back to these times. These Scottish settlers brought with them their Presbyterian form of worship and Cairncastle became the second Presbyterian congregation in Ireland, established here in 1646. Its first minister was Patrick Adair appointed by James Shaw of Ballygally Castle. Originally Presbyterians worshipped in the Church of Ireland, but conflict led to the erection of the first Presbyterian church in Cairncastle in 1667; the present Non-Subscribing Church occupies the site of that original building. Fixed to its wall is a sundial made by Andrew Snoddy dating back to the year 1779, the time of the American Revolution. In contrast to Cairncastle, by the late 19th century, Ballygally's only additions to its castle, were the Coastguard Station and cottages and the manse at the other end of the bay.

The Meetinghouse, Cairncastle

The house that was to become home was in the townland of Corkermain, Cairncastle, in the 'village' known locally as the "Meeting House." It was the pub at the crossroads, for generations in the ownership of the Moore family, that gave its name to the cluster of houses and public buildings which strung along this road junction half way between Larne and Glenarm; in earlier times the pub was believed to have been a Presbyterian house of worship. Around the crossroads at the Meeting House were two Presbyterian churches and two schools, a blacksmith's forge, an Orange Hall, a group of houses and on the hill beyond, St Patrick's Church of Ireland. The nearest Catholic church was four miles distant on the hill at Feystown.

Cairncastle had taken its name from the castle on the cairn or rock, that stood at the foot of Ballygally Head, a mile or so away on the coast. The Magill home (last occupied by my parents Peggy and John) where Charlie and Annie took up their abode, was a modest two roomed semi-detached cottage; it was one of the smallest in the area and was situated on the north edge of the village, beyond the blacksmith's forge. The ground floor room was partitioned to form a bedroom and, as usual in those times, the living area doubled up as a kitchen with the open fire providing the heating, cooking and baking for the family. It was two-storied, slate-roofed and had only three small windows at the front with two at the rear. The upstairs room was partitioned to form two bedrooms. Beside the house there were some outbuildings, a 'yard' or garden in which there was a vegetable patch, a midden and a stable. The Meeting House Magills did a lot of carting and road repairs and always kept a few horses. 'Carting' was the occupation of people who, in the age before the arrival of the motor vehicle, carried goods on horse drawn carts. Behind the house and alongside the Burnside loanin, they owned a field of little more than an acre where they grew hay for the horses. It was in this house over the next two decades, that 12 children were to be born and brought up. Land Valuation records going back to the 1860's, show that the Hunter family owned the house and it had been rented then by Mr. Andrew Little. It was the year 1886 when Henry Magill first took over the lease. Henry himself died two years later and then Charlie acquired the house.

It appears that originally there may have been one house but by this stage it had been divided into two houses. The Valuation Map of 1857, shows that the back garden of the house extended across the present Ballycoose Road to incorporate the field behind. Unlike to-day the road from Cairncastle to Feystown, started opposite Corkermain House (Brown's) and passed by the Peat Knowe (Petticrew's). It was a time when most of the land was owned by landlords and rented out to tenants. Much of the farmland around Cairncastle was then owned by the Agnew family of Kilwaughter. Squire Agnew's daughter had returned from Italy in 1897, having married an Italian nobleman and it was the Count and Countess Balzani, who became the landlords.

A Family of Twelve

First of the Magill family to be born in 1889, was Jane or Jennie as she came to be called. A second daughter, Mary, followed in 1891; then a succession of

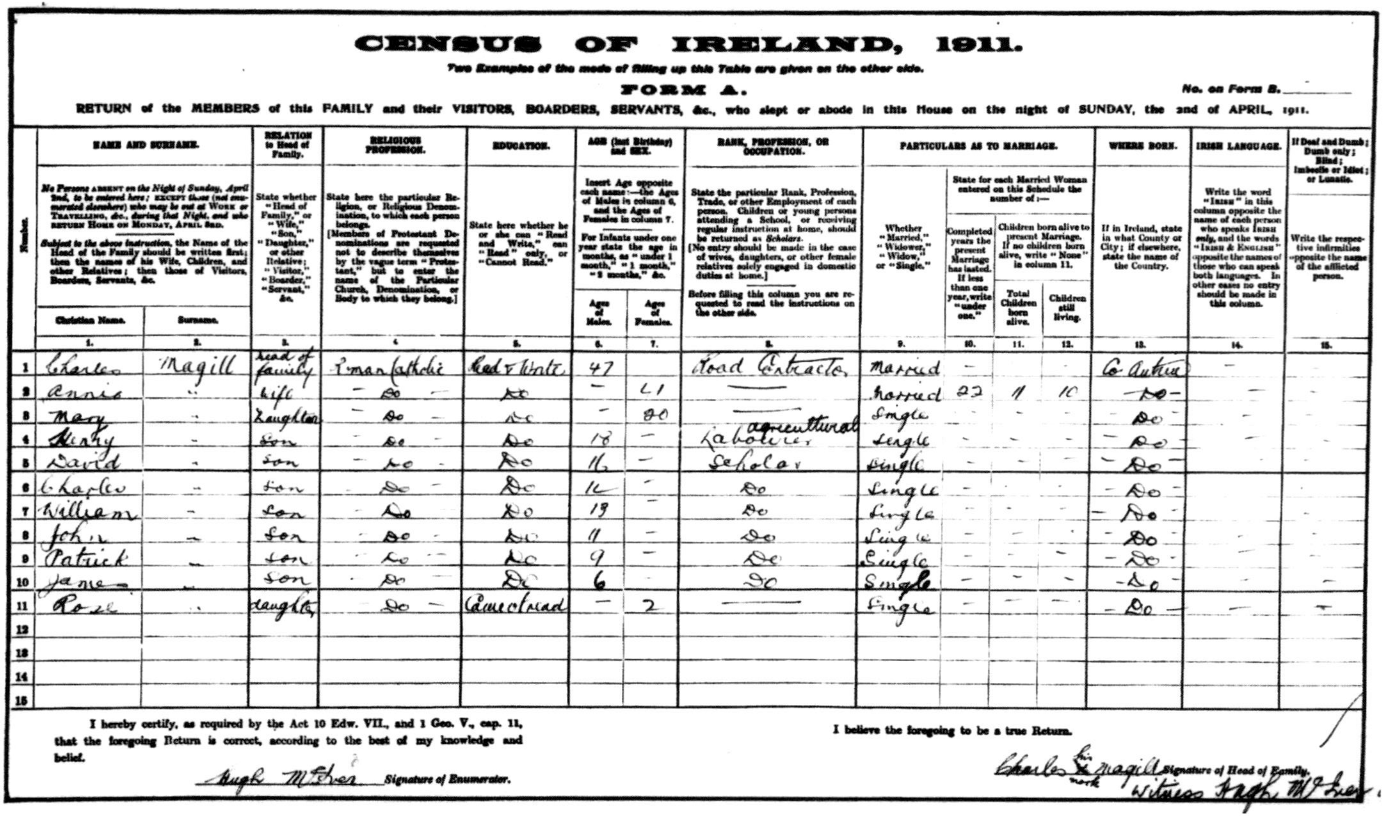

CENSUS OF IRELAND, 1911.

Two Examples of the mode of filling up this Table are given on the other side.

FORM A.

No. on Form B. ______

RETURN of the MEMBERS of this FAMILY and their VISITORS, BOARDERS, SERVANTS, &c., who slept or abode in this House on the night of SUNDAY, the 2nd of APRIL, 1911.

Number	Christian Name (1)	Surname (2)	Relation to Head of Family (3)	Religious Profession (4)	Education (5)	Age of Males (6)	Age of Females (7)	Rank, Profession, or Occupation (8)	Whether Married, Widower, Widow, or Single (9)	Completed years the present Marriage has lasted (10)	Total Children born alive (11)	Children still living (12)	Where Born (13)	Irish Language (14)	If Deaf and Dumb; Dumb only; Blind; Imbecile or Idiot; or Lunatic (15)
1	Charles	Magill	head of family	Roman Catholic	Read & Write	47		Road Contractor	Married	–		–	Co Antrim	–	
2	Annie	"	Wife	Do	Do	–	41	———	Married	22	11	10	Do	–	–
3	Mary	"	Daughter	Do	Do	–	20		Single	–	–	–	Do	–	–
4	Henry	"	Son	Do	Do	18	–	agricultural Labourer	Single	–	–	–	Do	–	–
5	David	"	Son	Do	Do	16	–	Scholar	Single	–	–	–	Do		
6	Charles	"	Son	Do	Do	14	–	Do	Single	–	–	–	Do		
7	William	"	Son	Do	Do	13	–	Do	Single	–	–	–	Do		
8	John	"	Son	Do	Do	11	–	Do	Single	–	–	–	Do	–	
9	Patrick	"	Son	Do	Do	9	–	Do	Single	–	–	–	Do		
10	James	"	Son	Do	Do	6	–	Do	Single	–	–	–	Do		–
11	Rose	"	Daughter	Do	Cannot read	–	2	———	Single	–	–	–	Do	–	–
12															
13															
14															
15															

I hereby certify, as required by the Act 10 Edw. VII., and 1 Geo. V., cap. 11, that the foregoing Return is correct, according to the best of my knowledge and belief.

Hugh McAleer Signature of Enumerator.

I believe the foregoing to be a true Return.

Charles his mark Magill Signature of Head of Family.
Witness Hugh McAleer

seven sons came: Henry in 1892, David in 1894, Charlie in 1896, Willie in 1898, John in 1900, Pat in 1902 and Jim in 1904. The first seven of the children, including John, had all been born in the Victorian era. The next child in 1907, was a girl, christened Anne, but tragedy struck when she died at the age of two years and three months, from "tubercular meningitis"; it was just three days after Christmas Day in 1909. The family was completed with two further daughters, Rose in 1909 and Annie in 1911. The naming of children in the past, often followed a set pattern. The first son was called after his paternal grandfather, the second son took the name of his maternal grandfather while the third son took his father's name. In this way there was Henry, followed by David and then Charlie. Similarly with daughters, the first took the name of the maternal grandmother, the second the name of the paternal grandmother and the third took the name of the mother. Later children were called after uncles and aunts. This pattern was strictly adhered to in the case of the boys, though it was not as closely followed with the daughters.

Considering the high level of infant mortality which averaged about one child in six in the early Twentieth Century, it might be said that the family was indeed fortunate that all but one grew into adulthood. The fabled 'three score and ten' was unattainable for most. Charlie's father, Henry, had reached 66 years, but David Connolly, Annie's father had been only 45 when he died. It is believed that as late as 1900 life expectancy for males in the UK was only 47. For many at the time it was the prevalence of diseases like Tuberculosis which brought with it untimely deaths. There was a stigma attached to the disease and many people, particularly in country districts, were frightened to even talk about it. 'Consumption' was the common name in the nineteenth century but in many cases the death certificates showed that the diagnosis was 'chronic bronchitis' or 'phtysisis.' There was much ignorance and prejudice about it and doctors did not know that it was caused by bacteria and that it was contagious until 1882. It was said that over 80% of those who contracted the disease, died from it. A headstone in Feystown Graveyard alongside the Magill burial plot, bearing the family name McKillen, records the deaths of four sons, Patrick, aged nine, James aged six, Michael, aged 3 and Hugh aged 16; all died between 25 October and 14 November 1882. It had been the year after Charlie's younger sister Mary had died at the age of 14.

The Magill family had been luckier than most with all, except one, of the twelve children surviving. Their home soon became a very crowded one, even by the standards of the time; the census of 1911 shows 11 of the original 14 still living in the house. The eldest, Jennie, had left for the USA in 1907 and the youngest child, to be named Annie after her dead sister, was yet to be born in May of that census year. As in most homes, there were few luxuries to go around; it was a struggle to clothe and feed such a large family. Willie, the fourth son, remembered that for the boys, it was often a case of *"whoever got up first in the morning got the pick of the clothes and boots."* In those days, Christmas was not the big occasion that it has become, but Willie recounted his excitement one year, when his parents returned from a shopping trip to Larne with a large parcel, only to be devastated when it was opened, to reveal two large shovels. There was much devilment among the boys growing up. Willie recalled that "*Once our Mother bought a barrel of apples in the autumn which was stored upstairs. In that period my young brother John developed an unusual behaviour of going to bed early - she discovered afterwards that he had scoffed all the apples in secret.*" As they grew older the mischief continued. The story is told how on one occasion, Henry, the eldest boy, was cutting the hair of a neighbour, 'Dan the Spaniard', (so called because of his luxuriant moustache) when suddenly an outstretched hand with scissors, passed through the open window and 'wheeked off' the owner's proud moustache. It was alleged to have been the hand of his younger brother, Charlie. Entertainment was cheap; at night-time the boys would fill a saucer with porter and enjoy watching the crickets appear on the hearth, to drink their fill with the inevitable results.

While there may have been few luxuries, the children were well fed and grew into healthy and strong youngsters. The father, Charlie had a steady income from his road contracting. It was the Grand Jury, a body of the main landowners of each county, which was responsible for such matters as road building and maintenance, before County Councils were set up in 1898. The record books of the Antrim Grand Jury show Spring and Summer payments to those local contractors who undertook to maintain the roads in their areas. The entry for 1891 reads *"to Charles Magill, half a year's payment, £24-3-9, to keep in repair for three years, 1480 perches* (about six miles) *of road from Larne to Cairncastle Meeting-house, between Poor-house (The Workhouse) main entrance and junction with Killyglen Road at Meetinghouse, including branch to Waterloo, in the townlands of Townparks, Greenisland and Ballygally, with 200 tons of stones and ten tons of gravel .... One man full time, entered into at Spring 1891."* In 1896 the entry reads *"to Charles Magill, to build a fence (wall) on 120 perches* (about half of a mile) *of road from Ballygally to Deerpark between said points, in the townlands of Drains Bay and Ballygally by 1st October 1896."* In Spring 1899, *"to Charles Magill to repair 1200 perches (about five miles) of road from Larne to Glenarm between Coast Road and Ballygally Castle, £38-9-0, by September 1899, 150 tons of limestone and 50 tons of basalt, one man full time."*

Annie kept a lot of pigs and chickens, was a good manager and put some of her money aside. There was nothing like the experience of the poverty experienced by other large families at the time. A namesake and contemporary of the family who also was one of 11 children, Patrick McGill (1891-1963), 'The Navvy Poet' - described an altogether harsher life at this time in his native County Donegal, in his 'autobiographical novel' "Children of the Dead End." In his case, formal schooling ended at ten years of age. Throughout much of rural Ireland, there was the hiring fair where boys and girls as young as 13 left their families for six months at a time and were auctioned off to wealthy farmers; " *We stood huddled together like sheep for sale in the market place in*

Strabane" recalled the author. When a few years older, these children graduated to the potato harvest in Scotland. Growing up in Cairncastle for the Magill family at that time was much kinder.

It was little more than a generation after the Great Famine but the level of malnutrition suffered by the working people in Ireland and Britain persisted and was exposed and highlighted when over a third of recruits for the army during the Boer War (1899-1902), were rejected as being unfit for service. As with all Irish families at the time, for the Magills of the Meetinghouse, the staple diet was potato, oatmeal porridge and wholemeal bread with milk, buttermilk and tea to drink. All cooking was done on the open fire over which hung the kettle, pots and the griddle. Baking bread was part of the daily ritual and butter was churned weekly. They kept their own chickens so they had a plentiful supply of eggs. They had a garden beside the house where vegetables were grown. There was a midden for manure alongside as was the custom of the time. The days were long past when the size of the midden outside the house was taken as a sign of the wealth of the farmer and was something of a status symbol, but ideas of sanitation and hygiene were still primitive. They kept several pigs which when slaughtered, provided the bacon, which was salted smoked and hung on the hooks from the wooden ceiling. The shotgun and snare were used to hunt for rabbits and hares which were used to supplement the diet. *'Your kitchen is in the hills'* was a saying of the time. Meat was not an everyday food-stuff except for the wealthy and even though they lived near the coast, fish was not a central part of the diet. When it was available, it was generally herring and mackerel. Ling was a much used fish at the time; it was salted and hung from the ceiling where it dried, before it was eaten. The family was largely self-sufficient in food and there was little reliance on shop bought products other than tea, sugar and the rare delicacy.

Mr. M'Neill. Won First Prize at the Feis in the Glens of Antrim 1904, and took Special Prize 1905 for best knit cycling stockings.

Among the neighbours were the families of Petticrew, Moore and Hunter, many of whose descendants continue to live there a century later. Others like Brown, Wilson, Crawford, McNeill have moved on. It was a village with its local characters, among whom must be counted the village postman, Johnny

McNeill (1871-1950) who was the village's link with the outside world. Johnny was one of a large family of five brothers and ten sisters. On his postal round he cycled 17 miles a day for the princely sum of five shillings (25 pence) a week. He was a man of many talents; among them he could count 'cooking, knitting and crochet work along with playing the organ in the Presbyterian Church.'

Alongside Johnny's house, was Petticrew's blacksmith's 'shop' which was the meeting place in the village for locals and farmers alike; many travelled from the surrounding countryside to get their horses shod and while there, they would quench their thirst in the Meeting House. The blacksmith's forge had come into the hands of the Petticrew family in the 1890's. James Petticrew had married Catherine Magill of Campbelltown and he built up a thriving business employing five apprentices. One of them was Charlie McGill of Aldergrove, who recalled 'serving his time' there, before like so many others, he left for Chicago. He spent much of his time in Charlie and Annie's house and stood for John as godfather, when he was christened in 1900. The family connection with Charlie continued when Charlie returned to Ireland and settled in Aldergrove.

The work of the blacksmith involved all kinds of iron-work from hooping cartwheels to making gates and mending farm machinery as well as shoeing horses. James Petticrew died in 1916 but his son Charlie, after a brief spell in the RIC, kept the smithy going over the next generation.

'Moey Gill'

A neighbour, Jean Armstrong (nee Petticrew) recalls how Annie or 'Moey Gill' as she came to be called by her children and friends alike, *"played many roles; wife, mother and worker. In the early days of marriage the help she gave her husband was legendary. Charlie, a road contractor and a farmer, had many mouths to feed and the work was hard, but Moey played her part. When Charlie was blasting in the quarry at Ballygally Head, Moey was by his side; she held the jumper while he sledged the hammer into the rock to make a hole for the dynamite to blast the stones. It was dangerous work but they were a team .... Moey was no stranger to farm work, helping at hay-time; she worked outside and inside. Providing the food, it was not unusual for Moey to be baking breads on the griddle at two a.m. and be out in the field early the next morning. She would round up the local*

Annie, ('Moey Gill') aged 65 in 1934

children for a ride on the hay lifter when bringing in the hay for winter fodder; of course they would have to partake of the tea ready for the men! Adults who were those children still speak so kindly of Moey who was born to share."

There was another side to Moey's work - apart from giving birth to her own 12 children, she also acted as the local midwife. In the days before the National Health Service came into being in 1947, this was the work of local women like Moey. As Jean writes:

"Moey in her role as midwife brought many children into this world; she had a wonderful way of putting people at their ease and when she would meet with a woman in trouble, Moey would say "Come in sure we are all women together." She delighted in showing the new baby to the other children in the family, telling them the proverbial "found below the cabbage leaf." She was still playing the role of local midwife when she was in her seventies.

The stories of her hospitality were legendary. *"Moey had an open door and ready fare for everyone. Between the wars the roads were busy with travelling people, some shell shocked from World War One. (*Some claimed that during the War, many were deserters who could only afford to spend two or three days at work in the one place, before they moved on.*) Moey brought them into the fire, gave them dry clothes and a meal; she would have darned their socks, put on patches and cared for their welfare. One dark night during frost and snow, a traveller after a couple of drinks at the pub, fell into a tub of water outside Moey's door. He was unable to get out owing to the drink. Moey heard the commotion and rescued the poor man from certain death, as the weather was severe and the frost harsh. Needless to say, he got the best of Moey's hospitality." (*Jean*)*

Growing up and Leaving Home

What was lacking in material wealth was more than made up for by the warmth of family life. A neighbour recalled *"It was a very happy home. All the neighbours, Protestant and Catholic called there and Annie made tea for them all ………… Annie had an open door for everybody. All the tramps called with her and she had a bowl of broth and a farl of bread to help them on their way."*

All the children in the family attended the local National School, of which there were two in Cairncastle; they sat alongside their Protestant neighbours and there they received their elementary education up to the age of 15 or 16. They acquired a good grounding in the "Three R's." But there was more besides. They also studied Geography and Elementary Science, Singing, Nature Study and Needlework. While pupils would have lived in fear of the cane, the Principal and her Assistant lived in dread of the School Inspector. *"I was not favourably impressed by what I saw on entering."* wrote Mr. R.W. Hughes, the School Inspector, after his visit on 31 October 1906. It was a day when there were 49 pupils present in this one room school. *"There were several girls standing at the gate outside: there was a class of small children at the fire, some lying on the floor, all of them idling. In the room there was din and confusion, a hen or two meandering about. Discipline, clearly is lax. The desks are covered with ink .... They are too flat and shaky."* On a later visit, the Inspector showed he was nobody's fool when he commented that *"a great many leaves have been cut out of the Exercise Books by the Principal. This is not a good sign."* Fortunately when he returned on 4, 5 July, 1907, he was more positive and concluded that *"Reading of juniors has improved. Composition, too is better than last year and the general appearance of the schoolroom is neater and cleaner than heretofore ...... On the whole the school is regaining the ground lost."*

Pupils memorised a store of poetry which never left them. Like many of his brothers, John as a boy was fascinated by the poems and tales of Robert Service about the Yukon and the vast wilderness of Canada. In old age, he would recite every verse of Robert Service's "The Shooting of Dan McGrew" and others from that time. Poems about local events such as "The Enterprise of Lynn," which described a local shipwreck at Ringfad near Garron Point in 1827, and "Tiveragh Hill," which told of the fairy folk who inhabited that hill near Cushendall, were all part of that repertoire for recitation, learned in childhood. It was Henry who made a name for himself in composing verses, which, as was the custom of the time, celebrated local heroes and castigated local villains in equal measure.

But schooldays were also often interrupted by the call of work. Children regularly had to leave the classroom to help the adults in the seasonal work of planting and harvesting. Attendance figures from the local School Register show that older pupils could be absent half of the school year. John would recall the hard work. *"The horse was the most valuable thing about the place."* His father would often "*spare the horse*" by removing some of the burden from the horse to put it on the shoulders of his able sons.

For children growing up, the surrounding countryside was steeped in history and legend which caught their imagination. Beyond the "Headless Cross" on the road to Feystown, were the "Giant's Grave" and the "Mass Rock" with stories of Redcoats and hunted priests. There were mysterious tunnels which apparently went the whole distance from the hill of Knock Dhu to Ballygally Head. There, stood the ruins of "O'Halloran's Castle" whose valiant prince in centuries past, had kept guard over his daughter against her suitor. Closer to home in the graveyard of Saint Patrick's was the Spanish Chestnut tree which was believed to have grown from the chestnut in the pocket of the shipwrecked sailor washed ashore at Ballygally, from the Spanish Armada in 1588.

As children, their imaginations were stirred by stories of fairies, good and bad, and characters with improbable names like 'Mag Wheesger' and 'Schenedrick,' who could only have been inventions of the mind. Such stories were adapted and passed down through the generations. Willie told them to his grandchildren and they crossed the Atlantic to America with Charlie. For Willie, 'Schenedrick' was a 'superman' figure, whose help could be called upon; when

Feystown Church

children were reluctant to perform a task, 'Schenedrick' could always be relied upon to get things done. By the time he had arrived in America with Charlie, 'Schenedrick' had been transformed. Charlie warned his children of the dangers of straying too close to the Hudson River. In America, the 'Schenedricks' had taken on a plural form, after they arrived from Ireland and along with other mysterious creatures, the 'Anktapuncti,' they lived in the rivers and the sea and would devour little children who disobeyed their parents and went out on the sea. *"Unlike the Anktapuncti, the very magical Schenedricks could be tiny and invisible at one moment, then larger and visible the next and finally so big that they could come up on to the river and creek banks. There, they devoured any children or dogs or cats or other living creatures they came upon during their hungry days. After their meals, they always spat out human hair and animal furs or even feathers, before shrinking down again into invisible creatures. Hair, feathers and furs could choke them or form wads of fluff in their stomachs, so they had to get away from them as soon as possible. These piles of evidence in the tides and water banks helped the authorities keep track of where the Schenedricks were living at any given time"* said Charlie. It was in stories like these that children would learn life's lessons.

Religion played an important role in everyday life. As in most Irish households, it was the mother who took on the responsibilities of bringing their children up in their Catholic faith. The practice of morning and night prayers was learned from an early age and Moey Gill taught them to recite:

"There are four corners on my bed,
Four angels 'round my head.
Matthew, Mark, Luke and John,
Bless the bed that I lay on."

Sunday saw the family start out on the four mile trek to attend mass in Feystown Chapel. It was all uphill and in those days a limestone roadway. They walked barefoot, saving their shoes till they got near the chapel; they had been fasting from the night before in accordance with the strict church regulations of the time. A family custom was that if there were any new clothes purchased, they would have to be worn to the chapel in Feystown first, as a way of giving thanks. When

Charlie aged 70, in 1934

the possibility of building a new chapel in Ballygally was first raised, Charlie offered one of his fields (opposite McKeegan's) but the offer was not accepted as it was believed there would not be room for an adjoining school. The new chapel was eventually built in 1944 at Ballygally, but without a school. Rose, for many years, taught the local children in a "Sunday School" after mass in the new chapel.

Yet alongside this religious belief there was an uneasiness with much of the religious intolerance of the time. As Charlie saw it, his children sat side by side with their Protestant neighbours in school. Neighbours did not ask about each other's religion when they worked with one another in the fields. He had several Protestant relations; among these were his aunt Jane Magill who had married Hugh Blair in 1857 and a cousin, Willie John Magill of the Howe. Tolerance and respect for his Protestant relations were values that were instilled in all the family. Over his life, Charlie had objected to the outdated practice of 'Offerings' at funerals, when the mourners' names and the amount they contributed, were read out before the congregation. His opposition was such that when it came to his own funeral, the priest would not officiate at the graveside and the prayers were led by the eldest son, Henry.

There was more to life than school, work and chapel for the children growing up. Living close to the coast, the sea was in their blood. Their father Charlie had been a successful oarsman in his earlier days and took part in gig racing; the local villages along the Antrim coast competed in rowing regattas. Living near the sea, they would go on occasional outings to the shore. It was to that part of the coast beyond Ballygally, known as Brae Head (possibly because it was nearer Charlie's mother's home at Crucie) that they went, not to swim, because they could not, but to bathe and paddle, collect dulse and whelks. Like all young boys they liked 'messing about on boats.' Stories are told that Davy as a young lad, made sails out of flour bags which he attached to a rowing boat and headed out to sea from Ballygally. Charlie, the third son, later told boyhood stories of going to sea as a cabin boy. However, it was Willie who as a young man made a name for himself in Ballygally's gig "The O'Halloran," winning many cups and trophies. Sunday afternoon was the day for walks and nothing was thought of a ten mile walk to Carnlough. Annie in old age would remember her father taking Rose and herself as children to check the quarry where he was working at Ballygally Head. She recalled his knowledge of the sea and nature and their delight on one occasion when he showed them a ring plover, a little bird that nested on the sand of the beach.

A Family Court Case, 1913

Belfast Quarter Sessions in the Courthouse, Belfast: David Magill of Cairncastle, a minor, by his father, Charles Magill, the Plaintiff: the committee of Larne Catch-my-Pal Total Abstinence Union the Defendants.

For the boys who were growing up fast, they naturally turned their attention to sport. It's not known when, but the barn or stable behind the house was turned into a makeshift gym and the brothers and their friends would spar there with one another. As a teenager Davy showed a special talent as a runner and first came to attention in the local area. Soon he was outpacing his adult rivals and in the local town of Larne, at the age of 18, he began to make the news. There was one incident in his early sporting career, which strangely enough was never mentioned in family folklore. The Larne Times carried a report on June 21, 1913, of a court case in which his father, Charlie Magill, contested the decision of the organisers of a race in Larne. His son's award for victory in an open competition in the race held on Easter Monday, 24th March 1913 had been withheld by the organisers, the '*Larne Catch-my-Pal Total Abstinence Union'*. The two mile race had been organized on a lap system and the judges and officials had got confused in their counting of the laps. In the end they decided to withhold the £5 prize money from the young athlete. It was a considerable sum then and would be worth closer to £500 in today's currency.

A working man with no visible signs of wealth and the father of a large family, Charlie challenged the decision of the organisers, whose membership read like a 'who's who' of the town. Among them could be counted some of the town's leading solicitors and auctioneers. The dispute went to court and at the Belfast Quarter Sessions in the Courthouse, Belfast, he secured a verdict in his son's favour. The Larne Times reported that *"the judge ruled that the officials had allowed the races to be muddled and mismanaged and the young man was entitled to the value of the first prize."* It was to be young Davy's first encounter with the harsh side of sporting officialdom. More than that, it was a remarkable example of a father's drive and determination for his son to succeed. If we are looking for clues for the sporting prowess of his sons, we only need to look back at events like the Ballygally Regatta of 1887 and this remarkable court case in 1913, to see where it originated.

2 The Magills at Home

Life got easier as the years went on. The home became less crowded as the older children 'flew the nest'. First to leave in 1907 to go to New York, was Jennie at the age of 18. Over the next decade the house gradually emptied. In 1911, Mary followed her older sister to the United States. In 1914 both Henry and Davy left to go to Dublin to join the Royal Irish Constabulary. In the following year, with World War One underway, the 19 year old Charlie enlisted in the North Irish Horse and would soon be in the trenches of the Western Front.

The New Farm

The Larne Times carried the following advertisement in November 1917 of the auction of a house and farm, which stood at the centre of the village. This was the second time in four years that it had come on the market. It was one of the most desirable houses in the area. It had been described in the first sale as *'recently built'* with 20 acres of good farmland; in addition to the buildings on this farm which were *'substantially built'*, there was a large range of *'Office and Outbuildings'*, a *'Cottier House'* and a *'Churning Machine'*. It had belonged to the Sheriff family, who were a well-to-do family in the area. (The road approaching Cairncastle is still referred to today by some as "Sheriff's Brae.") The owner, Joseph Sheriff, had died and the property had been sold at auction in March 1913, his son-in-law, Samuel Brennan of Carnfunnock, purchasing it for £650. Now in 1917, the latter was putting it on the market again, because, as the advertisement stated, *'he had acquired another farm'*.

Some family stories like that of the court case may have been forgotten with the passage of time but the story of the purchase of the house and farm was long

Larne Times, November, 1917

remembered in family folklore. It may well have been more than a century since the repeal of the Eighteenth Century Penal Laws which had forbidden Catholics to own land in Ireland, but the religious prejudice of the day still meant that often Catholics had to depend on the goodwill of their Protestant friends to bid for them when buying property.

According to the story, "*Old James Moore who ran the Meetinghouse Pub, said to Charlie, who was one of his best customers, that he should buy it and he would put up the money. They agreed on that and on the day of the sale, old James did the bidding and bought the farm. They all came back to the pub and had a good drink. Then James said to Charlie that they should go over to tell Annie about buying the farm. Old James told her and that the price was £1,000. (it was in fact, £905.) He said he was standing the money and over a bit of time she would be able to clear it. Annie said she had some money and she went upstairs and brought down a big wooden box with a chain and padlock and counted out the price of the farm on the table. Old James Moore said there was still some money left in the box. Annie kept a lot of pigs and poultry and she saved a lot of money. Old Charlie didn't know about it, for he and the boys were all hard drinkers."(Dan McKillion).* In many ways the buying of the new house was a 'rags to riches' story for the family. Just over 20 years before at the time of their marriage, Annie and Charlie had been 'servants.' They had struggled to feed a family of 12 in a very modest home. Now they had acquired one of the

James Moore and his wife Mary

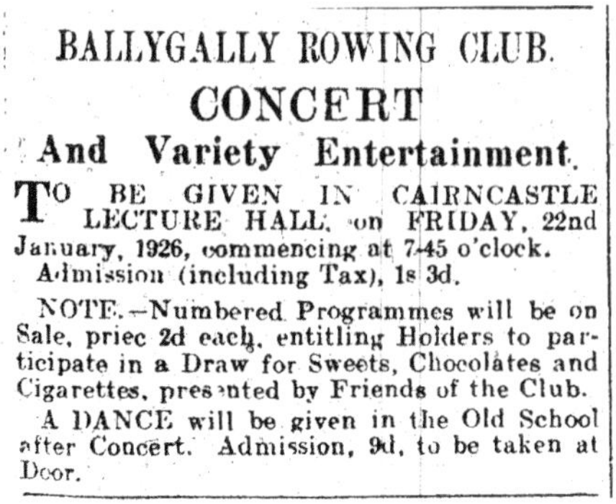
BALLYGALLY ROWING CLUB.
CONCERT
And Variety Entertainment.
TO BE GIVEN IN CAIRNCASTLE LECTURE HALL, on FRIDAY, 22nd January, 1926, commencing at 7-45 o'clock.
Admission (including Tax), 1s 3d.
NOTE.—Numbered Programmes will be on Sale, priec 2d each, entitling Holders to participate in a Draw for Sweets, Chocolates and Cigarettes, presented by Friends of the Club.
A DANCE will be given in the Old School after Concert. Admission, 9d, to be taken at Door.

more prestigious houses in the village and life would be much more comfortable. What was perhaps more incredible, was how Annie had managed to save such an amount. In 1917, £1,000 was a princely sum, amounting to nearly £70,000 in today's money. There had been no sizeable legacies we know of, but she had kept the accounts for Charlie over nearly 30 years and had always put money aside. Charlie and his sons had worked hard carting and repairing the roads, over the years. With good management, she had managed to fill that '*big wooden box with a chain and padlock.*' An old account book dating back to 1931, shows how meticulously Annie recorded the accounts of the carting business. Charlie had always kept a few horses and carried everything from coal from Larne to sand and gravel for the new houses being built at Ballygally and Drains Bay. Stone was quarried at Knock Dhu and Ballygally Head and seaweed carted from the beach at Ballygally. An entry for September 1932 reads *"16 loads of seaweed from the beach at one shilling (5* pence) *per load.*"

As in all rural communities at the time, the outside world rarely intruded on Cairncastle. In an age when the horse was the main form of transport and motor vehicles rare, Belfast seemed a faraway place. Life was marked by the rhythm

Back Row; William Hunter, John Hall, Bob Crawford (cox), Charles Hoffman, John Cane
Front Row: Dr. Crawford Blair, William Crawford, William Magill, Stanley Duffin, Alf McClelland, Willie Connolly

of the seasons; the lambing in spring, saving the hay in summer and gathering in the potatoes and crops during the harvest. The daily routines of milking the cows and tending to the animals continued to go on. The highlights of the farming calendar came with the Sheep Sales and for the Protestant inhabitants, the Twelfth celebrations. There was a strong sense of community which went beyond religious differences; the nature of farming required everyone to co-operate. This neighbourliness continued over the generations. It was a time when front doors were rarely locked, a world which was illuminated by the tilley lamp and not electricity. Yet it was far from a rural idyll. Work was hard with everyone in the family, including mothers and young children, expected to join in the toil, out in all seasons, whatever the weather.

But increasingly the family and people of Cairncastle found themselves drawn into the events of the outside world. Buying the new farm was not the only event in the news in the village that year. There was much talk of the War and the earlier enthusiasm had by this stage given way to concern for the soldiers at the Front. Many local lads had joined up and Charlie, the third boy in the family had joined the North Irish Horse Regiment and was posted to France. By now, the local paper was publishing lists of casualties.

"SUCCESSFUL ENTERTAINMENT TO PROVIDE XMAS PARCELS FOR CAIRNCASTLE SOLDIERS" ran the headline in the Larne Times, on Nov 10, 1917.

On Friday 26th Oct, 1917, a very successful entertainment was given in the Lecture Hall, Cairncastle...... In spite of the inclemency of the weather the hall was filled to its utmost capacity. Among the items were, ... "Lodgings to Let" by Cairncastle 'Black and White Minstrel Troupe', a magnificent sum of £21. one shilling and six pence being realised for the very worthy object of providing Xmas parcels for local soldiers and sailors."

Social life for most people involved visiting friends and neighbours, usually on Sunday, the day of rest from daily toil. There was of course the Meeting-house pub, but that was exclusively for men. Occasionally there were concerts, bazaars and dances organized in local venues. The Lecture Hall over the years was the venue for local social life as this advert shows. Concerts were also held in Feystown. The Larne Times reported on January 9, 1926 that "*An entertainment was held in the Young Ladies' Clubroom, Feystown, during Christmas week. .... "The Woodbine Brothers" from Feystown, gave a number of new dances, one in particular, "The Hunting Jig," evoking much laughter and applause. Mr. Henry Magill acted as M.C., and the music was supplied by Mr. Dan Hoey of the Feystown Jazz Band.*"

For the Magills of the Meetinghouse, their horizons were widening. Letters dutifully delivered by Cairncastle's postman, Johnny McNeill, came from Jennie, Mary and Charlie bringing the family news from America and from Pat in Australia. After 1920 the boxing exploits of Davy and later Jim brought a new celebrity to the family. The newspaper cuttings came from Belfast,

A youthful Jim displaying early trophies

London and New York. Davy became the popular idol of Belfast boxing fans and a film was shown in May 1923, in Belfast and Dublin of his gallant battle for the British Empire Light-heavyweight title in London. In turn, the youngest boy, Jim, would become the star of Irish amateur boxing. They would travel widely as boxing champions and draw the crowds to venues such as Madison Square Gardens in New York and the Royal Albert Hall in London.

Gradually the house filled with silverware and trophies, won by her athletic sons in running, rowing and particularly in the boxing ring. Moey Gill had a mother's pride in the success of her sons. It became a house filled with the comings and goings of visitors and well-wishers, from near and far who came to congratulate and share in the family's new found fame. Annie and Rose entertained family and friends who came regularly to visit. More important than this, the house was soon filled with the visits of the next generation of grandchildren.

Davy and Molly married 1924

Wedding of Henry and Sarah McNeill, 1926. John best man.

Wedding of John and Peggy Rooney, 1938. Lily Rooney, brides-maid, Jim, best man

Henry

John

Kathleen Matthews. Willie told Rachel and Rosemary that they were beautiful but not half as beautiful as their mother.

Marriage of Willie and Kathleen, 1942

Charlie and friend outside the Meetinghouse

Davy had married Molly Hynes in 1924. Their wedding in Saint Paul's, Falls Road, Belfast was reported in the press. Such was Davy's popularity at the time in Belfast, that it was said *"There were remarkable scenes of enthusiasm and rarely has there been a prettier wedding or a larger gathering to see it"... "A couple of thousand admirers."*

Boxing in the Twenties had great appeal and boxers like Davy were feted like film stars. Other weddings followed. Henry, the eldest brother, married Sarah McNeill in 1926 but it was not until 1938 that John married Peggy Rooney and 1942 when Willie married Kathleen Matthews. Finally in 1949 Annie married John McCafferty.

Changes of the 1940's

Annie, 'Moey Gill' and John

The War years were to bring big changes to the family. Tragic news came in February 1942 when it was reported that Davy, who had joined the Merchant Navy at the outbreak of World War Two, had been declared 'missing at sea.' The ship he was on board, the 'Ocean Venture,' a British owned steam merchant ship, was believed to have been struck by a German torpedo

David, Patricia, Tillie and Nan

and only 13 of the crew of 45 survived. Davy's widow Molly was left with five children. Later in the same year, on 21 November, Charlie himself died at the age of 78. The Ballymena Observer noted *"The passing of Mr. Charles Magill, Ballygally, removes a very popular and kindly man and a person of whom it may be said was one of nature's gentlemen. He was a successful farmer and well known on the Antrim Coast. In his early days he was a noted oarsman and a member of the Ballygally Rowing Club."*
The Larne Times reported in its obituary:

"Father Of Noted Boxers - Death of Mr. C. Magill"

"The death took place on Saturday last of Mr.Charles Magill, Ballygally, Cairncastle, Co. Antrim at the age of 78. He was an extensive farmer and in his younger days a keen oarsman competing in the early '90's at various regattas on the Antrim Coast.

He was the father of seven sons and four daughters. His second son, ex-Constable David Magill, R.I.C., attained fame in the boxing world. He was ex-heavyweight champion of Ireland and on the outbreak of war he joined the Merchant Navy. He was recently officially listed as having perished at sea, a victim of enemy action.

The seventh son, Constable James Magill, is ex-amateur champion of Britain, and was for six years European police champion. He is at present stationed in Queen Street R.U.C. Barracks, Belfast.

Ex-Head Constable Henry Magill, the first son, was well known in Lisburn, where he served for many years in the R.U.C.

Of Mr. Magill's other sons John is a constable in York Street Barracks, Belfast: Charles is a machinist in the U.S.A.; William is at home on the farm and Patrick is in Australia. Of the four daughters two are in America, one is in the accounts branch of the G.P.O., Belfast and the fourth is at home.

The deepest sympathy of a wide circle of friends is extended to the bereaved wife and family in their heavy loss.

The funeral took place on Sunday to the family burying ground, Feystown, Glenarm. There was a large attendance of neighbours and friends, including representatives of the R.U.C. and of the boxing world. The chief mourners were ex-Head Constable Henry Magill, Constable James Magill, Constable John Magill, and Mr. William Magill (sons). Rev. P.J. O'Keeney, C.C., Glenarm, conducted the services"

In his will, Charlie, had left the family home and farm to Willie.

Charles Magill 1864-1942

"I, Charles Magill of Ballygally, Cairncastle in the County of Antrim, Farmer ....I leave all my household furniture, furnishings and utensils to my wife Annie. I leave my farm situate in Ballygally aforesaid and containing about 18 statute acres together with all stock crop and farming implements to my son William. I leave my dwelling house garden and field in Corkermain to my wife Annie for the term of her natural life with remainder to my son John. I leave my small freehold property consisting of house and garden also situate in Corkermain to my daughter Rosy. All the rest, residue and remainder of my property I leave to my wife Annie. I appoint my said sons William and John to be the executors of this my will. As witness my hand this sixth day of March one thousand nine hundred and forty."

(Will of Charles Magill, 6 March, 1940)

Willie had been the son who remained at home to run the farm and work alongside his father. Dan McKillion recalled that "*Old Charlie had been a great battery builder along the Coast. He used the biggest stones possible - no good using small stones to turn the tide. He never had to tender for the work, the Council gave it to him because they knew that he always made a good job. He employed men and made money. His son Willie carted the stones from Ballygally quarry to where they were needed - hard work, a strong man.*" Like his brothers before him, Willie had gone off to Dublin and joined the RIC in 1920, but returned home to help on the farm and with the work, after six months of training.

He was 43 when he married Kathleen Matthews. *"I knew Willie would eventually marry"* his sister Rose allegedly commented when Willie and Kathleen announced their intention to marry. Marriage in those times was usually delayed until the son took over the family farm and was in a position to provide a home. The story was told that "*they honeymooned in a hotel in Belfast and Kathleen recalled her embarrassment when suddenly Uncle Jim appeared in their bedroom to visit them - an obvious lack of tact!"* When Willie and Kathleen married, they first went to live in the former home on Drumnagreagh Road and it was here that their first daughter, Rachel was born. After old Charlie died, there was an exchange of houses with Willie, Kathleen and Rachel crossing the village to live on the farm while Moey Gill, Rose and Annie would make their home in the old house.

Willie and Nelly in the Hayfield

"Their lives were around work, the chapel, the family and the ultimate prize .....getting to heaven." (Rosemary)

Willie's daughter Rosemary vividly recalls life on the farm as she grew up in the 1950's. She fondly remembers the long, hot summer days working in the hayfield *"our mother arriving with hot sweet tea in a big white jug and freshly baked soda bread."*

*"A major event in the village was the twice yearly Sheep Sales..........(*By the 1960's the Sales took place in Willie's field at the crossroads*) The farmers brought their sheep from the surrounding farms early in the morning and the village was alive and chaotic all day. Deals were made and celebrated in the pub and friendships were forged...... Indeed market days and funerals were always an excuse to exaggerate with the drink."*

There were events that stood out in her memory. *"Every year a pig was killed down the yard - Pat Magill (Pat A' Scroggie) arrived, knives were sharpened, kettles boiled and the poor old pig dragged, squealing to its death - mercifully it got stunned by a bang on the head before Pat cut its throat. When dead, the boiling water was used to scrape off the hairs and then it was hauled up by its hind legs. A line was made the length of the body with a sharp knife and the interior fell steaming into a bucket. All the children in the village witnessed the event with a mixture of fear and excitement - someone got the bladder which was used to squirt water on the others. The offal was distributed around the village, the stomach stuffed, boiled and then fried and the meat cut into portions and salted to be preserved for winter."*

Back: L-R. -?, Sam Moore, May Young, Willie Magill, Rosemary Magill
Front: L-R.: Mayanne Young, Charlie Magill,1948-'49

Willie was also the practical joker of the family and he enjoyed nothing more than telling jokes and teasing the children. A staged photo shows him outside the Meetinghouse posing as Cairncastle's "One Man and his Dog" Champion. In later years he delighted locals and visitors alike as he took to the roads with his donkey and cart. He had pet names for all his dogs, cats and cows. Life for Willie was in Cairncastle and centred round his beloved wife and four children. It was a struggle for small farmers at this time and the rewards from small farms were few. Every month the milk cheque was eagerly awaited as it was the only source of disposable cash. The hard work took its toll and it may have led to the rheumatoid arthritis that Kathleen suffered from in her last 14 years, when she was cared for by her daughter Rachel and the family. Willie lived all his days in Cairncastle apart from his time in Dublin training for the RIC. He was known widely for his humour and good nature. He was a man who could mix with all classes and creeds and was very much part of the Cairncastle community. His experience and knowledge gained him respect wherever he went. He died at the age of 80 on 24 February, 1978.

Willie and Laddie

L-R: Rosemary, Martin, Willie, Kathleen, Charlie and Rachel 1968

Willie and donkey returning home

Rose (standing) and Annie in their 'teens'

Rose, "an unclaimed treasure" (1909-1983)

Rose

Rose, who had worked in the Post Office in London in the Thirties, had been transferred back to Belfast and returned to live at the Meetinghouse. She made the daily journey by bicycle or on foot to the bus at Ballygally, and then took the train from Larne to and from her work in Belfast. She would often walk the four miles in and out of Larne and to the alarm of her family, carry the office petty cash with her in her handbag *'for safe keeping.'* In later years she stayed in a boarding house in Belfast before she finally left to spend her retirement in Cairncastle. Rose remained single throughout her life. There had been boyfriends in London and at home, but she never married. Her niece, Sheila, recalls how she had a wealth of stories and such a way with words. In her own inimitable way she described herself as *"an unclaimed treasure."* She had the knack of making everyone feel special and she became a favourite aunt to her many nephews and nieces. Their youthful indiscretions were excused by quips such as *"An old maid's children are always well brought up."*

Her niece, Rosemary in Brussels, remembers how "*she spoke with such precision and she often corrected our local Cairncastle dialect, by insisting that "an owl is a bird......." She also had a certain glamour having worked in London and Belfast - she must have been a role-model for us since Rachel and I both followed her into the civil service in the sixties."* Another niece in Vancouver, Anne-Marie, reminisced *"With my mother so involved with the farm and the daily chores, Aunt Rose really was the one who taught me so much, just because she simply had more time. It was sort of strange as I almost had two mothers. She let me away with murder and naturally I always wanted to stay with her when I should have been at the Drains Farm."* She clearly left her mark on all those around her in the

"Rose became a favourite aunt to her many nephews and nieces; she had the knack of making them all feel special."

The first of John and Peggy's ten children, Brian, Sheila and Sean c 1943

The youngest of Henry and Sarah's eight children, Rita and Harry

family but her influence went much further in the workplace and in the community. She even taught catechism before mass every Sunday in Ballygally Chapel to the local children who attended the primary school in Cairncastle.

Annie (1911-2006)

When Willie inherited the farm, he exchanged houses with his mother and sisters, Annie and Rose. It must have been an upheaval for the family leaving their home

Rebecca McCafferty, John McCafferty, Annie Magill, 'Moey Gill', Frank McCafferty and Rose Magill

Annie and John's three children,Sean, Therese and Anne-Marie

after 25 years; they now transferred to the house which would be home for Annie for the next 50 years. Born in 1911, Annie had been the youngest of the children. She was christened Annie after her sister Annie who had died four years before, and of course after her mother. 1911 had been the year her sister, Mary, had left for America when Annie was only five months old; she grew up with her sister Rose in a family of boys.

Unlike all of the others, she spent all her days in Cairncastle. She remembered her father taking her on childhood walks on Sunday afternoons, with Rose to Ballygally. One of her memories at the age of four, was her brother, Charlie, coming to tell Rose and herself, when they were tucked up in bed, that he was going off to war in 1915. She had been born in the old house in Corkermain and at the age of six, she moved with the family to the new home and farm in 1917. She had attended school just across the road and worshipped in Feystown Chapel. One of the rare occasions she left the Meetinghouse, was a visit to London. In 1934 when there, she remembered going to the Albert Hall to see Jim win the ABA title and being brought into the ring to be presented with a bouquet of flowers. In later years she and her husband John went to visit their daughter, Anne-Marie in Canada. Outside of that, she spent her entire life living in the village, except for her closing years when she could no longer cope on her own.

'Moey Gill' and Annie

Growing up, Annie had inherited much from her mother and became an excellent homemaker. She had all the practical skills of cooking and baking in abundance. Her friend and neighbour, Jean Armstrong, recalls "*The house was always filled with the smell of homemade bread. .... When Annie*

Charles and Annie, 1934

put the griddle on, all sorts of bread flowed off it; soda, wheaten, potato bread, potato oaten, potato apple, maize bread, then apple tarts in the oven. 'Save the flour at the mouth of the bag' she would say." She was a wonderful knitter too. As Jean says *"The knitting was never out of her hands; when she was out for a walk, the ball of wool was in her pocket.*"

She devoted herself to caring for her parents in their old age and in turn her sister Rose and brother Jim in later years. As a young lady she had many admirers. One young man summed her up as *'Beauty, Innocence and Sheer Simplicity,'* but it was John McCafferty who won her heart. Matters were not to be rushed and it was a courtship that lasted 19 years. Annie's nephew, Brian, can recall being sent as chaperone to accompany Annie and John when they went to the cinema. They tied the knot in 1949. John had been a successful footballer in his day and had been on the bench of Belfast Celtic. A family of three children followed and from that time on, Annie's life was shared between two homes, her own in Cairncastle and John's at his farm at Drain's Bay. "*She was happiest at the Drains farm. Every morning would see her make the journey from Cairncastle to the Drains in the Ford Van and she would spend the day helping with the farm work and preparing the food." (Jean).*

She had a wealth of stories, a memory that stretched back and remained alert and articulate well into her eighties. Because of her long lifetime in Cairncastle, she knew the seed and breed of everyone for miles around. In old age, Annie liked nothing better than company and a chat. Visitors and passers by, were equally welcomed to her fireside. Tea was offered, whether requested or not and buns and cakes appeared mysteriously and under no circumstances could they be refused.

In Annie's closing years in the nursing home in Larne, she showed great contentment and that acceptance of God's will that was the hallmark of her generation. In the words of Jean, she had been the "*last of the family to be born and last to die.*"

In so many ways she had kept family traditions alive and her passing at the grand age of 95 in the year 2006, clearly marked the end of the family that had started far back in 1889. It was indeed the end of an era.

3 Charlie in World War One

Private Charles Magill

"He told me he was caught in an explosion and buried alive, but managed to claw his way out of the earth. For years in America (where he emigrated in 1924) he never wore a turtle neck sweater or shirt, because he felt like he was suffocating. At Marne my dad said his leg was badly injured by shrapnel - he wandered, hidden in the woods with his leg injury and spotted a Salvation Army officer in a clearing and called out to him. He was taken by him to a field hospital, where they wanted to amputate his leg; but my father refused.
All his life, my father suffered tremendous leg pain, I think in his left leg from the shrapnel fragments. On damp and cold days, he often limped. Also, my dad said he was exposed to mustard gas" Kathleen Magill, (Charlie's daughter) New York, 2009.

Well, how do you do, Private William McBride,
Do you mind if I sit down here by your graveside?
And rest for awhile in the warm summer sun,
I've been walking all day, and I'm nearly done.
And I see by your gravestone you were only 19
When you joined the glorious fallen in 1916,
Well, I hope you died quick and I hope you died clean
Or, Willie McBride, was it slow and obscene?

"A Mounted Horseman in a Cavalry Regiment"

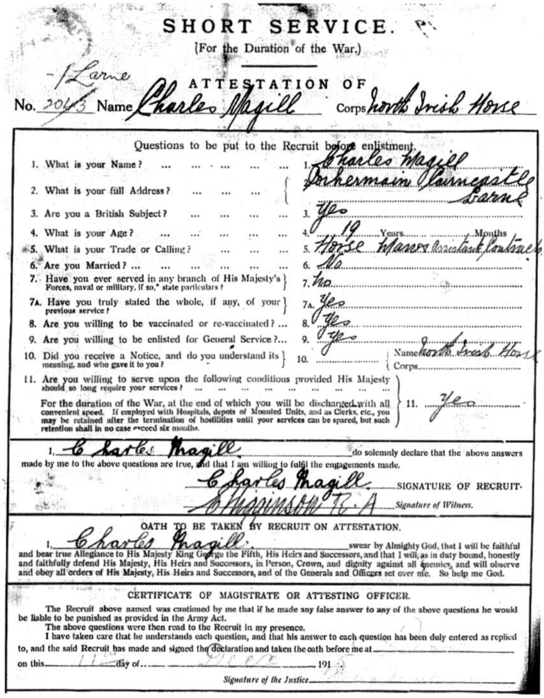

SHORT SERVICE.
(For the Duration of the War.)

ATTESTATION OF

No. 2043 Name Charles Magill Corps North Irish Horse

Questions to be put to the Recruit before enlistment.

1. What is your Name? ... 1. Charles Magill
2. What is your full Address? ... Dorhermain Cairncastle Larne
3. Are you a British Subject? ... 3. Yes
4. What is your Age? ... 4. 19 Years ... Months
5. What is your Trade or Calling? ... 5. Horse [illegible]
6. Are you Married? ... 6. No
7. Have you ever served in any branch of His Majesty's Forces, naval or military, if so,* state particulars? 7. No
7A. Have you truly stated the whole, if any, of your previous service? 7A. Yes
8. Are you willing to be vaccinated or re-vaccinated? ... 8. Yes
9. Are you willing to be enlisted for General Service? ... 9. Yes
10. Did you receive a Notice, and do you understand its meaning, and who gave it to you? 10. ... Name North Irish Horse Corps ...
11. Are you willing to serve upon the following conditions provided His Majesty should so long require your services? ...
For the duration of the War, at the end of which you will be discharged with all convenient speed. If employed with Hospitals, depots of Mounted Units, and as Clerks, etc., you may be retained after the termination of hostilities until your services can be spared, but such retention shall in no case exceed six months. 11. Yes

I, Charles Magill do solemnly declare that the above answers made by me to the above questions are true, and that I am willing to fulfil the engagements made.

Charles Magill SIGNATURE OF RECRUIT.
[illegible] Signature of Witness.

OATH TO BE TAKEN BY RECRUIT ON ATTESTATION.

I, Charles Magill swear by Almighty God, that I will be faithful and bear true Allegiance to His Majesty King George the Fifth, His Heirs and Successors, and that I will, as in duty bound, honestly and faithfully defend His Majesty, His Heirs and Successors, in Person, Crown, and dignity against all enemies, and will observe and obey all orders of His Majesty, His Heirs and Successors, and of the Generals and Officers set over me. So help me God.

CERTIFICATE OF MAGISTRATE OR ATTESTING OFFICER.

The Recruit above named was cautioned by me that if he made any false answer to any of the above questions he would be liable to be punished as provided in the Army Act.
The above questions were then read to the Recruit in my presence.
I have taken care that he understands each question, and that his answer to each question has been duly entered as replied to, and the said Recruit has made and signed the declaration and taken the oath before me at ...
on this 11th day of Dec 1915
Signature of the Justice ...

Page 1 of Service Record of Charles Magill

World War One had begun in August 1914 and Charlie volunteered and joined the North Irish Horse at their camp in Antrim as Private 2043 on 16 December 1915. Conscription had not and would not be introduced in Ireland during the war. Like young William MacBride in Eric Bogle's famous anti-war song "The Green Fields of France," Charlie too was a young man of nineteen; in fact his nineteenth birthday had just passed ten days before. The oldest of the family at home, now that Henry and David had gone to Dublin to join the RIC in 1914 and Jennie and Mary were in the USA, he was probably keen to become independent and see the world. No doubt he was attracted by the glamour and prestige of joining a cavalry regiment. So, like countless numbers of other young men at the time, it was in an army uniform that Charlie would first see the outside world.

Throughout the country there was a mood of enthusiasm for the war. The local press kept its readers informed through "The War in Pictures every week." The Larne Times reported on the public sympathy for the plight of Belgian refugees. A house to house collection was taken up in the town and the Larne Relief Committee offered hospitality to twenty five refugees till the war was over. The report added that "one of the Belgian refugees, a priest, at present stopping at Glenarm Castle, conducted Divine Service in Glenarm Catholic Church." The newspapers were full of thrilling stories of war and the victories of patriotism against the odds. Readers were kept up to date with "Letters from the Front" every week, like that from an officer serving in the North Irish Horse:

"*23 September 1914. We have been here for the last ten days .... We were only about twenty miles from Paris, and I had hoped to be able to go in and dine there, but we were away again .... I had far rougher times in South Africa*

North Irish Horse, Antrim 1915

(The Boer War) than in this show. They feed the troops splendidly ...... We are living in great comfort in a chateau ..... Our mess includes wine, costs one franc fifty cents a day." (Larne Times)

We are fortunate that Charlie's service record has survived as over half of these have perished, ironically due to German air raids during World War 2. His enlistment papers describe the young man of nineteen as "*horseman and assistant contractor - five feet nine inches in height and weighing eleven stone*." Coming from a background of working with horses he was well suited to a career as a mounted horseman in a cavalry regiment and the rate of pay of one shilling per day was attractive to any young man. The belief on all sides at the time was that the war would be over soon, hence the "Short Service" enlistment form. Irishmen, Catholic and Protestant, nationalist and unionist in their thousands (estimates range from 200,000 to 250,000) joined up during the course of the War.

Much of the following year was taken up with training and preparation. On the day after arrival in the camp at Antrim, Charlie and the new recruits were issued with a rifle, sword, saddle, blankets and each was given a horse. They were introduced to the daily routines: Reveille at 5.30 a.m., make beds, sweep floors, then fall in at 6 a.m. for physical jerks, then 6.15 a.m. to stables. There, the horses were exercised, watered and groomed while the stables were cleaned out. After breakfast, it was time for riding school, when the recruits were taught the rudiments of cavalry training. Recruits were also trained in sword and rifle drill. Training and preparation went on for much of the year 1916 and Charlie didn't leave for France until 26 November 1916, when he sailed from Southampton and disembarked at Rouen. The North Irish Horse had been drawn up in support of the 36th Ulster Division in the disastrous attempt to break the stalemate at the Battle of the Somme starting in July 1916.

The war of movement planned by the generals in which cavalry would play a leading role didn't materialise; the countryside of France and Flanders had been so ravaged by artillery fire that it was impassible to men on horseback. Instead of cavalry charges the rival armies dug in and faced each other in opposing lines of trenches which stretched from the Channel ports to Switzerland. This was the situation when Charlie arrived in France.

The regiment had moved to the Ypres sector in Flanders, spending most of November 1916 to June 1917 there. Most of Charlie's first 6 months were spent quietly, mainly at Boeschepe. The regiment was in support at the Battle of Messines before being withdrawn to Aix-en-Issart near Etaples and not a great distance from Boulogne, where the Regiment was dismounted and trained as infantry.

With the role of the cavalry now redundant, the men of the North Irish Horse went into the trenches and took on the menial tasks of infantrymen. Over the next years Charlie like many young men, saw and experienced at first hand the horrors of the war. Of course there were the routines of parades, guarding bridges and storage dumps, providing stretcher bearers and burying parties often under shell-fire; worse was digging trenches on ground that had already been fought over with what was described as "*dead bodies in varying stages of putrefaction lying about all over the place.*" In the end, the decision was taken in August 1917 to convert the North Irish Horse from cavalry to infantry.

Voyage to Egypt, 1917

Francis Joseph MacMahon

Charlie's service record shows him embarking for Egypt on 25 August 1917, from Marseilles on the "Bohemian" conducting horses, since these were no longer required by the North Irish. Egypt was then part of the Ottoman Empire and Turkey had joined the war on Germany's side. One of Charlie's comrades in the North Irish Horse, Francis Joseph MacMahon from

On right, Charles Magill in Egypt

Newry, later wrote a detailed account of his experiences in France and described the journey from Marseilles.

"We entrained the horses for Marseilles (we never knew where we were going until we got there) with an officer [Lieutenant T.H.M Leader] and some men were put in charge of the horses, we ultimately arrived in Marseilles where an Indian regiment officered by English officers took the horses from us, we hung around Marseilles for 2 weeks, then joined a ship with 850 horses as usual destination unknown.

We set sail with the ship overcrowded with indentured Indians, returning home. We had 2 Japanese destroyers as escort for the ship, conditions were really tough, bad food, grooming horses and cleaning out the manure at night time, it was essential it was done at night, because the manure floated on the sea and it was a real give away for German submarines. We arrived at Malta but were not allowed ashore, after taking on stores and water we sailed again and finally arrived in Alexandria (Egypt) where the Australians took over the horses. After a short time in Alexandria we boarded a Ship (destination unknown). Arriving at some Greek islands we lay up by day in these islands and sailed at night (submarine scare), arrived at Salonika in Greece, then Taranto in Italy, entrained in Taranto, crossed Italy by train, held up at Farenzo? [probably Firenze] whilst the brass discussed using us as reinforcements on the Pavo [probably the Piave River], then back through France to Le Havre, transferred to a famous Irish Infantry regiment, then up into the trenches. [The "famous Irish Infantry regiment" was the 9th (Service) Battalion Royal Irish Fusiliers, part of the 36th (Ulster) Division. The Battalion had suffered severely during the Battle of Passchendaele, and absorbed much of Frank's Regiment, becoming the 9th (North Irish Horse) Battalion Royal Irish Fusiliers.]

(Diary of Francis Joseph MacMahon)

Royal Irish Fusiliers

After he returned from Egypt on 5th October 1917 Charlie was transferred to the 9th Royal Irish Fusiliers as Private 41592, at cavalry rate of pay. (according to Army Form B.218P His Majesty's Army: Weekly Rates Of Pay. Cavalry of the Line drew 8/2 on enlistment and 9/11 to 11/8 after 2 years service. By way of comparison, Infantry of the Line drew 7/- on enlistment and 8/9 to 10/6 after 2 years service). The regiment drew its recruits mainly from the counties of Armagh, Cavan and Monaghan. Most of its members were originally from a Protestant and unionist background, but perhaps because of the great losses incurred by this stage, they now included Catholics like Charlie and Francis Joseph MacMahon and an increasing number of English soldiers. One in six of those 300 members of the North Irish Horse, who transferred with Charlie were to lose their lives in the war. Charlie himself would survive the year with only minor ailments, suffering "*contusion* (swelling) *of the knee*" and "*Pyrexia* (High temperature) *of Unknown Origin*." The Regimental Diary gives a vivid picture of the war experienced by the soldiers:

The Trenches

	"trenches very badly flooded .... Our artillery active day and night."
December 3-4	*Batallion left Metz at 8 p.m. - arrived in support trenches 5.30a.m. Enemy artillery very active -casualties - heavy shell ing.*
December 8	*Enemy aeroplanes very active over our lines, flying very low.*

December 18 *Marched through deep snow to our billets... Moved through shell-shattered country...Distance between enemy and our front line averages 1,000 yards.*

February 1918 *On patrol nightly in No Man's Land - no enemy encountered and wire found good. Officers in front line seen observing our lines through glasses."*

Gunner in 22 Light Tank Battalion

According to Phillip Tardif, historian of the North Irish Horse, Charlie and the Royal Irish Fusiliers saw some serious military action during the Battle of Cambrai 1917. This was the first major tank battle of the War. Charlie and some 23 of his NIH/RIF comrades joined the Tank Corps immediately after the Battle. It is likely that following the losses suffered by the Tank Corps at Cambrai, they called for volunteers from the infantry. Charlie and the other former cavalrymen would have been only too happy to leave the infantry (not to mention the attraction of the winter months spent in England in training). The nature of combat was changing with the introduction of tanks to break the stalemate caused by trench warfare. They had gone into action for the first time on 15 September 1916 on the Somme battlefield. By the end of December of 1917 Charlie had been transferred to the 22 Light Tank Batallion with the rank of Gunner in a machine gun base. He returned to England, to military camp at Oswestry in Shropshire where training in tank warfare took place from 28 December 1917 until 26 April 1918.

When his training was completed, he returned to active service in France before the end of April and here he saw military action until August. This was the beginning of the Allies 'Advance to Victory' campaign but by the end of August he was admitted to the Field Hospital at Rouen, wounded. His service record bluntly states "GSW Foot R" meaning "Gun-shot wounds to the right foot." He returned to England on the "Panama" on 23 August 1918, where he remained in hospital before going to camp at Bovington, Dorset. He was finally demobilised 13 March 1919. In all he had served a total of three years and ninety three days, half of it in France. On return to Ireland he joined the RIC in December 1919, when he was posted to County Roscommon. It was a transfer from the Western Front to the guerilla conflict of the Irish War of Independence. After the demobilisation of the RIC in 1922, he returned to civilian life and in the following year, he emigrated to Canada and then to the United States where he died in 1972.

4 Emigration to USA, Canada and England
- five of the family leave Ireland.

"Those of my family, who had arrived in America .... were all willing to 'tough it out' here in the New World. A few went back on boats for visits, but no immigrants in my immediate family ever stayed in the old country after living and working in America." Kathleen Magill. They became Americans.

Kathleen Magill

First to leave home and go to America was the eldest, Jennie, at the age of 18, in 1907. She was followed by Mary, aged 20, in 1911; both sisters spent the rest of their days in New York. Charlie, who had served in France from 1916-1918 and had travelled to Egypt, Greece and Italy, during World War 1, ended up in New York too; he had come to the United States after originally going to Canada in 1923. Davy had travelled to box in New York in 1923, but unlike many other Irish fighters, he decided not to stay and returned to Ireland where he was to marry Molly Hynes. Pat left in 1926 for Perth, Australia, where he remained for the rest of his life. Rose was the last to leave; she went to London at the end of the Twenties but returned just before the outbreak of World War 11.

The Magill family was not unique in its experience of emigration from this area. The story of emigration in the 19th and early 20th centuries and its impact on the surrounding countryside has been documented by Felix McKillop in "*Townlands, People and Traditions" 2006.* Abandoned houses and deserted town lands, all tell their own stories. The advertisements appearing in the Larne Weekly Reporter in 1907, promised '*To Canada for £3,*' '*guaranteed work and good wages.*' Those who could afford the cost of the voyage left, but some relied on the help of others as one of the provisions in the will of a cousin of the Meetinghouse Magills, John Magill of Ballyruther, who died in 1894, shows: *"I bequeath ....to Rose Annie Magill a legacy of the sum of £15 to be expended in providing an outfit and paying her passage to America."*

The statue of Liberty which was the first sight to greet immigrants coming to New York

Most people from this part of County Antrim left to go to the USA, especially Chicago and New York, but many went to Canada; a lot also ventured farther to Australia and New Zealand while others moved to England or Scotland. The year Jennie arrived in the United States, 1907, was the year in which immigration to the USA peaked at 1.25 million. Four years later in 1911, when Mary was to follow her, a writer in the Larne Times in January 28, noted that *"The tide of emigration has set in on the Antrim Coast and many are crossing the Atlantic to friends or relations in either the USA or Canada. The country around has been greatly thinned during the last few years, owing to emigration and in a short time there will be few left, except the very young and the very old. As a result of this emigration, land is going out of cultivation, houses are becoming dilapidated, and those who remain behind seem downhearted and lonesome."*

It is easy to understand the reasons for such an exodus, both in terms of the poverty and lack of opportunity in this part of County Antrim and the promise of a better life when they arrived on foreign shores. Nor was it so unusual at the time for a young single girl of eighteen like Jennie, to be making the journey. Studies show that while males dominated as immigrants among other nationalities, Irish females, especially young and single, were just as numerous as Irish males. Eldest sons in Ireland usually stayed at home to inherit the family farm but there was no similar incentive for females. In the years after the Great Famine, there was a reluctance to split up family farms and marriage prospects in Ireland had diminished in the years after the Great Famine, as males increasingly postponed or even avoided marriage. Besides, Irish girls were much in demand as maids for the American middle-class.

Jennie, aged 19

For those who went to the USA, it must have been a major culture shock coming from rural Ireland to live in the cosmopolitan urban centres of the United States. There were those like Moey Gill's cousin and classmate in the school at Feystown, Richard Campbell (1870-1935), who went and succeeded; he left Deerpark at the age of seventeen and ended up a Supreme Court Judge in the United States. Undoubtedly there were winners and losers and many failed to realize their dreams.

S.S. Caledonia

From Cairncastle to New York - the Voyage to America in 1907

Jennie left Derry on May 4th, 1907 on the SS Caledonia. The voyage at that time had been cut to nine days, as the trans-Atlantic liners competed to make the quickest crossings. Her travel papers show that she was travelling in the company of a group of local young men who were all heading to Chicago. Among them were Daniel Feeney, James Mulvenna, Hugh McAlister and two brothers, Ned and James Magill, from nearby Loughdoo, who were travelling on to Chicago to join their brother Daniel. Before her departure, Jennie filled in the questionnaire that all immigrants had to complete for inspection when they arrived in the United States. It provides us with a brief description of the young eighteen year old. She was five foot six in height, with fair complexion, dark hair and blue eyes. In her travel trunk she carried her belongings and some mementos of home like the amber glass bread plate, with the words *"Give Us This Day Our Daily Bread"* around its rim; it had been given to her grandmother as a wedding gift. In later years Jennie kept the plate wrapped in flannel cloth in her steamer trunk before eventually it was put on display in the "Treasures from Home" exhibition in the Ellis Island Immigrant Museum. Apart from that, the total cash in her possession amounted to $22.

The S.S.Caledonia on which Jennie travelled, was a new vessel, just launched in 1904; it was 500 feet long and 9,223 tons. It held a total of 1,468 passengers, of whom 869 were 'steerage' or third class, who were confined to the lowest of the three decks. Jennie travelled 'steerage' which was overcrowded and proved to be a nightmare experience for many passengers. In later life she told her niece, Kathleen, that *"the people in steerage became very sick and the smell of human sweat and vomit filled the stale, still air."* She recalled that a man lay dying in a separate section from the women, and she could stand it no longer. She changed into her Sunday best and made for the top deck which was reserved for first class passengers only. Trembling that she might get caught, she was dizzy and nauseous from three and a half days at sea but she was determined to get some relief from the smelly, dark, bumpy bottom deck of the ship. While standing there, a young American couple who were first class passengers, came along and sat on the deck chairs behind her. They struck up a conversation and they invited her for tea. They soon became friends and every afternoon, for the rest of the voyage, Jennie was asked by the *"Yankee couple"* to join them. She would remember their kindness for the rest of her days.

Ellis Island

On arrival, Jennie and the 3rd class passengers were taken by barge from their vessel to be processed in Ellis Island, the Immigrant Station. It had been only 15 years since the first immigrant had passed through its doors, a 15- year old Irish girl, Annie Moore from Cork, accompanied by her two brothers, in 1892. Now it was the turn of the young 18-year old Jennie from Cairncastle. Henry Roth, the Jewish American writer, painted a vivid picture of the human flood that surged into the New World. He set his classic immigration novel "Call it Sleep" in the very month and year when Jennie arrived, May 1907. *"All that day, as on all day since spring began, her decks had been thronged by hundreds upon hundreds of foreigners, natives from almost every land in the world, the jowled close-cropped Teuton, the full-bearded Russian, the scraggly-whiskered Jew, and among them Slovack peasants with docile faces, smooth-cheeked and swarthy Armenians, pimply Greeks, Danes with wrinkled eyelids. All day her decks had been colourful, a matrix of the vivid costumes of other lands, the speckled green-and-yellow aprons, the flowered kerchief, embroidered homespun, the sliver-braided sheepskin vest, the gaudy scarfs, yellow boots, fur caps, caftans, dull gabardines. All day the guttural, the high-pitched voices, the astonished cries, the gasps of wonder, the reiterations of gladness had risen from her decks in a motley billow of sound."* On one day alone in 1907, over eleven thousand passed through the doors of Ellis Island.

In the Registry Room of Ellis Island they were fumigated, checked for contagious diseases, and their papers were inspected to see they were in order. For those who were turned down, Ellis Island became "Heartbreak Island." According to the Ellis Island records, Jennie along with several other young females who had been on board were selected for further interrogation (the authorities were determined to ensure that single females were of *'high moral standing'* and would not fall into prostitution.) Eventually they were given their landing cards and permitted to continue on their way. It was 13th May, 1907 when Jennie first landed in America. Ahead of her lay her future life in the New World.

New York in 1900

Arriving in New York

We can only hazard a guess at the thoughts that raced through the young Jennie's head when she came ashore. The New York that she arrived in was a bustling city, with a population of over four and a half millions; it was already greater than the entire population of Ireland. It was a world away from the Cairncastle that she had left. As early as October 1904 the city had acquired its first Subway. It was already the most culturally diverse city in the world.

On her immigration papers, she had stated that she was going to stay with a friend, Mrs. Frank Walsh, who had sponsored her and lived at Greenpoint, Brooklyn, New York. Mrs. Walsh or 'Tessie' as she was called, had been a cousin of the Wilson family who lived beside Jennie's family at the Meetinghouse; Jennie and later, Mary and her family were to continue their friendship with the Walshs during their years in America. Mr. & Mrs. Frank Walsh later lived in a brownstone house in Manhattan. Jennie's niece, Rose remembered vividly visiting it with the family when she was a little girl. They also had a house in Espous, in upstate New York. The family also would visit Mr. & Mrs. Walsh in their Espous house as they were growing up. Jennie and Mary remained eternally grateful to them for having enabled their arrival and settlement in the USA.

It was shortly after arriving, that Tessie Walsh introduced Jennie to her friend, Kate Lipsett Hagerty, who lived in the Bronx. Soon Jennie met one of her sons named Hugh. They fell in love and married in September, 1908 and

Hugh and Jennie Hagerty, at the time of their marriage September 1908

Hugh and Jennie

set up home in Warburton Avenue, Yonkers. Yonkers borders the New York City borough of the Bronx and is two miles north of Manhattan. Hughie was employed in the city as a steam fitter, working with industrial piping systems.

Mary Arrives 1911

On 21 October 1911, at the age of 20, Mary left the port of Liverpool on board S.S. Campania. It was just six months before the ill fated voyage of the Titanic, which met its fate in April, 1912. S.S. Campania was one of Cunard's major passenger liners, launched in 1892. Accompanying her on the ship was Elizabeth (Lizzie) Wilson who had lived next door in the Meetinghouse. Lizzie, aged 26, was described as "*dressmaker*" on her immigration papers and she had been in New York previously in 1907. She, Mary and Jennie remained very close friends for the rest of their lives in New York and Lizzie was always known as 'Aunt Lizzie' to Mary's children. Aunt Lizzie later married Arthur McGill. On arrival, Mary and Lizzie went to the Walshs in Greenpoint, Brooklyn, just as Jennie had when she first came.

The two sisters, Jennie and Mary, were now reunited on American soil and their lives would be close for the next sixty years or more. Shortly after arrival, each of them had found positions of employment where they could live in with their employers. Domestic Service was the usual role for Irish females when they arrived in America. Both Jennie and Mary, took great satisfaction in their work and

Mary, aged 22

appreciated that they had better opportunities and were more favourably treated by their employers than they would have been at home. Mary's granddaughter, Pat Kelly, writes "*I remember Grandma telling me of taking care of a professor's elderly mother in Glen Falls, New York and how very nice the family was to her and what a beautiful house they owned.*" Apart from providing better opportunities of employment, America also offered greater freedom for young Irish females seeking male partners. They were now free from the constraints of parents and home. Like Jennie before her, Mary met her future husband, John Matthews, within a year of arrival. John was an Irish immigrant too, having originally come from Derry.

"Life revolved round family, neighbourhood, school and church." Pat Kelly

Pat Kelly

In 1913 Mary and John Matthews married and they settled down in Brooklyn, New York where he worked on the subway system. Upon marrying it was the custom for Irish women in America to stay at home and give up work. Married women had to raise their families and seldom worked outside the home. Mary gave birth to 11 children, among them two sets of twins. Eight of the family, four boys (Jack, Charles, Hugh and Thomas) and four girls, (Mae, Anita, Dorothy and Rose) survived childhood, but she lost a second set of twin boys; they were very small and both died within 24 hours of each other when they were almost three months old. Her last child, Kathleen, died when she was a year old. Mary's grand daughter Pat recalls Mary in her later years. "*Very rarely did Grandma ever talk about her life in Ireland. She was the type of person*

S.S. Campania

Sr. Lawrence Marie (Anita)

who lived for the present and her children and grandchildren. Grandma was a great cook. I remember her telling me how she learned how to make spaghetti and meatballs on her own and that it was so good, her Italian neighbour liked Grandma's better than her own. There was nothing she couldn't make. I had so many favourites – especially her ginger snaps and shortbread cookies."

There were hard times for many during the Depression Years of the 1930's, but these were particularly difficult times for both Jennie and Mary. Both lost their husbands within a few years of each other and as a result, they both had to go out to work to make ends meet. Jennie's husband, Hughie, went off to work one morning and collapsed on the sidewalk and died of a stroke. They had been unable to have children and Jennie was left on her own. She found work as a housekeeper - first for the clergy in rectories, then later for wealthy couples on Fifth Avenue. During her lifetime as a maid in glamorous Manhattan, she had many marriage proposals but declined them all. It was in 1934 that Hughie had died. Three years later, Mary's husband, John, died. Both sisters had been widowed in their mid forties.

Pat recalls *"Grandma spent most of her time taking care of her large family. When Grandpa died in 1937, circumstances changed drastically for Grandma and she had to clean office buildings and movie theatres during the evenings and early morning hours, while the older children took care of the younger ones. Even though it was during the Depression, Grandma would never have considered taking any help from any welfare organization; instead Grandma, the three older boys and Mom, all worked to support the family. Grandma was a very independent, self-sufficient person. Of course, after Grandpa died money was tight, but Mom told me they had plenty to eat and great clothes. Grandma could sew, crochet, knit, everything. She would make a lot of the girls' clothes, even coats and suits. They always looked smart. She lived in a six family apartment house on Stewart St. in Brooklyn for many years and I have many fond memories since I visited her constantly there.*

Sr. Jean Dorothy

I spent many weekends with my Grandma and always was ready to pack my little suitcase and go over. My brothers would rarely stay with Grandma – they wouldn't leave Mom. I can actually visualize the Stewart St. house. It was the design

Mary and John Matthews at the time of their marriage, 1913

John and Mary Matthews with sons Jack, Hugh and Charles

Row 1: Jackie Matthews
Row2: L-R. Mary, Bridget Matthews, Jennie and Kathleen Lipsett
Row 3: John Matthews, Charles Magill

of what we call a railroad apartment. You entered the dining room and to the right was the kitchen and to the side a bathroom. Going through the dining room was one bedroom after the other – I believe three and then you went into the living room……. We always would have Christmas Eve with my father's mother but Christmas was always with Grandma."

Religion played a very important role in the life of Mary, as it did in all Irish American communities. Pat remembers, *"Grandma was very religious and attended for years one of the most beautiful churches I can remember. It was called Our Lady of Lourdes. My Mom was married there and though the pictures are in black and white, I can remember how gorgeous it was. The ceiling was hand painted with different saints, the altar was marble and the grotto in the back of the altar was so very beautiful. How I loved going with Grandma to this church*." Two of Mary's daughters, Anita in 1939 and Dotty in 1941, became nuns and entered the Order of Saint Joseph.

World War 11 brought further changes to the family. Pat writes "*Mom and Aunt Rose both mentioned when Uncle David Magill came over to visit the family in New York during World War II and how much they enjoyed his visit when he stayed with the family in Stewart St. As you know, unfortunately his ship was sunk going back."* All four of Mary's sons served during World War II in the Army and fortunately all came home safely. Tom was the last one to enter at 17. The older three were all sent overseas but Tom stayed in the U.S.

Coming Home

Jennie and Mary kept in regular contact with home through letter writing and heard all the news from the Meetinghouse. Over the years there had been visitors from home. At the end of 1923, one of their young brothers, Davy came from Ireland to stay with Jennie in Ash Street, Yonkers during his six month boxing campaign in New York and he met up with his new American nephews and nieces; by this time Mary had a family of 6 children. It must have been a busy house with the comings and goings of friends and fans. The sports writer Jim Edgar who had followed Davy's boxing fortunes in New York, recalling the farewell party before Davy's return to Ireland, wrote *"I had quite a social night at the home of Davy's sister, where our hostess was the acme of lavish Irish hospitality. The sports writers, who had been boosting Davy to the clouds, shed many an inky tear over his leaving."* Davy's younger brother Charlie, had already arrived in Canada in 1923 and he too would eventually cross to stay in New York.

For Jennie and Mary, they looked forward to returning to visit the Meetinghouse. The local press reported their visit home in 1954. *"Homeland Revisited after Forty Years" "Mrs. Jane Hagerty and her sister, Mrs. Mary Matthews, sisters of Constable Jim Magill, the well known boxer, are on a visit home from New York. It is over forty years since their previous visit to Ireland,"* reported the Ballymena Observer on August 13, 1954. That was true in the case of Mary, but not for Jennie who had returned earlier.

Davy in New York, 1924, with his nieces Mae, Dotty and Anita

Back row L-R: Breige (Mary's sister-in-law), Anita (Sr. Lawrence Marie), Jennie, Joan (Mary's daughter-in-law), Mary, Dotty (Sr. Jean Dorothy), Rose, Mae and Helen Holidak (friend of Jennie)
Front row L-R; John, Pat and Robert (1954)

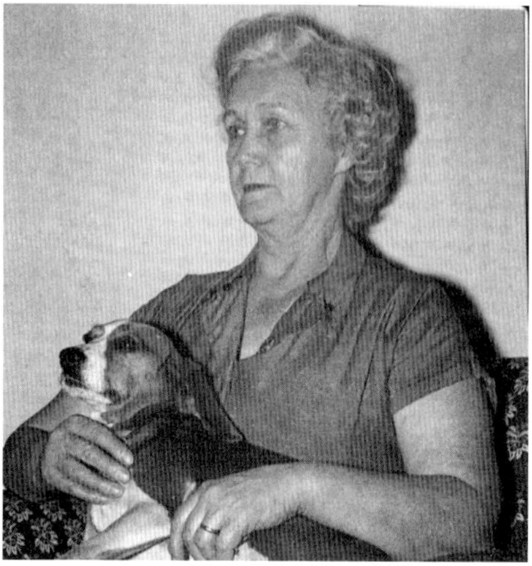

Jennie, posing with her employer's dog in his apartment off Fifth Avenue, mid-town Manhattan

Jennie and Mary in Old Age

Pat recalled *"As previously mentioned Aunt Jennie was a constant in Grandma and her children's lives. She always spent her time off with Grandma so it was natural that when she retired from her position in 1973, she moved in with Grandma and the two ladies lived together for many years."* They were a great source of comfort to each other in their closing years. Mary became very ill in her late eighties and died at the age of 89 on 22 November, 1980.

Aunt Jennie then went to a nursing home called Jeanne Jugan which was run by the Little Sisters of the Poor. *"What I best remember about Aunt Jennie was the blue dye she always had put in her pure white hair, her generosity, taking trips to Ireland, and she was the best pastry cook in the world. She made deserts to actually die for. She loved Grandma and Uncle Charlie's families and spending time with them was her great joy.* She is fondly remembered by her niece, Kathleen, as *"a warm, energetic, intelligent and a good looking woman; she got along with everyone and was much loved. Aunt Jennie was very pro education and one of the most positive and hopeful people I've ever known."* Jennie died on 20 October, 1985 and at the age of 96, she had lived longest of all the family. As the eldest, she had always been the matriarch of the family. She was above all the person who united the Magill family on both sides of the Atlantic.

"Moey Gill" and Jennie

Charlie in Canada

Charlie, the cowboy, riding a steer in Canada at the Bunk House where he stayed as a harvester

Charlie arrives in Canada

It was August 1923, a few months before Davy would set out on his boxing campaign in New York, that his younger brother Charlie arrived in Canada. He was already well travelled. He had served in France, Belgium, Italy and Egypt during World War One. When the War ended, he had returned to Ireland and joined the RIC but a year after the force was disbanded in August, 1922, he determined to go on his travels again.

At the age of 27, he crossed the Atlantic on the S.S. Canada, leaving the local port of Larne, on August 12th, 1923, bound for Quebec, Canada. There were few opportunities at home for work. The family farm was not large enough at twenty acres to support anyone else and labouring wages on his father's road works could not match his earlier earnings. The Canadian authorities were keen to attract immigrant workers and the local press carried adverts like the one opposite, offering free land, work and golden opportunities for farm-workers. The voyage across the Atlantic lasted a week and he landed on August 19th. at Lake Erie and was ferried to Buffalo and from there on to Quebec. On his 'Ocean Arrival' form which all entrants to Canada had to complete, Charlie declared that he was going to Winnipeg, which was a railroad journey through the vastness of Canada of nearly 2,000 miles. Coming from a farming background, he stated that his intended occupation was *'Harvester.'*

Farm Lands in Canada

THE

CANADIAN PACIFIC RAILWAY

Colonization Department

MAKE IT EASY

for the farmer and farm worker

TO SETTLE IN CANADA.

Easy terms of payment spread over 20 years if desired. Loans to approved settlers in certain districts towards the cost of permanent improvements.

Excellent land within easy distance of schools, churches, markets, towns, etc. Farms can be selected in the best agricultural districts.

CONDUCTED PARTIES TO VIEW THE LAND AT FREQUENT INTERVALS.

Regular steamship sailings from Liverpool, Glasgow and Southampton.

Money transferred at lowest rates

For full particulars and illustrated pamphlets apply to:

The Canadian Pacific Railway,

Colonization and Development Department,

41-43 Victoria Street, BELFAST, or 62 Charing Cross, LONDON, S.W.1

Advertisement, Larne Times, 1923

Charlie's daughter, Kathleen, recalls that *"In the 1920's my father found it difficult to find work in Eastern Canada. He lived for a time in Toronto and I have pages from his yellowed notebook, listing members of the athletic association as well as names and addresses of acquaintances he made while in the city. One picture of him there shows him wearing what looks like a black beaver hat and coat for protection from the Canadian frost." "In search of steady work, he migrated to the Canadian mid-west. ..... he decided to say he was a Scotch Presbyterian when*

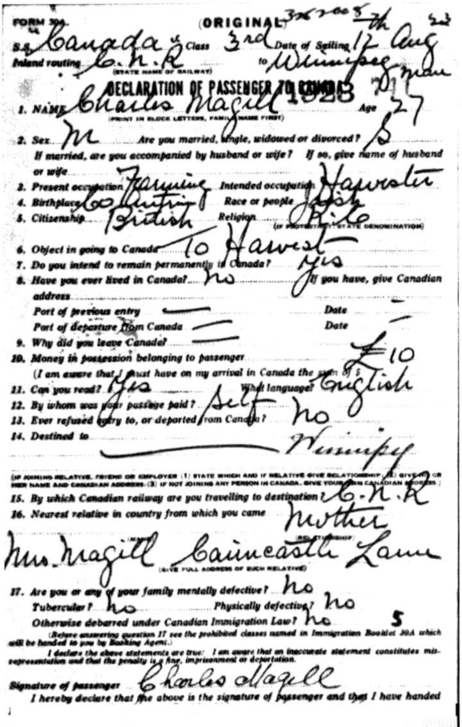
FORM 30A (ORIGINAL) 326005 7th 23

S.S. Canada Class 3rd Date of Sailing 17 Aug

Inland routing C.N.R to Winnipeg Man

(STATE NAME OF RAILWAY)

DECLARATION OF PASSENGER TO CANADA 1928

1. NAME Charles Magill Age 27

(PRINT IN BLOCK LETTERS, FAMILY NAME FIRST)

2. Sex M Are you married, single, widowed or divorced? S

If married, are you accompanied by husband or wife? If so, give name of husband or wife

3. Present occupation Farming Intended occupation Harvester

4. Birthplace Co Antrim Race or people Irish

5. Citizenship British Religion

(IF PROTESTANT STATE DENOMINATION)

6. Object in going to Canada To Harvest

7. Do you intend to remain permanently in Canada? Yes

8. Have you ever lived in Canada? No If you have, give Canadian address

Port of previous entry — Date —

Port of departure from Canada — Date

9. Why did you leave Canada?

10. Money in possession belonging to passenger £10

(I am aware that I must have on my arrival in Canada the sum of $)

11. Can you read? Yes What language? English

12. By whom was your passage paid? Self

13. Ever refused entry to, or deported from Canada? No

14. Destined to Winnipeg

(IF JOINING RELATIVE, FRIEND OR EMPLOYER (1) STATE WHICH AND IF RELATIVE GIVE RELATIONSHIP, (2) GIVE HIS OR HER NAME AND CANADIAN ADDRESS. (3) IF NOT JOINING ANY PERSON IN CANADA, GIVE YOUR OWN CANADIAN ADDRESS.)

15. By which Canadian railway are you travelling to destination? C.N.R

16. Nearest relative in country from which you came Mother

Mrs. Magill Cairncastle Lane

(GIVE FULL ADDRESS OF SUCH RELATIVE)

17. Are you or any of your family mentally defective? No

Tubercular? No Physically defective? No

Otherwise debarred under Canadian Immigration Law? No

(Before answering question 17 see the prohibited classes named in Immigration Booklet 30A which will be handed to you by Booking Agent.)

I declare the above statements are true: I am aware that an inaccurate statement constitutes misrepresentation and that the penalty is a fine, imprisonment or deportation.

Signature of passenger Charles Magill

I hereby declare that the above is the signature of passenger and that I have handed

Canadian harvesters - Charlie 4th from left

Harvesting Canadian wheat

he settled in Edmonton to make it easier to get a job as a ranch hand.... In Edmonton he was called 'Scottie' by his bunkmates." He found work as a farm-hand in a place called Retlaw, (Walter spelled backwards), so called in honour of a railroad official named, Walter R. Baker. Once a bustling settlement, it had been bypassed by the new water canal and by the 1920's had become a ghost town.

Life in the Canadian prairies was tough. Charlie had been there just about a week, when he experienced a locust plague and was terrified, thinking it was a tornado. Winters were hard in Alberta and temperatures could drop to under -50 degrees Centigrade; summer temperatures could reach as high as 40 degrees Centigrade. It was here that Charlie found work on a cattle ranch as a cowboy. He had grown up accustomed to working with horses in Ireland and had joined the army as a cavalryman in 1915. Now he was a cowboy in Canada, herding cattle on horseback and carrying out the normal routines of the farmhand, from branding cattle to mending fences.

Charlie arrives in New York, 1929

Among the many exhibits in New York's Ellis Island Museum which document the arrival in the United States of the teeming millions of immigrants, is item number 78 representing Irish immigration; it is a pony shoe, poignantly labelled:

"Father's gift to emigrant son before Leaving Cairncastle, Charles Magill.

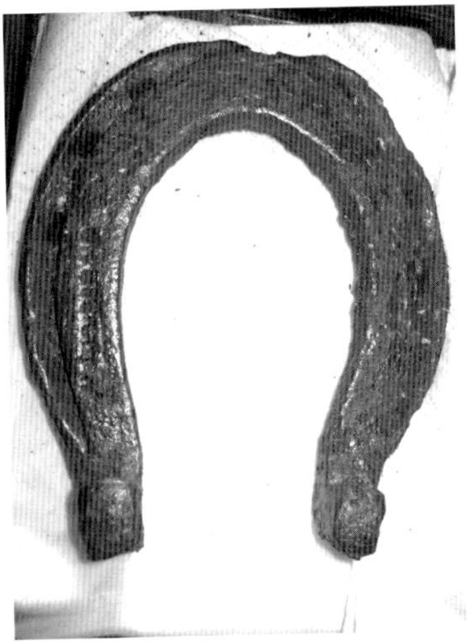

It was some five years after he had arrived in Canada, that Charlie crossed the border and came to the USA. Friends of his sister Jennie, Delia and John Lipsett, had moved to Greenwich, Connecticut and Charlie was invited to meet up with his sister who had left Ireland when he was just a ten year old boy. Not only was Charlie delighted to meet up with his sister but he was also introduced to Kathleen, a niece of the Lipsetts. She was an American girl of Irish parents who was training to be a nurse. Charlie later said that it was love at first sight and whether or not it was helped by his big sister's match-making, they fell in love. They planned to marry after Kathleen would graduate as a nurse. Charlie didn't meet with universal approval from the Lipsett family. Some disapproved as he was twelve years older, probably gassed or brain damaged in World War One and an immigrant without formal education. But the marriage went ahead and they married in Saint Mary's, Greenwich, Connecticut in 1929. Charlie and Kathleen went to live with Jennie and her husband in their apartment on Warburton Avenue in Yonkers and in January 1934, he became an American citizen. This was how Charlie came to live in the United States. If he hadn't met his wife, he later claimed that he would never have left Canada.

The Immigrant's Experience

The year 1929 was also the year of the Wall Street Crash and the beginnings of the Great Depression. Unemployment in the U.S.A. reached 12 million and times were desperate. "*My parents*" wrote Kathleen "*went hungry many times during the Depression Years before their children were born. ..... there were long lines of impoverished people waiting on Broadway in Manhattan for free soup and kitchen food... my father worked as a janitor for the Knights of Columbus, collected glass bottles for deposits and did odd jobs wherever and whenever he could find them.*" Times improved when he found regular employment as a machinist in the Otis Elevator Company.

Life was tough for immigrants in other ways. There was much prejudice and bigotry directed against them. Charlie had been in Canada at the time but he remembered how the execution of the two Italian immigrants, Sacco and Vanzetti, in 1927, had a chilling effect on him as an immigrant. The Ku Klux Klan was active in its violence against Blacks, Jews and Catholics. Nearer home was the Yankee contempt for the newcomers. The more overt forms of anti Irish bigotry with the 'No Irish need apply' signs and cartoons ridiculing the impoverished Catholic Irish may have lessened but prejudice was still very real.

Charlie as he appears on his citizenship papers in 1934

Immigrants like Charlie flocked into the city of Yonkers. As his daughter Kathleen recalls "*Italians claimed the construction industry, the Irish the liquor and bar business... The Chinese had laundries and restaurants. Blacks and Hispanics were scattered in low paying jobs in the hotel, restaurant and tourist industry. Like the majority of Irish immigrants in Yonkers, most of the Italian migrants were poor, Catholic, had big families and worked at unskilled and semi skilled labouring jobs. -though they often lacked the English language.... As an Irish immigrant in Yonkers I felt intimidated by Yankees later known as Wasps, but felt a close alliance with Jews. The Irish Catholics and the Russian Jews were on the same side in most political battles for power and prosperity in the city of Yonkers. The Yankees looked down on us both.*" At least the Irish immigrants had the advantage over the other national groups, of having English.

Kathleen paints a nostalgic picture of the long twilight evenings of her childhood in the forties in her neighbourhood, in Yonkers. Since electricity was expensive, people sat in the dusk of evening without electric lights or the background noise of the radio. "*We listened to the adults talking and joined them in singing Irish songs and reciting poetry and sayings. Often we heard our neighbours laughing, talking and singing. I thought the Russian men sounded beautiful as they harmonized songs in a language that was distant and mysterious to me as the moon and the stars. Our Italian neighbours could be heard on very still nights dancing and laughing at summer wedding gatherings on the tiny streets off Elm. Their Neapolitan love songs and dramatic opera solos touched my heart and tingled my nervous system. I wondered what the words meant in English and believed that such beautiful music must have wonderful words to accompany it. Sometimes the "colored" people in the building two houses down from my own on Locust Hill Avenue, used to sit on the front stoop (steps) and sing joyous and sad songs in tumbling profusions and often people passing by them would stop and listen and clap in approval. Some of the blues songs had slowed down Irish melodies while others had a throaty, sobbing rhythm that almost broke my little girl's heart, especially the one that said, "Sometimes, I feel like a motherless child."*

Charlie in Yonkers

Charlie took an active role in the community and in trade unionism. He was an ardent member of the CIO (Congress of Industrial Organizations) and actively campaigned for workers' rights. He was much in demand as a speaker at union meetings and rallies. Kathleen remembered marching in the picket line with her father and travelling with him many times to Harlem, New York, on union business. *"At that time,"* she recalls *"blacks (called coloreds) were discriminated against by companies and unions. My father and his wonderful Scottish boss, Mr. David Barbour, had managed to transfer one black man to their floor at the Otis Elevator Company in Yonkers. Over-qualified as a college graduate, he had previously been relegated to clean the latrines by the company. After one year of experience as a machinist on Dave and Charlie's floor, they helped the young man to secure a management position in another company."*

When the AFL (American Federation of Labor) and the CIO considered joining together into one larger and more powerful union, Charlie spoke at workers' gatherings all over the city. Kathleen watched him actively persuade members of both unions to accept their amalgamation into one union. Eventually the workers voted for the merger and the new AFL-CIO was born.

He was active in the local community. During World War 11, he volunteered to act as an air warden. When the sirens warned of unidentified aircraft overhead during the night, he would rush from his bed and go to patrol the streets to enforce the 'blackout' and escort people safely home.

"My father was friendly, courteous and accepting of other people's cultures" Kathleen recalls. *"He helped found the Irish Unified Society for Irish Catholics, Jews and Protestants in Yonkers. Women and men were officers and I was the first female assistant to the Grand Marshall of the Saint Patrick's Day Parade our society organized in the city of Yonkers. Two elderly Russian Jewish ladies*

Charlie in his Otis Elevator work clothes, showing his AFL-CIO union badge

who were honorary members, enjoyed the forbidden treat of having American pork hot dogs during the celebrations. During the McCarthy Era in the US after World War 11, when people were being labelled communist and there was growing suspicion of our Russian neighbours in Yonkers, my father would calm his frightened neighbours explaining to them that our Russians in Yonkers, New York, were devout Orthodox Christians. He helped the Russian immigrants to mainstream, once they spoke English, to explain who they were and their ancient venerable Orthodox faith."

He became a popular unofficial mediator of local disputes. He had a remarkable ability to understand different points of view, a talent that may have been due to the values he grew up with in Cairncastle as much as to his travels and experiences in adult life. On one particular occasion he helped to dissipate a riot between the 'coloureds' and the Italian born immigrants. His achievement was all the more remarkable because the blacks and Italians, probably only understood half what he said in his Northern Irish accent.

Charlie was above all a family man. His first child, Mary Patricia, was born six years into the marriage in May 1935, and then Charles, Kathleen and James followed to complete the family. As Kathleen recalls, *"He taught us the songs and stories of Ireland and frequently recited poetry from memory. He was a great joke teller and people were attracted to his humour and warmth. He told us we came from a land of saints and scholars, but due to our deportment wouldn't be saints "but by Jesus I'll have scholars." Some of us became scholars - but no saints so far."* It was a home which placed great emphasis on education. When he became angry with his misbehaving children, he would sigh *"Is this what I crossed an ocean for?"* He would take the children fishing off the pier and for long Sunday afternoon walks. It was around the kitchen table he would draw on his wide repertoire of stories; these would range from the legends of Finn MacCool and Irish mythology to stories of his travels in Egypt and other exotic lands. But these were stories that would teach lessons and hand down the wisdom of one generation to the next. It was a household that talked politics and history. The course of American politics and world events, were followed closely and discussed round the kitchen table. In the thirties, it was Roosevelt who was hailed as a hero and his New Deal supported enthusiastically. Then it was the turn of the War, Senator McCarthy and Civil Rights but "Ireland" seldom left the kitchen table.

Kathleen, Mary Patricia, Kathleen, Charles

Like most families they had their good and bad times. Tragedy struck in 1965 when Mary Patricia, the first child and now a maths teacher, died of a brain tumour when she was only 33. Charlie himself died in 1972, at the age of 76, and his wife Kathleen in 1986. But to repeat what his daughter Kathleen said "*Those of my family, who had arrived in America .... were all willing to 'tough it out' here in the New World. A few went back on boats for visits, but no immigrants in my immediate family ever stayed in the old country after living and working in America.*"

In many ways the lives of Jane, Mary and Charlie were similar to the experience of all immigrants throughout history. They had left Ireland and settled in America, but if their heads told them that their future was in their new country, their hearts drew them back to the old country. "As an immigrant you always have one foot stuck in both countries" (Anne-Marie). This nostalgia for home is well captured in the following poem of Charlie's daughter, Kathleen.

James and Charles

Mary Patricia

Kathleen, Charles, Charles (sen), Kathleen, James

Memories Of The Light Under The Kitchen Door

They all clung together in that kitchen,
Weathering the storms and calms of the non-Celtic
world surrounding them.
They were Irish, Welsh, Cornwall English and
Scottish,
With accents, pauses, phrases and words that held
exotic sounds and rhythms.

Their ritualistic drinking of cups of tea celebrated
all rites of passage.
Sorrows were shared and hushed and soothed over
those teacups.
Shame was dissipated in quiet stirrings of the
sugar lumps.

Joy and triumph were poured into rounds and rounds
of hot steaming liquid.
Scones and soda bread helped to satisfy deep longings
for the tastes of home.

The kitchen light was unable to match the brilliance
of their conversations about travel, history,
literature, religion and politics.
The light was tolerant of their shady stories about
Con O'Neill, Mary Never Wed, church scandals,
subway robberies and Celtic rogues.
Sarcasm, wit and mysticism flashed by in quick
succession in songs, sayings and many a
conversation about Yeats, Pearse, Burns and
Jefferson.

Sometimes brooding thoughts sprung from the hearts
of the immigrants,
like black seeds of pain in aching places.
But hope was always at that table and shared,
as they passed the butter and described their dreams and triumphs.
How lucky I was to sleep in the bedroom next to the kitchen!

Through the slit of the closed door I felt their
warmth and heard their laughter.
I gloried in the sounds of words like Sallagh, Dundee,
Drumnagreagh, Ballygally and Carnlough.
Utterly content, I would drift off to sleep amidst
their Celtic charms and gentility.

1983 Kathleen A. Magill

Rose

Peggy Rooney, 1938

Rose (1909-1983)

Rose was born in April 1909, the second girl after a succession of seven boys. Just three days after Christmas in that same year, her two year old sister Annie had died. In 1911 there was another addition to the family when another daughter, also called Annie, was born. Six months later, the eldest girl at home, Mary, left to join her sister Jennie in America, leaving Rose and Annie, the two baby sisters, to be brought up in a home of seven older brothers.

Rose was a bright, intelligent girl who had a flair for mathematics and possibly this led to a lifetime career. She passed the exam to gain entry to the Post Office and just like many others before her in the family, Rose too had to leave home to find work. She went to London to work in the Accounts Branch of the Post Office. There, like many other Irish girls who had just arrived, she found lodgings in Hammersmith Convent.

At the Post Office, she recalled having met the two elderly sisters of Michael Collins, who were still working there in the 1930's. She soon had a wide circle of friends. One of her closest friends was Nan McGill whose father John had come from the Braid and had joined the Metropolitan Police. This was a friendship that was to last for the rest of their lives.

Peggy Rooney and Rose

She soon befriended Peggy Rooney, a girl from Belfast, who had also come to work in the Post Office as a shorthand typist.
London in the Thirties was an exciting city to live in. The young ladies visited all the sites and got to know its attractions. It was also a world away from home. Peggy used to relate the story of her introduction to Hyde Park as an innocent Irish Catholic girl. On her first visit, sitting on a bench, she was accosted by a 'lady of ill-repute' who ordered her to move on 'as that was her patch'. For Rose and Peggy, one of the highlights of their weekend was their Sunday trip to Speakers' Corner in Hyde Park where they would hear the various orators and hecklers; Fr. Vincent McNabb was one of their heroes.

Jim was a regular visitor to London in the thirties where he was one of the star attractions in the boxing ring at the Albert Hall. There were frequent meetings with him at Euston Station when he was either arriving or departing for home. Peggy would soon get to know the Magill brothers. It was Jim who first won her attention. They went out on a date but it was on a visit with Rose back to Cairncastle that she was introduced to his older brother, John, and love blossomed. Peggy was fond in later years of recalling her first meeting with her future father-in-law, Charlie. The young city girl was taken aback when he asked "*Can you make a shirt out of a flour bag*?" (In those days flour bags had always been put to good use by the resourceful farmer's wife who would bleach them, remove the stitching and make them into sheets, pillow cases aprons or even shirts). Cairncastle was indeed a world away from London but Peggy left office life there to marry John in 1938; Jim was to be best man, a role he fulfilled on many occasions.

Rose was keen to return home too as her parents were getting on in years and she was able to get a transfer back to the Post Office in Belfast.

5 Pat in Western Australia

In the Perth suburb of Karrakatta in Western Australia, there is an unusual two -sided headstone in the cemetery there. On one side the inscription reads: "CONNOLLY" and on the other "MAGILL." This was Pat Magill's final resting place and therein lies a story. What follows is an attempt to piece together Pat's life, after he left Cairncastle. At the age of 24, Pat sailed from London to Fremantle, Western Australia on October 14, 1926 on the S.S. Beltana. A steamship built in 1909 specifically for the Peninsular & Orient Service, which specialised in the emigrant trade, it carried about 1,100 passengers, over 200 of whom were children. The "Beltana" had basic cabin accommodation for up to 350 3rd-class passengers and temporary dormitories for an additional 750 emigrants in the hold; this would be removed to make way for a cargo of frozen meats and dairy products on the homeward voyage. She carried a crew of 260.

The Passenger List for the S.S. Beltana describes Pat as a *"farmer, age twenty four."* He had been born a week before St. Patrick's Day on 10 March, 1902, coming between John and Jim in the family. The majority of his fellow passengers were also young men in their twenties, labourers and tradesmen who were travelling in the hope of finding a better life. There were some wives and families accompanying their husbands and other unattached females who worked as cooks, waitresses and embroiderers. The economic situation in Britain and Ireland in the years after World War One had made work difficult to find. The demobilisation of troops returning from war and the closure of wartime industries caused painful adjustments to the economy. The 'Land fit for heroes' did not materialise and 1926, the year of Pat's departure, was the year of the General Strike. Pat had experienced the hard times. After he left the RUC, 2 August 1924 he had gone to London and in a letter home to his brother John, dated 3 January1925, he noted that he "*had been sick for four days and lost my job through a lack in trade.*" He added that he had to postpone a fight due to this illness. We next hear of him on March 3, 1925 in a bout in Leipzig in Germany against Sabri Maher (Turkey) and in May 20, 1926 against Joe Crampton (Oldham) in Liverpool. But boxing too was affected by the hard economic times in the early twenties. Promoters were having difficulties paying purses and staging bills at a time when unemployment was hitting attendances. Five months later Pat had left for Australia.

The Voyage to Australia

On 14 October, 1926 S.S. Beltana left London. The voyage would take nine weeks and three days before it reached its final port of Sydney. While most vessels now took the shorter route through the Suez Canal, this ship went via Lisbon to the Cape of Good Hope and then across the Indian Ocean to Fremantle, Melbourne and Sydney. Along with Pat were three other Belfast men, Samuel Murray, Thomas Monaghan and William Saunders. All four told Mr. Albert J. White the Superintendent in charge of Migrants on board, that they wanted 'bush work' when they got to Australia and they wished to be placed together. The Australian authorities were keen to attract tradesmen and farm workers after the loss of so many Australian men in World War 1.

Conditions on board for the third class traveller were spartan. One passenger told how "*The upper deck was First Class passengers, and us common migrants had the main decks. All our cabins were built around the cargo space, four bunks on each side of the cabins, two high.*" There was much overcrowding, with eight people to a cabin and the absence of proper ventilation led to an unhealthy atmosphere which at times was unbearable. Mr. White reported that "*Seasickness was prevalent in the first week of the voyage and a handful of the passengers continued to suffer especially when the sea was slightly rough.*" There were two deaths on board and both were buried at sea. But for the majority of passengers, the biggest problem of the nine week voyage was boredom. To relieve the monotony, all sorts of entertainments were organized. Open-air concerts, fancy dress balls and evening functions such as dances and parlour games were performed. Mr. White wrote that "*A boxing ring was set up, where many interesting boxing exhibitions took place, to the great delight of the passengers.*" No doubt Pat was one of the star attractions.

On 11 November, Armistice Day, a service was held and everyone observed the "two minutes' silence." "*On the morning of 22 November last, the weather being fine, we were able to have a close view of St. Paul's Island.* (a volcanic island halfway between South Africa and Australia in the Indian Ocean) *This occasion was greatly appreciated by the passengers,*" noted Mr. White in his report. Finally they arrived at Fremantle 21 November, 1926. Pat and his fellow passengers all arrived safe and sound after their ordeal, with the exception of one unfortunate young man. On leaving the Beltana, he was interrogated by a Customs Officer, as his clothing appeared unusually bulky. When searched he was found to have two blankets, the property of P.& O., round his hips under his trousers. He was sentenced to two months' imprisonment.

Passengers aboard S.S. Beltana, 1926

Ahead of the migrants was an unknown world. Mr.White had reported that *"a very great number of the migrants were intensely interested to know more about the country to which they were going."* Emigration from Ireland to Australia at this time was a big challenge. The United States was closer and known as a prosperous country where there were close contacts, but Australia was much farther away. Australia in the 1920's encouraged immigrants, especially from Britain, in its "white Australia policy", through assisted passage schemes where passengers were given £6 to cover half the cost of the minimum passage.

Having arrived in the port of Fremantle, twelve miles south of Perth, Pat and the new arrivals went to the Migrants' Hostel where they boarded as they awaited final instructions to proceed to the country. West Australia was vast, covering an area that was about half the size of the United States. There is no record of his experience in the Bush but from the little we know, Pat later ended up in Perth. A report in the press in December of 1927, describes him boxing there and over the next years he became well known in the boxing rings of Perth. Some of his bouts were reported in the pages of the local newspaper, "The West Australian." Frequently fighting several times in one week, he often spent more time in the ring in brutal contests than in the gym. He was up there with the top heavyweights in Perth, West Australia, but was unable to break into the top rank; he would spend the next years as a 'journeyman boxer,' willing to take on any challengers in the boxing venues of Perth.

Kalgoorlie Goldfields

"Some made their fortune, thousands did not and many died trying"

On 21 January 1933, Pat married Edith Bennett in Perth. His marriage certificate shows him described as "Prospector." His wife Edith was six years older than he was, at 36, and had been born in Auckland in New Zealand. They are both listed in the Electoral Roll of 1936 as living in Coolgardie, where Pat is recorded as a "Miner" and Edith as "Home duties."

His last appearance in the ring that we know of, seems to have been in March 1933, and with his boxing career at an end, Pat had gone to live and work in the gold mining area of Kalgoorlie. It was almost 400 miles northeast of Perth, on the edge of the desert. It was a new town which had grown up around the gold

fields there; these were opened up in the Gold Rush which started after three Irishmen, Patrick Hannan, Tom Flanagan and Dan O'Shea had noticed signs of gold in the area in 1893. They were followed by hundreds of prospectors swarming into the area in search of fortune. During the 1890s, the Goldfields area boomed as a whole, with an area population exceeding 200,000, mainly prospectors. Of those who travelled to the Goldfields, it was said, some made their fortune, thousands did not and many died trying.

Life in these mining towns was tough. Kalgoorlie had all the appearances of a frontier town in the Wild West and gained a notorious reputation for its bandits and brothels. The small mining town of Coolgardie where Pat settled, was some 24 miles from Kalgoorlie. In its heyday Coolgardie had a population of 15,000, but the gold soon began to run out and by the First World War many of its residents had left for other towns where the gold was still plentiful. Its population slipped to around 200 and it became a virtual ghost town. As if to illustrate this decline, in March 1896 Coolgardie's main street had been lit by electric light, but by April 1924 the same street was lit by four hurricane lamps.

Many of the first miners had died of typhoid from drinking contaminated water and miners fell victim to respiratory diseases from breathing in the dust in the mines; they often had to endure extreme temperatures which ranged from 100 to 30 degrees fahrenheit. They were constantly working in the water of half flooded shafts. In 1926 the government ordered that all mine employees should be x-rayed. A great number of workers were found to have tuberculosis and had to leave the mines immediately. Many had come there to seek their fortunes but few succeeded and many perished. Such work and his lifestyle would take its toll on Pat himself.

MAGILL: On May 26, 1950, suddenly, at Scarborough, Patrick Magill, dearly loved son of Mrs. Annie Magill (of County Antrim, Ireland), and the late Charles Magill, fond cousin of W. (Bill) Connolly, of 35 Clarence-street, Mt. Lawley; aged 47 years.
R.I.P.

Notice in the "West Australian"

On July 10, 1941, at the age of thirty nine, he joined the Australian Army at Claremont, West Australia but already his health was breaking down. Years of hard work and hard living had taken their

William (Bill) Connolly, Perth, 1938

toll and he was admitted to hospital suffering from bronchitis. He was discharged from the army after little more than six months, on January 16, 1942, as medically unfit. His service record confirms that his wife was Edith and that they had one child, who according to some sources was a daughter. It also provides us with the only surviving photograph of him. It appears that he returned to Perth and was living in the suburb of Scarborough. Pat's condition deteriorated in the following years, though his death at the age of forty eight, on May 26, 1950, was regarded as sudden. The death certificate tells us that he died of lobar pneumonia, a condition which many miners fell victim to. Sadly, it records that there was no known next of kin.

Throughout his days in Australia, one close friendship that remained to the end was with his cousin William (Bill) Connolly. When Bill's father had died in 1919 and his mother Agnes re-married, some of his family had left Belfast to go to live with their aunt, 'Moey Gill' at the Meetinghouse. As their late father's only sister, she looked after the boys and both families had got to know each other well. Bill had come from Ireland in 1928, two years after Pat and he too settled in West Australia. It was Bill who made the funeral arrangements and placed his death notice in the 'West Australian' newspaper.

Pat Magill in Australian Army, July 1941

Writing early in 2009, Bill's daughter, Mary-Attracta Connolly takes up the story:

"I am thinking that Pat and Dad would have caught up with each other if they were in Perth at the same time – our Dad used to move around for work in his early years here - but I am not sure how close they were. However, I recall that my Dad always spoke very fondly of the Magill clan so I imagine that he and Pat would have been close. I am also sure that Dad would have felt a keen sense of kinship, as Pat's only family in Australia, to make sure that his funeral and burial were attended to properly.

Regarding Pat's name on the grave headstone, this was not actually something that Dad had put in his will; it was something my brothers and I did. When our Mum died in 1992 and both Mum and Dad were interred in the same grave, my brothers and I decided that it was important, when we erected a headstone, to acknowledge that Pat Magill was also buried there. I recall making some attempts to find out if Pat had any family in Kalgoorlie at the time but, as we had no names to go by, nothing was discovered. However, we thought that by putting Pat's name on the gravestone that, should a relative of his do some investigating one day then they would be able to at least find his resting place .... the headstone is double sided, our parents' names are on one side and Patrick Magill's is on the other."

6 Seven Sons, Seven Policemen

While this was a boxing family, it was also a police family. If not unique it was certainly unusual that all seven sons joined the police. Together their careers spanned the years 1914 to 1962, policing in all parts of Ireland, north and south during some of the most turbulent times in the 20th Century. They saw service in the R.I.C. (Royal Irish Constabulary) before 1922 and then the R.U.C. (Royal Ulster Constabulary).

If there had been a family tradition, it was limited and fairly tenuous. A cousin of Charlie's on his mother Rosie's side, himself called Charles Magill of Crucie (Ballyruther), had been a member of the police. RIC records show that he had joined in February 1879 and had been stationed in County Cavan. However his service was short lived and he retired in July 1882. (He was pensioned, unusually after such short service and died in 1890). Whether or not that had any influence on them, the two eldest boys, Henry and David joined on the same day, 15 July 1914. In the coming months thousands of other young men throughout the country would flock to join the Army but at that time a career in the R.I.C. offered considerably better prospects for young men. For the vast majority of people at that time, it was not a decision affected by any overt

R.I.C. Phoenix Park Depot, 1920

religious or political sensitivities. In the Ireland of 1914, Catholic and Protestant, nationalist and unionist had few qualms about joining the R.I.C. In fact, some eighty per cent of the rank and file came from a Catholic background. It was a career that promised secure employment with reasonable wages. For the sons of many Irish tenant farmers, it was better than staying on the farm or facing the unknown world of emigration.

In 1914, recruits to the R.I.C. were required *"to be of good character, fair physique and have a certain standard of education."* The height qualification of five foot nine inches was to be reduced to five foot eight in that year, in an attempt to increase the number of applicants. It has to be remembered that in the early 19th Century, people were much smaller than today. It has been estimated that among recruits to the British Army during the First World War that average height was five foot five inches, chest measurement 34 inches and weight about 140 pounds. Neither Henry at over six foot one nor Davy at five foot eleven, had any difficulties meeting the physical requirements for entry into the R.I.C. New pay scales were also introduced in 1914 to award trainees ten shillings (fifty pence) a week and constables would start with twenty three shillings a week, rising to thirty one shillings a week on completion of twenty years service. From this there was a deduction for barrack accommodation. Only single men were allowed to join but they were allowed to marry after seven years with the permission of their superiors. Training for the new recruits took place in the Depot in Phoenix Park, Dublin and continued for six months. There, the recruits learnt the rudiments of policing. Great emphasis in the training of constables was placed on drill, weapon handling and strict standards of deportment and dress. Bob McKillop, a friend of Henry's and a fellow recruit, recalled how the high necked collar of the recruit's tunic often had pins inserted in it to ensure the recruit held his head upright at all times. The recruits lived in spartan conditions - straw bedding was used for mattresses. Hours were spent in the classroom memorising rules and regulations. The morning began with an hour of parade and drill, was followed by school and gymnasium, ambulance instruction and stretcher drill.

HENRY AND DAVID

On 9th February 1916, both Henry and David were posted to County Donegal. It was R.I.C. policy that a policeman was not to be stationed in the county of his birth, nor indeed in that of his wife's; this was to ensure that there would be no strains on his independence or loyalties. Policemen had to reside within the police station and for those with wives and families, there were married quarters.

Soon Henry got involved in the wider area of union or representative matters. A letter he wrote from Letterkenny as a District representative of the men, shows his strong views on several aspects of policing at the time, in particular the grievances of the ordinary policemen. He singled out the men's complaint of not being allowed to wear plain clothes when off duty and the Divine Service

Henry Magill, R.I.C. 1921

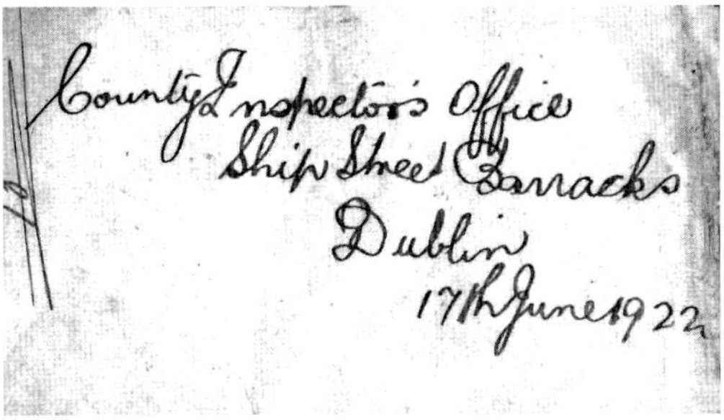
County Inspector's Office
Ship Street Barracks
Dublin
17th June 1922

parades, a practice in which it was compulsory for R.I.C. members, Catholic and Protestant to march in uniform to church on Sundays. He complained of the fact that serving policemen were not allowed to vote and were now being required to pay income tax. "*We either are or are not citizens,*" he insisted. *"If the former, we are entitled to a vote, to the protection of the law and every right which is afforded to civilians. We have none of these. Even to the last drop of our blood, we are by statute bound to zealously guard the life and liberties of every member of the community. We are also prevented from exercising the Franchise, surely here we have 'Taxation without Representation' in its vilest form.*"
He welcomed the decision of the official representative body to demand fifteen years' added service in the event of disbandment, but he challenged the fact that these representatives had not been properly elected by the men whose views up to this were being ignored.

While these letters tell us much about policing at the time, they also reveal something of the character and intellect of Henry himself. He was a man with no formal education beyond elementary school and had been recorded as an agricultural labourer in 1911 according to the census of that year, but he possessed a formidable memory and grasp for figures. It is remembered that he put his photographic memory to good use in his spare time in becoming a formidable draughts player, who had the ability to recall every move in earlier games. Through wide reading and self education he won the respect of his fellow policemen; moreover he was a man of strong opinions and he was never afraid to articulate them.

The move to County Donegal in February 1916, meant that neither Henry nor Davy were in Dublin to witness the Easter Rising, April 1916, but Henry was sent back to Dublin in October 1916 to be stationed in Dublin Castle. He was to remain here over the following momentous years which saw the War of Independence, the Anglo-Irish Treaty 1921 and the eventual disbandment of the R.I.C. The political settlement of 1920 and 1921 had created two separate states, the Irish Free State for twenty six counties and Northern Ireland for the six northern counties. The R.I.C. was disbanded in the summer of 1922 and each state had its own police force, An Garda Siochana and the R.U.C..

We can get occasional glimpses of the challenges to policing in these times from one of his surviving letters. Writing in 1922 on the eve of the disbandment of the R.I.C., to Bob McKillop, his friend and now retired colleague who had returned to Glenarm, he enquired *"Is there any sign of hostility to ex-policemen in that part?"* Reminiscing about their earlier days when they were stationed in County Donegal, he wrote "*I'm sure it must be a terrible change from the grand old days in Letterkenny. Times were better there than we knew and God knows if we will ever see the likes of them again .... I do not know exactly when I'll go home, but I'm nearly fed up with this place.*" We can get a sense of the atmosphere in the final days of the R.I.C. in Dublin.

"As you will see from above, I'm still here.... Larkin took his departure about a fortnight ago for Belfast. I suppose you heard that he joined the Ulster constabulary. He is now in a CI's office and stationed in Omagh. Mr. Foster left us on Thursday last to take up the position of Paymaster at Newtownards Camp (the new R.U.C. training depot) *and we have Mr. Ryan from Lurgan in his place. The latter appears to be a worthy successor to a great predecessor..... Kinny went home about a week ago so only O'Brien, O'Donnell and O'Shea and your humble servant remain ...... I don't go out much and generally get a game of cards, and as you know, I'm in my element at that."*

Enquiring of his two brothers who like Bob also had by now left the R.I.C. and returned home to Cairncastle, he asked *"Do you see Pat (*Pat had joined in June 1920*) or David at all? I haven't heard from them for ages. I suppose they are gradually becoming acclimatised and accustomed to the customs and mannerisms of the country folk."*

Henry's career in the R.I.C. ended in July 1922 and like many of his colleagues, he joined the R.U.C. As much as fifty per cent of the new R.U.C. force drew its numbers from former R.I.C. men. He was first sent to Belfast where his leadership abilities were soon recognised and he was promoted to sergeant in November 1926. He showed a quick mind and did not suffer fools gladly; he had an imposing presence, being the tallest of all the brothers. As sergeant he was sent to Armagh and then seconded to the R.U.C. Depot at Newtownards, County Down, for six months in 1927. He returned to Armagh for five years and after promotion to Head Constable, (it was said that at the age of forty one, he was then the youngest Head Constable in the R.U.C.) he was transferred to Lisburn in February, 1933. He continued his interest in representative matters and was elected to the Representative Body in the year 1937-1938. At the outbreak of the war in 1939, after a short time spent in Tyrone, his career came to an end when he resigned in January 1940 and he entered the R.A.F.

DAVY IN R.I.C.

While Henry had been stationed in Dublin, in the closing years of the R.I.C., Davy was transferred after a brief spell in County Donegal to Dover Street Barracks in Belfast in October 1916. Increasingly he was showing his sporting ability in cross country running. He won several major competitions and given his athleticism and physique, he was encouraged to take up the sport of boxing. As a member of the R.I.C. he made his ring debut at the age of twenty five on January 1920, in the Ulster Hall against Constable J. McHale. Before the year was out he had won a reputation for himself not only locally but in England, as the most promising Irish heavyweight for a generation. In November 1921, he won the heavyweight championship of the R.I.C. with a victory over Con. Llew

Williams in a two day R.I.C. tournament in Enniskillen. As a way round police regulations, he boxed in England under the name of *"Dave Connelly* (Connolly being his mother's surname) *of Derry"*, but soon he was to make the decision that he would become a full time professional boxer. With the R.I.C. facing disbandment, he finally left in May 1922.

It was during these years stationed in Belfast that he was to meet his future bride, Molly Hynes. The circumstances surrounding their first meeting were later published in the Irish Independent, on the day after their wedding on May 5, 1924, in St.Paul's Church, Falls Road, Belfast.

Irish Boxer's Romance (Irish Independent)

"A rare degree of romance lies, says the "Daily Herald," behind the marriage yesterday in Belfast of Davy Magill, the noted Irish boxer, and Miss Molly Hynes. Two years ago when mysterious tragedies were frequent in Belfast armed men raided the public house owned by Mr. Hynes, father of the bride, in Falls Road."

"Mr. Hynes was taken out to the street, and preparations were made to shoot him when Magill, then a constable in Belfast, intervened and saved his life. His gallant act was the beginning of the friendship with Miss Hynes, which was followed yesterday by the marriage."

While the story may have been embellished for the benefit of the readers, the armed men in question were Black and Tans. This was the nickname given to the new recruits from England who were raised in 1920 by the British government to boost the ranks of the R.I.C. in their efforts to counter the IRA. This sudden influx of men led to a shortage of R.I.C. uniforms, and the new recruits were issued with khaki army trousers and dark green R.I.C. tunics. They had been recently posted to Belfast and were making a name for themselves in the area.

Though Davy had turned professional in 1922, he did not lose all contact with the police. In 1927 he was offered the position of trainer to the newly established R.U.C. boxing team; in this role he was to lead them to great success.

CHARLIE, WILLIE AND PAT

While Davy was embarking on his boxing career, still a member of the R.I.C., three other brothers followed him into the police. With the end of World War One, Charlie, the third son at the age of twenty three, enlisted in December 1919, and was posted to County Roscommon. It was in the middle of the Troubles or what had been subsequently called the War of Independence, which had broken out in January 1919. It was a guerrilla war in which the main struggle was between the 'flying columns' of the IRA and the R.I.C. Having experienced the worst of conflict on the Western Front, he was now in Roscommon, later transferring, to Westmeath and finally to Gormanstown, County Meath. He left

Pat c 1920

in August 1922 when the R.I.C. was disbanded and soon decided to head for Canada.

The next brother to enlist, Willie, left home in March 1920 at the age of twenty two to begin training at the Depot in Phoenix Park, Dublin. However, his service was short-lived, as in August of the same year he was to resign from the force as his record stated *"he was required at home."* At the age of 18, one of the younger brothers, Pat, joined in June 1920. He had been considered as 'the wild one of the family' and found himself ill-suited to the rigour and disciplines of the police force. He was stationed in the then Queen's County which became County Laois and served there until disbandment in April 1922. He then transferred to the R.U.C. in October 1922, but finally left in August 1924. While he too had embarked on a boxing career, he did not meet with the same success as his brothers, Davy or Jim, but went on to London and from there emigrated to Australia, where he was to spend the rest of his days.

By the end of 1921 the War of Independence from Britain had ended but violence re-emerged in the newly created Irish Free State, in a Civil War between the rival IRA forces loyal to Michael Collins and Eamon De Valera. At the same time the new state of Northern Ireland was to face continuing IRA attacks and to be convulsed by outbreaks of sectarian violence. It has been estimated that one in twenty R.I.C. men were killed in the conflict of these years and many times more, injured. The Magill brothers, all five of them, could count themselves fortunate not to have been included in those figures.

JOHN

John in R.U.C. 1923

For the two remaining brothers, John and Jim, their time in policing was not so short lived. John, aged twenty three, joined the recently formed R.U.C. in April 1923 and Jim, aged twenty two, followed in June 1926. They both became career policemen, John serving the longest of all the Magills, for thirty nine years and Jim, thirty three years.

The worst of the Troubles was over when John joined the police in 1923. Whereas his brothers before him had gone to the R.I.C. Depot in Phoenix Park, Dublin, John trained in the new Depot in Newtownards. He recalled the spartan conditions and the straw mattresses for beds in the accommodation blocks. The R.U.C. Depot there was a far cry from the Georgian elegance of the Phoenix Park Depot. He had an early introduction to the harshness of the regulations when just weeks after his appointment, he was refused leave to see the film of his brother Davy's British Empire title fight in May 1923, which was on show in two Belfast cinemas. John himself was later to have a short stint in the ring, when he boxed in the R.U.C. tournament in the Ulster Hall in December 1927. It was the same tournament that launched his younger brother, Jim's career. He won his two bouts in style and became novice light-heavyweight champion of the R.U.C. However a subsequent injury received in sparring put an end to his boxing career.

John spent his entire policing days in Belfast and in the same area of the Docks and North Belfast, in the barracks of York Street, Henry Street, Glenravel Street and Antrim Road. It was a part of the city which continued to experience poverty and unemployment and the sectarian tensions which came to characterise much of Belfast. There were the normal routines of policing, break-ins, assaults and dealing with road traffic accidents. Traffic was different in those times. One of the first road accidents John as a new constable recorded in his police notebook was when on 29th of July 1924, a man on a bicycle collided with a pony and trap coming down York Street from the direction of Royal Avenue! Over time the type of vehicles in the city centre would change.

He married Peggy Rooney in St. Patrick's Church, Donegall Street in November 1938 and on the day of his wedding the Irish News carried a piece about "*another R.U.C. man meets his fate.*" John laid down his roots in the north of the city where he and Peggy reared a family of ten children. He remained at the rank of constable all his 39 years in the police, saying that promotion would have meant being moved and uprooting his family. There were difficult times, especially during the Blitz when that part of the city suffered the brunt of the German air raids. On the night of Easter Tuesday, 15 April 1941, two hundred bombers of the German Air Force attacked the city. One thousand people died as a result of the bombing and raids and half of the houses in Belfast were damaged or destroyed. Outside of the city of London, this was the greatest loss of life in a night raid during the Blitz. The most heavily-bombed area was that which lay between York Street and the Antrim Road where John was stationed. Half the population fled the city and corpses lined St. George's Market, Falls Baths and the Mater Hospital. Peggy in later life recalled that night when she had left the city to stay with her newly married sister, Lily in the comparative safety of Andersonstown; she went into the centre of Belfast on the following morning to see if her husband, John, who was on duty throughout the day and night, was alive or dead. Wheeling a pram with her two babies, Brian (eighteen months) and Sean (two months), the distance of about ten miles there and back, through smouldering ruins, she felt overwhelmed by the smell of burning and the sight of hundreds of refugees leaving the city.

But there were also better times when the sight of policemen in uniform, attending mass in the local church, was not considered out of the ordinary. Policing was less contentious in those times than it would become after the '60's. There were many policemen, some former R.I.C. men, who had made their home in the local area in Belfast and the accents of Kerry, Sligo and farther afield were to be heard whenever they would meet up. Like John, they were in the main, countrymen living in the city and most had their vegetable plots, possibly as a way of keeping their contact with their rural backgrounds. John was at his happiest there, on his police bicycle or walking the beat on the streets of Belfast. He knew it was time to leave the police force when squad cars were introduced and contact with the local people was lost. At the age of 62, he finally retired. After a few years, his family now grown up, he returned "home" with his wife Peggy to the house he had been born and reared in, at Cairncastle. He enjoyed a long retirement and died in 1991 at the age of 91.

Belfast Blitz, 1941. St. Anne's Cathedral in background

Jim c. 1926

Jim

Jim, the youngest brother, had joined the R.U.C. in November 1926, at the age of 22, after several successful bouts as a paid boxer. All Jim's days in the police were spent in Belfast too. His first station was in College Square North, but it was closed soon after he arrived. Within a year the barracks of Queen Street, which had previously been a children's hospital, opened and he spent practically all his service there. It was a career that lasted thirty three years and saw him reach the pinnacle of success in Irish and International boxing. He has gone down in history as one of Ireland's greatest ever amateur boxers and the man who put police boxing on the map. Indeed it was often said that he did more for recruitment to the police than any of their official campaigns.

As a single man he spent a lifetime living in barracks. An old friend, Jimmy Harkin, (now 91 years of age) who was stationed with Jim in Queen Street in the 1950's, remembered him vividly. Single men lived in the station in those days and he and Jim had adjoining rooms in Queen's Street. Conditions were fairly basic and they all shared a communal kitchen where everyone cooked their own food. Their 'beat' was the city centre and life was busy. Even as late as the 1950's there were no traffic lights at Castle Junction in the centre of Belfast and Jim was a policeman known to many as he stood in the middle of that busiest of roads on points duty, directing the traffic. Jimmy recalled that St. Mary's Chapel Lane was the local church and Jim and himself were regular worshippers there in their police uniforms.

Jim was well known too in the city as a boxer. His reputation was often enough to defuse a row but there were occasions when he had to use his skills. During the War there were often cases of over exuberant soldiers on leave causing trouble. Jim was remembered on more than one occasion, single-handedly 'taking on' American GI's who were creating havoc in Smithfield and hauling them back to the station. His colleague, Jimmy Harkin recalled how one night Sergeant McAvoy said there was a 'bad row' in the Washington Bar and

Jim Magill on left

asked for help. There was a group of Canadian soldiers causing a rumpus and when Jim arrived in plain clothes with the accompanying police party, the soldiers turned their attention to Jim, whom they thought was an interfering civilian. According to his friend who witnessed the scene, Jim knocked out five of the soldiers in a row. It was later learned that one of them had to be detained in hospital until he recovered. The following day, the commanding officer of the Canadians arrived at Queen Street Station. There was naturally some trepidation until the officer announced that he was there, not to condemn the policeman involved, but to congratulate him.

There were incidents of another kind to deal with. Nearby was Amelia Street, notorious in Belfast for its ladies of the night and part of police routine was dealing with the kerb-crawlers who frequented the area and sorting out the disputes that often erupted in the street. One night, one of the well known ladies of the street came across to Queen Street Station and complained that her landlord would not let her into her flat in his house which stood at the corner of the street. Jim and his colleague went to the house, knocked on the door and demanded admittance. At this, an upstair's window opened and a hand appeared holding a chamber pot which was duly poured over the two policemen below. In the court proceedings that followed, Jim and his friend were compensated by the payment of costs for two new coats. Jim retired from the police in June 1959 after an extension of service in Templemore Avenue in the Commissioners Office.

THE HEADLINES

They Were The Glorious 'Bobby' Boxers!

Davy Magill

By E. J. SLOAN

A policeman's life may not always be a happy one, but the Magill brothers—boxers who, between them, shared more than 250 fights without suffering a knock-out — certainly lived gloriously.

Below our contributor recalls many of the feats performed by both Davy and Jimmy Magill, and highlights some of the greatest professional fights in which Davy was engaged.

Ireland's Saturday Night, July 16, 1955. **3**

164 bouts—seven defeats

HE PUT POLICE BOXING ON "THE MAP"

GREATEST ever Irish amateur boxer and the man who put police boxing on "the map" is due to retire shortly from the R.U.C.

He is Constable James Magill, Queen Street Barracks, Belfast,

How a fight in the Ulster Hall saved a soldier at Dunkirk ...

RUC CHAMPIONS 1928

THREE BROTHERS

DAVY

JOHN

JIM

Constables Rothwell, Hyde, McIntyre, Gibson, McCartney, Herbison, Sgt.Crawley.
Hd.Const. Murphy, MM., Constables Patterson, Weir, Fyffe, John Magill, Lappin, McVicker, Hughes.
Sgt. Twaddle, Constables Quigley, Jas. Magill, Ashfield, Kennedy, (Davy Magill Trainer), Constables Heaney, Blair, McCormack, Doherty.
Hd. Const. Colhoun and Campbell, Dist.Insp. Wm Lynn, F.A. Britten Esq., B.A., O.B.E. Commr. and D.I.G.,Lt. Col. C.C. Wickham D.S.O.Inspector General.
Co. Insp. R.W.D. Harrison, O.B.E., Capt. T. D. Morrison, M.C.,B.L.,D.I., Capt. R. T. Hamilton, M.C.D.I.,Dist.Insp. J. Stratford.

The Fighting Magills

The Magills in the Ring

- Davy, Jim, Pat and John

The Fighting Magills

Belfast Boxers' Contribution to Ireland's Sporting History

Poster on display in the Belfast Boxing Exhibition, held in the City Hall, Belfast, 6-30 September 2010 to honour Ireland's sporting heroes.

Davy Magill

1894-1942

Photo by R. Clements Lyttle, Belfast

DAVY MAGILL.

(Heavy-weight and Cruiser-weight Champion of Ireland.)

- LEARNING THE ROPES - THE IDOL OF BELFAST
- 1923 YEAR OF THREE TITLE FIGHTS
- 1923-1924 MADISON SQUARE GARDENS
- IRELAND'S MOST POPULAR BOXER IN THE TWENTIES
- A THIRD IRISH TITLE - RETIREMENT AS UNBEATEN CHAMPION
- 1935-1936 THE COMEBACK

LEARNING THE ROPES - THE IDOL OF BELFAST

Early Years

Davy was born on 31 December 1894 in the small County Antrim village of Cairncastle, situated near the Antrim Coast and about 20 miles north of Belfast. He was the second son of a family of 12 children, seven boys and five girls (one of whom, Anne, died in infancy) born to Charles and Annie Magill.

As a teenager David showed a special talent as a runner, first coming to attention in the local area, soon outpacing his adult rivals. Boxing was also beginning to fire his imagination and part of the stable behind the house was rigged out as a makeshift gym. There was no shortage of sparring partners in a family of seven boys and their pals from the local area and in time the young Davy and his brothers were winning a reputation for their boxing skills.

In July 1914, just two months before World War One broke out, along with his elder brother Henry, he joined the RIC, which was the current police force in Ireland. After training at the RIC Depot in Phoenix Park in Dublin, he was posted first to County Donegal. From there he was transferred after a few months to Dover Street Barracks in Belfast; it was there that he joined the Ulsterville Harriers. His athletic prowess soon gained recognition on the running track and in cross-country running. He won the Four Mile Cross-Country Championship and as vice-captain of the club, won the Victory International Race, organized to mark the end of the War, at Glandore Avenue, Belfast. He became one of the best one to four mile runners in Ireland. It was while training with the Harriers at Windsor Park that he first met Billy Campbell, the groundsman and Irish distance walking champion. Billy held the Irish record for the one mile walk of 6 minutes 39.2 seconds. He saw Davy's potential in the boxing ring. At that time, he managed a small gym and the young policeman became a frequent visitor. Billy became his trainer and mentor and a lifetime's friendship followed. He introduced him to George Sayers, who was to become his manager, and it was this partnership of two amateur sports enthusiasts that was to guide Davy throughout his career. So began a training programme which day after day for six months would lead to Davy's debut in the Ulster Hall, on January 22, 1920.

Davy Magill was 25 years of age before he threw a punch in the ring.

His introduction to boxing had come at the relatively late age of 25 while he was a serving member of the police. His physique and athleticism showed potential from the beginning in the ring. He was five foot 11 in height and weighed inside 12 stone seven, the light heavyweight limit; height and weight in the 1920's were less than today. Jim Coffey, the so called 'Irish Giant,' was six foot one. World champions, like Gene Tunney and Jack Dempsey, measured six foot and six foot one, respectively. Unusually for a man of his size, Davy was a guy who could move fast. His first appearance came in a ten two minute round contest in the Ulster Hall, Belfast, against Constable McHale of Enniskillen on Jan 22, 1920. The press report praised him on a marvellous display and noted that he carried a powerful left. The referee stopped the boxing in round six to save his opponent. He returned to the ring on March 10 for a six rounder with Harbour Constable McCappin.; once again the referee stopped the contest in round six. *"He will soon be christened "The Butcher" if he finishes his opponents as in his last two fights"*, was the opinion of one seasoned commentator. A succession of opponents went the same way during the next year. Davy had become one of the most popular boxers in Belfast since he exploded on to the local boxing scene. "*He represents the best type of boxer - clean and effective in his deliveries and defence, smart on his feet and quite "tame" when outside the ropes*" wrote one reporter.

His first real test with a cross Channel heavyweight opponent was against Wally Buckley of Liverpool on December 29, 1920; Buckley had won seven out of his last eight contests. The bout was considered to be the fastest and most cleverly fought contest yet witnessed in Belfast. A vicious right dropped Buckley in the fourth and a KO followed in round five.

"Dave Connelly, a hitherto unknown Irishman"

While he was well known in his adopted city as '*Dave Magill the RIC man,*' it was decided initially to fight under an assumed name when boxing across the water. This was possibly a way round police regulations, as he was still a serving member of the RIC - he boxed under the name *"Dave Connelly* i.e., Connolly with an "e". His mother's maiden name had been "Connolly". On occasions he would box under the name of "*Dave Connelly of Derry,*" or on others as "*Dave Connelly, Glasgow,"* creating a stir at the National Sporting Club in London where a right to the jaw toppled Harry Knight of Marleybone in the seventh.

Another local victim came when he knocked out Stoker McCormick in the second round in the Ulster Hall. (15 March 1921) A return match did not last much longer, McCormick being stopped in the third round. March 28, 1921 saw him in action in the Victoria Club, Glasgow where "*Connelly of Derry* beat Sid Burns (Aldgate)" - it was reported that Connelly was too guilty of sending the right without first making an opening, but when he sent the left, he had more success and Burns was fought to a standstill with a KO before the first round ended.

"Up and Coming Irish Boxer - Dave Connelly of Derry has a future" wrote the sportswriter John S. Barron - *"A fine upstanding athlete with tapering arms, legs and torso and a mouth that told any casual observer that here was a fellow with a will of his own. Connelly's is a fighting face if ever there was one. With proper tuition, perseverance and well chosen opponents, Connelly should go far.... I don't dub Connelly a world beater but I think he might make fistic history."* Barron was not alone in recognising the raw talent of the novice and the exciting prospect he had become. Some fans thought he resembled Jack Dempsey in physique. Dempsey was the current world heavyweight champion who had become the idol of his generation. Fight fans in Davy's adopted home city of Belfast and across the Channel warmed to

CAIRNCASTLE BOXER IN ACTION.

HE PRINCIPAL CONTEST AT THE SUCCESSFUL BOXING TOURNAMENT HELD ON THURSDAY AFTERNOON AT EWTOWNARDS CAMP WAS BETWEEN DAVY MAGILL (BELFAST), IRISH HEAVY-WEIGHT CHAMPION, AND EX 'OKER M'CORMACK (U.S.C.) PHOTO SHOWS M'CORMACK (LEFT) AND MAGILL (RIGHT). THE LATTER WO IN THE THIRD ROUND.

his aggression and his all action style. His first seven opponents failed to make the distance, with KOs in rounds 6, 4, 2, 1 and 2; the towel was thrown in twice in rounds 6 and 14. It had been some time since Belfast had a big hitting fighter in the heavier weights and the fans took him to their hearts.

Davy's successes gave them plenty to cheer. A 15 round bout on April 1, 1921, against Albert Brown (Otley) turned out to be disappointingly brief, when Brown was knocked out in round two, but the crowd was delighted at the popular policeman's decisive victory over such an experienced opponent. Davy was enthusiastically cheered on leaving the arena. In a bout on 23 April, 1921, staged by Linfield Football Club as the first of a series of open air tournaments to be held over the summer, Joe Dixon of Leeds, managed to last fourteen rounds, but the bout turned into what was called a "*massacre*" as Magill relentlessly punished his opponent. The towel was thrown in before the referee had counted him out in round 14. Timekeeper (John Caughey in Ireland's Saturday Night) wrote "*the boys have not stopped talking yet of the gameness of Joe Dixon, Leeds who covered 14 rounds against Constable Davy Magill, with the latter an obvious winner from the second session. Magill's success was very popular and the boys were not backward at letting him see their delight when he finished so effectively.*" But Timekeeper also pointed out that he was up against a rather slow opponent and that "*he had taken some risks that made spectators hold their breath ...... Davy could well be advised to develop his cover while polishing himself up in other branches.*" He went on to confide in his readers that chatting with Louis Ruddick after the fight, the Leeds feather-weight told him that "*if Davy Magill was with a certain camp in England, he would be British champion within a year.*"

There was plenty of advice for the novice from outside the ring. *"Good Irish Boxer - Where Connelly Goes Wrong"* wrote John Barron. *"Connelly is at this very moment just a promising piece of raw material. Ever so promising, but ever so raw......Connelly, being inexperienced, showed us that he had a whole string of faults which he will have to get rid of. One of these is the bad habit of failing to put his whole weight behind his blows. Also he makes the bad mistake of sending the right far too often when he has no earthly chance of landing it. He has another very crude habit of leaving himself absolutely unprotected when close in. I think he must be having a lot of practice that is of very little use to him at present. ....I think Connelly is one of the most promising big fellows in all Britain today ......Connelly will be heard of soon in London....."*

First Setback Roland Todd (Doncaster) May 9, 1921

"The best heavyweight contest ever witnessed in Belfast"

The venue selected by the promoters, Messrs. Rice and MacAnerney, was Belfast's Music Hall, the Empire Theatre. It was full to the brim and at least 1,000 were turned away.

Davy had a considerable advantage in poundage, though the reporter Ringside let his readers know that *"I was not pleased to see him in the Turkish Baths in the morning getting down to 12 stones."* Roland Todd may have been a middleweight and two years younger than Davy, but when it came to craft and experience, he was the master and Davy the novice. With little more than a year's boxing behind him, Davy was fighting the second best middleweight in Britain. Todd would have a run of almost 40 fights unbeaten and would go on to take the British, Empire and European titles from Ted Kid Lewis in February, 1923. Would the novice be ready for such a challenge or was he going to be out of his depth?

From the beginning, Todd showed his superior speed and excellent footwork, managing to avoid fighting at close quarters with Davy, whose heavier punching would have taken its toll. Todd's left leads to the face built up a lead which Davy was unable to overcome even though after the tenth round, he landed repeatedly. It had been a thrilling fight and many believed that had Davy boxed as in the last four rounds, he would have stood a big chance of getting the decision.

Davy sparring with Roland Todd

It was Davy's first defeat after a run of seven inside the distance wins, but there were no regrets. He had had the experience of being up against class and learned more than in a dozen contests against second raters. He showed that he could go the distance of 15 rounds and take some punishment into the bargain. Todd's manager had said that he could, in six months perfect Magill to beat any cruiserweight in Britain. It had been apparent when Todd stabbed home his left that Davy was too open. Had he the same defence as Todd, how far would he go, asked one reporter. It had been the best heavyweight contest ever witnessed in Belfast and the referee claimed that it was the most scientific contest between heavyweights that he had ever had charge of.

Like the good pupil he was, Davy was to learn from his mistakes. From this on, he and Roland Todd were to come together as sparring partners and they were to embark on a road that would eventually take them both to the USA. He would now learn some of the defence tactics that Todd had mastered and shown to such effect in his victory in Belfast.

Royal Irish Constabulary Heavyweight Title, 1921

A two day tournament in November 1921, held at the RIC Depot in Enniskillen, brought him the RIC heavyweight title when he defeated Con. Llew Williams in the third round. Williams was reputedly a native of Australia; a return in December in Dublin with Williams was won in the second when the referee stopped the fight.

Over the next year, Davy was to be matched with all the leading light heavy and heavyweight contenders in Britain and Ireland in his journey to the top. He would fight in Belfast, where he was a firm favourite of the fans and became a big draw in all the major boxing cities across the Channel, from Liverpool to Glasgow and London.

If peace is maintained in the City, there is a good prospect of a revival of boxing.

However it was in his adopted city of Belfast that his career was launched. The Belfast of 1921 was a city in the throes of rioting and sectarian violence. Boxing's correspondent, J. MacAnerney noted *"Owing to the situation here, now, there is very little sport, in a city which boomed in past years ... plenty of fighting but not with the gloves, the weapons being more deadly."* By June, 1922 he noted that "*Last Saturday the first open air show (*Where Davy Magill stopped Sergeant Palmer at the start of the second round*) was held at the Oval football grounds .... There was a good crowd in an area which is hard to reach from across the city."* The situation was improving. Already he was looking forward to more open air shows that summer and there was talk of staging a fight between Davy Magill, now retired from the police, and Sergeant Pape. "*If peace is maintained in the City"* he wrote in September *"there is a good prospect of a revival of boxing. Since the shooting commenced, boxing which was then booming has been practically wiped out. A big promotion was abandoned last year owing to military occupation of the Ulster Hall..... the club shows twice weekly are crowded out."* On top of political disturbances, Belfast promoters had to face the general problems of economic hardship. *"Since Christmas last"* MacAnerney wrote in 1923 *"money has been scarce and the workers are no longer able to afford prices from 5 to 15 shillings."* Some promoters were blaming their financial straits on the excessive demands of the younger generation of boxers, when older fighters contented themselves with smaller purses.

One of those who first saw the chance of a revival of boxing in Belfast was Jim Rice, turf accountant and promoter. Alex Maskey (senior) writing in the Andersonstown News on November 1988, claimed that "*Jim Rice took boxing from the back streets and presented it in grand style awarding championship winners with gold and silver belts. He presented boxing at Celtic Park, Donegall Road and Grosvenor Park, the Ulster Hall ....and in theatres and picture houses."* Along with Jim MacAnerney he showed great enterprise and promotional flair in bringing top class boxing to Belfast. He saw that Davy Magill was a fighter who would bring in the fans. In the year 1921 alone, Davy would appear no less than eight times in Rice promotions, topping the bill in venues which ranged from St. Georges Market, the Empire Theatre and the Opera House.

Among his first victims in the year 1921 was Tom Berry (Custom House). Just ten days after his defeat at the hands of Roland Todd, Davy was back in the ring again. He defeated the Londoner on points on May 20 in Belfast and again in a return at Holland Park Arena, London, on July11, 1921. (Berry was himself to go on to win the British title.). Still boxing under the name of *Dave Connelly,* Davy was making a big name for himself in cross Channel boxing circles. Already there was talk of matching him with the champion, Jack Bloomfield. One reporter wrote *"When eulogies were being delivered across the water as to the surprisingly good form shown by a hitherto unknown Irishman..... I was asked who was Dave Connolly but for the time I wished to preserve a little secret. I now have pleasure in letting you know that Belfast's favourite Davy Connolly Magill, has found his feet."*

Wild Burt Kenny

On Aug 13, 1921, he met Wild Burt Kenny (America) in Belfast. The American came with a reputation but he was now past his best. He had wins over Battling Levinsky and three years before had gone ten rounds with Jack Dempsey and in June 15 with Frank Moran. A long time was occupied in the preliminaries as a glove could not be found large enough for the American's right hand. Tension mounted as Davy waited nervously in his corner. Kenny lived up to his reputation of having an unorthodox smashing style. He rushed at his opponent, flailing like a hurricane but Davy evaded him with clever footwork and countered with straight lefts. In the third round Kenny was disqualified for a swinging low blow. It was the first of several victories over seasoned overseas campaigners. Over the next few years he would see off the challenges of Australian, Canadian and Belgian champions.

It was not all plain sailing. On 19 December 1921 he had the first of several meetings with Harry Drake. It was a keen contest in which Drake built up a strong points lead. Excitement was intense as the last round started. Davy fought fiercely, landing lefts and rights almost at will, with the Englishman lucky to survive. But a strong finish by Davy failed to win the decision and a section of the audience gave vent to their displeasure by booing. "*Drake was beaten to a frazzle in the fifteenth round*" according to 'Boxing's' reporter, but Davy had left it too late.

He soon got a chance to redeem himself when on December 28, 1921, he met Alf Bright, an English heavyweight at Windsor Park. Thousands braved the elements to see Davy's third important contest inside a fortnight. This London heavyweight had not taken the full count in a hundred contests and was a good stone heavier than Davy. He had fought two 15 round contests with Harry Reeve and Tom Berry in the ten days before, just as Davy had fought two with Harry Drake and Llew Williams in the same period. On this occasion it was all over in the sixth round when Davy crashed across his right and Bright failed to beat the count. Davy had given him his first experience of a knock out and this inside six rounds. It showed to one and all that Davy carried what few of the cruiserweights or light-heavyweights of the day possessed a convincing right punch. The opinion formed by good judges everywhere was that he would beat all the present day light-heavyweights:

1922 "Magill is the idol of Belfast and has the backing to fight any cruiser or heavyweight in England and his backers do not throw their money away." Boxing's Belfast correspondent.

Davy's progress continued in the next year as his style developed. He was now fast maturing from the exciting natural fighter who had been launched on the boxing scene two years before into a more complete boxer who had been acquiring the defensive skills learned from sparring with Roland Todd. He was to defeat all his opponents in rapid succession and most inside the distance in the course of this year. Among them were - March 21, 1922 - Con. McCappin WR4, April 25, 1922 Cyclone Billy Warren (Australia) WR2, and on June 3, 1922 Sergeant Palmer - KO 2. On May 10, 1922 he retired from the RIC, which was about to be disbanded in August, and decided to become a full-time professional boxer.

Gipsy Daniels

Magill unlike many of his predecessors in the ring in Ireland carries his conquests farther a field than his native soil.

It was in Liverpool on July 20, 1922, where he had the first of several encounters in a 15 round contest with Sergeant Pape (York). The fastest contest he had ever handled was the verdict of the referee after the main bout in Liverpool. Up to meeting Davy, the Yorkshireman had had an unbeaten record. There was some heavy hitting from both men in the early rounds and Davy had his right ear damaged early in the bout. (Later he

sported a cauliflower ear). A right hand split Pape's lips; it turned out to be a gruelling contest. *"Both put up a wonderful fast slam of a thrilling nature. They mixed it in whirlwind style round after round, and the crowd was in a state of pandemonium"* wrote the reporter. The hall was seething with excitement and the cheering continued even through the interval between rounds. It appeared that the bout would go the full distance, but in a dramatic ending in the twelfth, Davy swung a right which put Pape down for the full count. The return was set for Liverpool Stadium, Aug 28, 1922 and the Liverpool crowd were not to be disappointed with their new hero. This time the contest went the full 15 rounds but once again *"Davy after fighting like a Trojan"* emerged the winner. Both men were at their best and again it was proof if it was needed, that Davy had arrived.

There were more scalps to be taken before the year was out. On September 18, 1922, he met the Welshman Danny Thomas who rejoiced in the boxing name of "Gipsy Daniels" of Newport, on account of his swarthy appearance, in a 20 round bout. Daniels in time was to become champion of Britain and the British Empire at light-heavyweight. He would be remembered for his first round knock out of future World Heavyweight champion, Max Schmeling, in 1928. In Liverpool, Davy won a strenuous and fast encounter on points, taking the £100 side stake. On October 23, 1922, he met Harry Drake again. In their last meeting in Belfast, about a year before, Drake had won on points, but this time a much improved Magill, reversed the decision. Timekeeper wrote that *"Fight Fans in the city are talking yet about the thrilling clash between Magill and Drake, who is one of Carpentier's chief sparring partners."* After the contest Drake paid tribute to Magill's prowess *"I never had such a pasting in my life"* he said.

On November 2, 1922 he met Frank Moody (Pontypridd), another Welsh star, in Liverpool. The attendance of over 4,000 was a record for the Stadium. Moody was the hot favourite, five to two on, but the Liverpool-Irish crowd fancied Davy. It was a fierce struggle but Davy had the best of all the work at close quarters and one key feature of the fight was his much improved defence. The decision went to Magill amidst scenes of great enthusiasm among the crowd. Before the bout, Mike McTigue, Irish America's light-heavyweight

The Working Class Turkish Baths
Donegall Street, Belfast: advertisement, 1861

ADVERTISEMENTS. 183

TURKISH BATHS,

112, DONEGALL STREET,

BELFAST.

THESE improved TURKISH BATHS are in constant operation, Sundays excepted.

These Baths were built by Dr. Barter, on his patent principle, and are managed by proved attendants from Blarney, under his directions, the same as at Dublin, Cork, Limerick, Waterford, Sligo, Bray, Killarney.

TERMS.

FIRST CLASS.

	s.	d.
From 6 to 8 a.m.,	1	6
From 6 to 8 p.m.,	1	6
Shampooing,	0	6
Subscription Ticket for 12 Baths at the above-named hours,	15	0
From 10 a.m. to 4 p.m.,	2	6
Subscription Ticket for 12 Baths,	24	0
Shampooing,	0	6
Subscription Shampooing Ticket for 12 Baths,	4	0

SECOND CLASS.

	s.	d.
From 6 to 8 a.m.,	0	6
From 6 to 8 p.m.,	0	6
From 10 a.m. to 4 p.m.,	0	9
Shampooing, with the use of Sheet,	0	3

Children under four years, Free to the Baths.
Children under ten years, Half-price.

Come, and take "THE BATH."

ENTRANCE TO FIRST CLASS, 112, DONEGALL STREET.
ENTRANCE TO SECOND CLASS, 40, LITTLE DONEGALL STREET.

M

Albert Lloyd,Heavyweight champion of Australia

Davy (2nd left) training with Bridgewater

Victor McLaglen

hope was introduced to the crowd and challenged the winner. However he did not return from the USA to make good his promise but instead was to go on to win the Word Light-heavyweight title in Dublin, on Saint Patrick's Day, 1923.

The year ended with further dramatic stoppages. In November 1922 he finished off the Canadian Harold Rolph inside six minutes. Then on December 7, 1922 in Liverpool, he met Harry Drake for the third time, both previous contests having been in Belfast. On this occasion he punished him so severely, driving him from pillar to post, that Drake retired in the ninth round. This had been Davy's sixth appearance in the Liverpool Stadium since the end of July that year. He had won them all and four of them inside the distance. The reporter concluded that

"It can now be truly said that Liverpool boxing enthusiasts have taken Davy Magill to their hearts... He is hailed as a heavyweight who can punch with both hands and move about the ring with the speed of a bantam weight."

"There is no stopping the successful run of the Belfast ex-policeman ...The Irishman has developed his punch wonderfully and in addition his speed has improved."

Finally in December 18, 1922, he fought Albert Lloyd the touring Australian heavyweight champion. It was a popular victory for Davy who gave away about a stone, though he had the advantages of height and reach. Boxing against heavyweights, while Davy weighed about 12 and a half stone, would always put him at a disadvantage. Besides, it was learned at the conclusion of the Albert Lloyd fight that Davy had been in anything but a proper condition to box, having a temperature of 101.8 just before entering the ring. But he went ahead with the fight and won on points. A return in April 1923 with the Australian champion over 20 rounds, ended in a draw. An earlier 15 round points victory on April 9 over heavyweight, Arthur Townley (Birkenhead) at Liverpool, left Davy's unbeaten record in Britain intact. Townley had famously knocked out future film star Victor McLaglen in the seventh round of what proved to be McLaghlen's last fight on October 11, 1920. McLaglen would go on, more than thirty years later, to earn more for his screen fight with John Wayne in the classic "The Quiet Man."

1923 - YEAR OF THREE TITLE BOUTS

By now, Davy had defeated most of the top men in Britain. He was the first to knock out Alf Bright and Sid Pape, twice defeating Harry Drake, Sid Pape and Tom Berry. He had also defeated Gipsy Daniels, Frank Moody, the Canadian champion Harold Rolph and the Australian champion Albert Lloyd. And so the list went on. He had never been knocked out. Yes, he had been beaten by Roland Todd, but that was as a novice. His defence had improved vastly since, after working with Todd. This had been obvious for all to see in his return bout with Harry Drake and again when he fought Frank Moody.

He was unbeaten in England and was now acknowledged to be the fastest and strongest light-heavyweight in the country. So far, he had fought 29 contests, winning 17 by KO and ten on points. The only two light-heavyweights he had not yet met were Jack Bloomfield, the reigning Champion and Dublin's Boy McCormack, the former title holder. So the stage was set in May 1923 for a clash with Jack Bloomfield.

Davy vice-captain of the Ulsterville Harriers - winner of the Anderson Cup, the Craig Cup, the two mile flat and the Victory International Race, pictured in his early running career.

In little more than two years after stepping into the ring, the cross country runner was fighting for the championship of the British Empire. .... In little over three months in the summer of 1923 he was to take part in three sensational title fights. In May he was to make his bid for the Light Heavyweight Championship of the British Empire, in June the Heavyweight Championship of Ireland, and in August,the Light-heavyweight Championship of Ireland. The end of 1923 was to see his arrival on the stage of Madison Square Gardens, in New York. It was to be a momentous year.

Rest and Relaxation before the Bloomfield Fight

The Bloomfield Contest
Venue London Olympia

Ringside underlined the significance of the event by invoking the memory of the epic fight at the Curragh of Kildare in 1815. *"It is over a hundred years ago since Dan Donnelly and Ned Cooper an Englishman, fought for a championship. We have not had an Irishman since fight a championship battle till Davy Magill on Thursday night last."* (The mummified arm of Dan Donnelly had been acquired in 1904 by Beau (Texas) McAlevey, Belfast's celebrated bookmaker and bar owner, and put on display in his premises, the Duncairn Arms.)

Freeman's Journal reported that there had been something of a political sensation in the lead up to the fight, in Belfast sporting circles. The Council of the National Sporting Club, boxing's governing body at the time, had ruled that Davy was ineligible to fight for the British title and Lonsdale Belt on the grounds that he was not born in Great Britain. Having been born in County Antrim and being a former member of the RIC, this naturally gave rise to political debate. It was argued that "Boy McCormick" had been born in India of Irish parents and yet he had not been barred from holding the British title. However the decision held and it was for the championship of the British Empire that Davy would fight.

The pre-match build up saw reporters visit the boxers' training camps. Davy was training at the Peggy Bedford Hotel, Colnbrook, Longford in Middlesex. It was a quiet rural spot about 20 miles from London. Not far away was Jack Bloomfield's camp where he was training at the Dumbell Hotel, Taplow. From the outset, it could be seen that Bloomfield's camp had stolen a march on the Irish visitors. They had snapped up the services of Tom Berry, Harold Rolph, Sid Turner and George Hetherington, the top light-heavyweights around, as sparring partners for Bloomfield; the object was to defeat Magill from having the assistance of these men and to learn how the Irishman fought, for Davy had beaten each of them before. So Davy suffered from a lack of suitable sparring partners. Helping him prepare were Ken McLaglen of Australia (younger brother of Victor, once a boxer and now a hero of the screen) and a couple of lighter men. The reporter noted that *"The three sparring partners worked hard and fast, but were nothing more than chopping blocks."* It was a serious training handicap going into a bout with the champion, Jack Bloomfield, originally known as Sol

Jack Bloomfield- signed copy to Jimmy Magill

Blumenfeld. He was one of the many Jewish fighters in these years who were competing at the very top in British and American boxing. Not one of his previous seven opponents had gone the distance with him; six hadn't got beyond the sixth round. He had a devastating punch and was a highly regarded champion who had proved himself. Jack Bloomfield was the clear favourite in London's boxing circles.

The Title Fight, Olympia, London,May 17, 1923.

OLYMPIA, THURSDAY, MAY 17, at 8.
(Under the direction of J. ARNOLD WILSON.)
BOOK NOW FOR THE
GREAT CHAMPIONSHIP TOURNAMENT.
LIGHT HEAVY-WEIGHT CHAMPIONSHIP OF BRITISH EMPIRE.
Jack BLOOMFIELD v. Dave MAGILL
LIGHT-WEIGHT CHAMPIONSHIP OF EUROPE.
Seaman HALL v. Harry MASON
BANTAM-WEIGHT CHAMPIONSHIP OF EUROPE.
Charles LEDOUX v. Bugler LAKE
AND OTHER SPECIAL CONTESTS.
BOOK AT Major WILSON'S office (2nd floor), Faraday House, Charing X rd. (phone Regent 1758): PAGETS, 40, Aldersgate st. E.C.1 ('phone Clerkenwell 2840): SELFRIDGE & Co., Ltd. (Sports Dept., 2nd floor), New Building, Oxford-st ('phone Gerrard 1): SPALDINGS, 317, High Holborn, W.1 ('phone City 9808), 78, Cheapside, E.C.2 ('phone City 446): FORTNUM & MASON (Sports Dept.), 169, Piccadilly, W.1 ('phone Regent 41), and usual agents
PRICES (including Tax): 5/9, 12/-, £1 4/-, £2 7/-, and £3 10/.

From the beginning, Bloomfield, using his advantage in height (6 ft. 1)and reach, boxed with the confidence of a champion and outscored his opponent. But increasingly Magill was getting through Bloomfield's defence with lefts to the face and right handed swings. He quickly recovered from a knockdown in the third to get to the champion. Magill's cover-up frustrated the champion and made it difficult for him to penetrate his guard. Bloomfield hurt his right hand by hitting Magill four times on the top of the head in the third and Magill, seeing what had happened, forced the pace and took the next rounds. The crowd began to rally behind the underdog and he was cheered again and again. It was anyone's fight. And so it went until the high drama of the twelfth when Magill was on the point of causing a mighty upset, by winning the contest. Bloomfield was a battered man. Magill's attacks were taking their toll and Bloomfield began to rock and staggered to his corner in a groggy condition at the end of that round.

Round 13 turned out to be a sensation and certainly proved unlucky for the challenger. At the opening of the round, Magill rushed at Bloomfield but dropped his guard and was caught by a terrific left hook to the jaw. Davy dropped to the floor but got to his feet at the count of six. He fought back desperately, but was caught by another right from the champion and went down again. This time just before the referee counted him out, as he struggled to his feet, the towel was thrown in from the Irishman's corner. Bloomfield's finishing was clinical and showed why he was the champion.

Bloomfield (left) v Magill

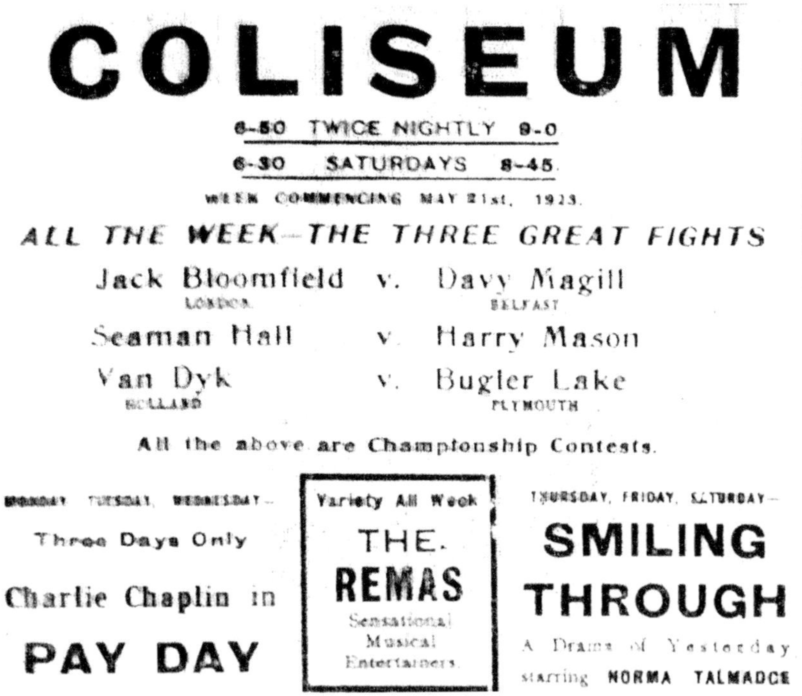

COLISEUM

6-50 TWICE NIGHTLY 9-0

6-30 SATURDAYS 8-45.

WEEK COMMENCING MAY 21st, 1923.

ALL THE WEEK—THE THREE GREAT FIGHTS

Jack Bloomfield (LONDON) v. Davy Magill (BELFAST)

Seaman Hall v. Harry Mason

Van Dyk (HOLLAND) v. Bugler Lake (PLYMOUTH)

All the above are Championship Contests.

MONDAY, TUESDAY, WEDNESDAY—

Three Days Only

Charlie Chaplin in

PAY DAY

Variety All Week

THE

REMAS

Sensational Musical Entertainers.

THURSDAY, FRIDAY, SATURDAY—

SMILING THROUGH

A Drama of Yesterday

starring NORMA TALMADGE

Coliseum cinema, (1915-1959), situated on Grosvenor Road and Durham Street, Belfast

But the next day's headlines summed it up:
"*Davy Magill Does Great Work - Cheered by the Londoners*"- by Ringside ....
"*How Magill Missed Championship*"
"*Splendid effort to wrest the title from Jack Bloomfield......*" Davy's display had surprised the sporting critics, who at the outset had predicted an easy victory for the Londoner who outreached the Irishman. Fred Dartnell, the Daily News boxing correspondent, said Magill had given Bloomfield for 13 rounds the hottest fight he had ever been in.
B. Bennison wrote *"he could have won in the ninth round. At the latest, victory would have been his in the twelfth"*
Timekeeper was soon writing that Davy was back again in Belfast as fit as the proverbial fiddle, and with not a mark save a slight cut over one of his eyes. For Davy's fans at home, they had the chance to see the fight on film.
Timekeeper told how *"The picture of the Davy Magill Jack Bloomfield scrap (when the Irishman gave such a brilliant display) has been drawing good crowds to the Alhambra and the Colliseum this week, and every move that showed Magill's superiority over the champion was loudly cheered. A pleasing incident took place at the Colliseum on Monday evening last. Just before the fight film was shown on screen, and when the stage was in full darkness, Mr. Gibson Bradley, the manager of the hall brought Magill to the front of the platform, and a spotlight was thrown on the boxer."*
Davy's tremendous popularity was proved by the warmth of the welcome he got.
"*The house rose and cheered him to the echo, but the modest ex-policeman, as one would expect from his retiring nature, turned and fled into the wings from such a rousing ovation.*"
The film of the fight was also advertised in the Irish Times as showing in the Masterpiece Cinema, Talbot Street, Dublin, on Monday, May 21, 1923.

Later Davy claimed that when he had boxed Bloomfield, he didn't know enough about the game. *"I had Jack in difficulty up to the 13th round when he caught me with the "Heel" of his glove ...... I am after him for a return fight and when I get him in the ring with me again am certain to wipe out that defeat."*
However there was now another more pressing matter .... a meeting in Belfast with Bartley Madden.

Bartley Madden

— AT —

CELTIC PARK, BELFAST.

CHAMPIONSHIP OF IRELAND,

HEAVY-WEIGHT TITLE.

SATURDAY, JUNE 23, 3 p.m.

DAVY MAGILL (BELFAST)

(Who gave Bloomfield the fight of his career for British Empire Title).

V.

BARTLEY MADDEN (DUBLIN)

(Who beat Bill Brennan, and fought the latter three times;

Fought Fred Fulton last March a great ten rounds, no decision;

Also met Gibbons, who boxes Jack Dempsey on July 4, and Battling Levinsky).

TEN-ROUND CONTESTS—

JACK HUGHES v.
LEN OLDFIELD (Darwen).

JACK NEWELL v.
BILLY MOON (Leeds).

M. ROSE v.
BILLY MANCHESTER (Salford).

BOY WHITESIDE v.
LEO KELLY (Manchester).

SIX-ROUND CONTESTS—

PAT LOGUE (Crumlin) v.
FRANKIE BURNS (Belfast).

TWO RESERVE BOUTS.

All for 3/-; Stand, 3/- (booked); Ringside, 800 at 5/9 (booked).

Tickets and Bookings at Messrs. Leahy, Kelly and Leahy's, or Jim Rice, 6 Pottinger's Entry, Belfast.

ACCOMMODATION FOR 20,000 SPECTATORS.

The Irish Heavyweight Title 1923

"At two minutes past five, the men shook hands and the fight began"

The fight had originally been scheduled to take place at Lansdowne Road, Dublin on May 26, but the venue and date were changed, on account of the Bloomfield fight.
The Magill - Madden Bout, when it finally took place on June 23, 1923, was described at the time, as the most important open air boxing tournament ever held in Belfast. Long before two o'clock on the Saturday of the fight, huge crowds were reported to be swarming up the Donegall Road and the Falls Road and by the time of the opening bout, *"the ground was packed by a seething mass of humanity."* Up to 15,000 were reported to have come to Celtic Park to see the clash. According to the Belfast Telegraph *"All records for attendances at city boxing shows were broken."* Opposing Davy was Bartley Madden, an experienced Irish American who laid claim to the title as he had a KO victory over Jim Coffey, "The Irish Giant", in the USA in 1917. Madden had been keeping in condition, training with Mike McTigue, the newly crowned light heavyweight champion of the world. The pre-match tension had been building up for weeks as Madden and Magill exchanged challenges and this was thrown into the mix with the customary rivalry between Belfast and Dublin. The tension in Celtic Park that day was palpable.

"The crowd had grown to enormous dimensions when the hour arrived for the big fight. Madden was first to make his appearance and was followed in a minute by Magill. If the Dubliner could be said to have won a rousing reception from the crowd, it was a thunderous ovation which greeted the Belfastman. Madden appeared to have a clear advantage in weight and reach. Magill looked ghastly pale when he rose to be introduced, while his opponent smiled on all and sundry. At two minutes past five the men shook hands, and the fight began."

The first round began with Madden taking the initiative trying to get to close quarters and taking some punishment to the head. His American style from the beginning was puzzling Magill and drawing the attention of the referee who cautioned Madden for his use of the head as early as Round 2. Madden's attacks were met with Magill's counters. In Round 5 Madden was again cautioned, this time for hitting low. Things were slowly hotting up and the ninth round was the best yet. Each managed to put in telling blows. In Round 11 there were allegations of low punching by Madden and in the twelfth, the referee cautioned him again. In Rounds 13 and 14 it appeared Madden was edging in front. Magill went down for a count of six in the thirteenth, but recovered well. By the 14th it seemed he was tiring. Round 15 opened with a sharp exchange when suddenly the referee had to caution Madden for a low blow as Magill dropped to the canvas. The way the fight ended added to the unbearable crowd tension. Amid scenes of uproar and confusion, when seconds and officials invaded the ring, Madden was disqualified and the fight was awarded to Magill. Madden protested and demanded that Magill should be examined. A doctor (Dr. McSorley) was called for, but even though his examination revealed no injury, the referee's decision stood.

Madden issued a challenge to meet Davy again with a side stake from £100 to £1000 for a contest in Dublin. Mr. Murphy, the Dublin promoter, offered to stage the return on July 7, only a fortnight away. Madden was due to sail for America in a couple of days so he postponed his departure.

The controversy over the referee's verdict did not end there. A bitter correspondence followed in the letter pages of the Irish Independent between one of the promoters, Mr. J. McAnerney and the reporter "WPD" (Belfast) who criticised McAnerney's usurping the function of the referee "*by his demand for a doctor's examination of Magill, after the referee's decision had been given*". McAnerney's actions have to be seen in the context of the allegations of referee bias which were still fresh after the verdict in favour of Mike McTigue over Battling Siki in Dublin on St. Patrick's Day, that year. In his letter, McAnerney stressed that "My one bogey has been favouritism of locals by a great majority of referees, and I have tried every referee of note across the Channel. On this occasion a Welshman who did not know the principals or Belfast, Mr. Morgan, erred. But I don't allege he showed favouritism. The ringsiders ragged him over low hits, all of which save one in the second round, were legitimate body blows. The reporter took issue with McAnerney's claim that the referee should not have given a decision when Madden protested and before a doctor's examination was carried out. In response the reporter WPD, asked "*What would be the consequences if every defeated pugilist had the prerogative of calling in a medical practitioner after the referee's decision had been given.*"

HAMPION HONOURED.—Mr. J. Murphy (right) presenting Mr. Dave Magill (Belfast), Irish cruiser and light heavy-eight champion of Ireland, with the Murphy gold belt at the banquet held at Barry's Hotel on Saturday night last. —Cashman.

APH, MONDAY, JUNE 25, 1923.

SATURDAY'S BOXING AT CELTIC PARK.

MAGILL, BELFAST, TRIES A RIGHT TO THE STOMACH, AND BARTLEY MADDEN, DUBLIN, COUNTERS WITH A LEFT TO THE FACE.
WAS MR. MORGAN, OF PENYGRAIG. (2) MADDEN SHORT WITH A LEFT LEAD. MAGILL WELL OUT OF DANGER. (3) MADDEN T
AD PUNISHMENT. (4) WORK AT CLOSE QUARTERS. NOTE MADDEN'S EFFECTIVE COVER OF HEAD AND BODY. MAGILL WON ON A

Cruiserweight Championship of Ireland

August 20, 1923

The Only Irish Championship Ever Fought Outside the Country

Fierce Fistic Battle

A third championship battle followed in Liverpool Stadium. It was to be fought over 20 three minute rounds, between Davy and Boy McCormick. McCormick had been born in India and now lived in Dublin. He represented the Free State and was the fancied contestant. He came with a great reputation. In his tour of the USA he had defeated Tommy Gibbons, Gunboat Smith and Battling Levinsky. He had formerly been the cruiserweight champion of Britain but his long lay off after his return from the USA was not the preparation needed. Davy was presented to the crowd as representing Belfast. In the pre-match war of words, they could not agree on a suitable venue in Ireland, so Liverpool was picked as neutral ground. It was to be a real needle match.

Both men went all out from the beginning in thrilling toe to toe exchanges. The pace increased in the second and third rounds and no quarter was given. It was in the fourth that McCormick was the first to crack as he took a right swing to the jaw and took a count of eight. Magill's caution soon gave way to aggression.; it was a ruthless, clinical performance. In the fifth, the Dubliner took another couple of counts as Magill went after him relentlessly. He was beginning to look grim and battered. Magill drove his man from pillar to post in the eighth and ninth and McCormick could not escape Magill's heavy swings which

dropped him for nine. When he came out for the tenth it was plain that he had no chance and the towel came in before the end of the round.

Davy was now the indisputable champion of Ireland at Cruiserweight as well as at Heavyweight.

The headlines stressed the emphatic nature of the victory *"Fierce Fistic Battle." "Magill Trounces McCormick" "Magill Outclassed His Opponent In Every Way", "Belfastman's Magnificent Display*". Nothing like it had been witnessed on Merseyside for years. In later years Davy was to say that this had been his best victory. His trainer, Billy Campbell agreed. Looking back more than 20 years later he told Ireland's Saturday Night, 17 February, 1945, "*Magill knocked out McCormick in the 10th round. ....One of the best fights I ever saw."* Our Own Correspondent concluded that "*Magill is one of the best boxers ever Ireland produced - In Davy Magill we have found a champion who will take some of the high honours in the boxing world."* A further victory over Guardsman Penwell in October in Doncaster, when he was disqualified in round 12, underlined Davy's ascendancy.

However there was to be one disappointment before the year's end. On Oct 29, 1923, he met George Cook, the Australian heavyweight, at the National Sporting Club. Cook got the verdict after a close and disappointing bout. The verdict was not too popular with the crowd. When the referee awarded the fight to Cook, there was a good deal of hissing. Criticism of Magill's change to defensive tactics and more infighting, followed from the pundits. The famous referee, Eugene Corri, openly criticised the influence of Roland Todd, who had been in Davy's corner. He argued that it was not a good idea to teach a man well advanced in the boxing business any new tricks. The Irishman had shown himself to be a good natural fighter and Todd's stylish defensive boxing would not be to his benefit. *"...had he been allowed to develop on his own lines, he might have grown into a very tough fighter, even if he lacked the polish that Todd is trying to put in his boxing."*

Trevor Wignall wrote that it takes at least ten rounds to warm Magill up .... "*his fighting blood did not begin to swirl until the fight was nearly over.*" 'Boxing's' correspondent did not mince his words. Magill should cut out the boxing lessons he has been given and revert to his natural style, he complained "*Magill Has Been Misemploying His Time. Some well-meaning, but most unwise person, has been apparently engaged in the quite harmful labour of supplying Magill with instruction in the Noble Art .... for the Irishman faced Cook in a style which was quite foreign to anything we have seen from him before. Instead of walking in with his face smothered and fists held in readiness to start a flashing attack, he stood up straight, and had seemingly made up his mind that his surest method of winning would be by boxing on the defence and trying to make progress by counter-hitting."*

MADISON SQUARE GARDENS

Davy goes to USA - The Golden Age of Boxing - Dempsey and Tunney

"This Magill is an emphatic wow."

The Twenties were the heyday of boxing in America, the age of Dempsey and Tunney. Jack Dempsey, born in 1895, the year after Davy and like him too, one of a family of 11 became one of America's first great sporting heroes. His defence of the Heavyweight title against France's Georges Carpentier in 1921 was the first ever million dollar gate and his first bout with Gene Tunney in 1926 would draw over 120,000 fans. This was the America, where Davy arrived on 23 November 1923. He had sailed from Southampton on the Berengaria with Roland Todd and his wife, Annie. While Davy would stay with his sister Jennie, who had been in New York since 1907, at her home in Ash Street Yonkers, the Todds booked into the luxurious Waldorf Astoria. It was in Madison Square Gardens, the mecca of American boxing where Davy was to have three bouts with the ultimate prize being a chance to meet with Gene Tunney, the Light-Heavyweight Champion of the World.

The New York Times announced his arrival:
"Dave Magill, fresh from the Old Sod, with the peat smoke still in his hair, made a wonderful impression. Most of the men who have come to us from across the water have proven false alarms, but this Magill is an emphatic wow."

He trained at the Columbus Sport Club in Yonkers alongside Roland Todd, English middleweight champion, who would be fighting Tommy Loughran in the Garden, Davy was being seen in the press as Ireland's best bet for title honours.

SAILOR MAXTED, Dec. 21, 1923

He made his American debut with a 4th Round KO of Sailor Tom Maxted of Newark. He had made a very favourable impression. Giving away ten pounds and what was not known by the public was that Davy had only been given five days notice before the fight and had been ill. He achieved prominence overnight. The fans back home had to rely on what they picked up from the reports by American journalists but one of the best descriptions sent to "The Saturday Night" from New York, was given by Belfast's Joe Devlin (ex Celtic FC trainer) who was in Magill's corner. He told how Davy had caught a chill the Tuesday before the fight through a sudden change in the weather and had to spend a day in bed. Mr. Bridgewater, Roland Todd's manager who was accompanying him, wanted

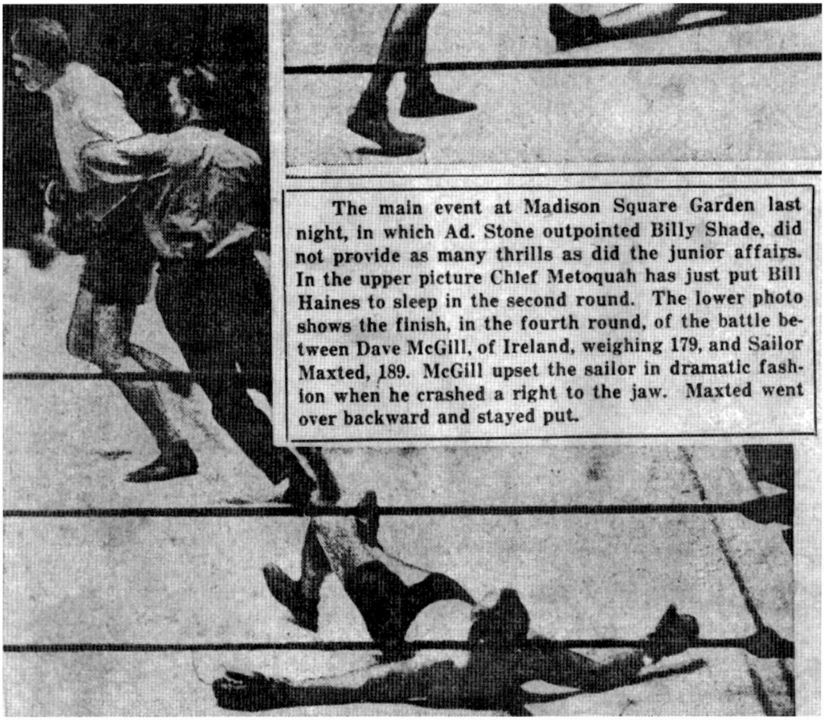

The main event at Madison Square Garden last night, in which Ad. Stone outpointed Billy Shade, did not provide as many thrills as did the junior affairs. In the upper picture Chief Metoquah has just put Bill Haines to sleep in the second round. The lower photo shows the finish, in the fourth round, of the battle between Dave McGill, of Ireland, weighing 179, and Sailor Maxted, 189. McGill upset the sailor in dramatic fashion when he crashed a right to the jaw. Maxted went over backward and stayed put.

him to postpone the fight. Davy never considered the suggestion, and decided to see the thing through.

Devlin said that "*His opponent was six ft one" in height, broader than Davy, and nearly a stone heavier. He was knocked out by Firpo in seven rounds, but was a very dangerous opponent, and could hit very hard. He rushed in at the first, with the result that Davy was put off his boxing, but about the end of the round, Magill began to land. He amazed the crowd with his two-handed work, and they could hardly believe he could hit so hard with both left and right. Davy was looking a lot better in the second round, and attacked the sailor fiercely. He went in very fast, landing his left to the body so fiercely that Maxted doubled up like a concertina. In the third he was fighting like himself, and now had the crowd with him. His punching was a treat, both hands, one as hard as the other, scarcely ever missing. The fourth and last round was short and fast. Davy went after the sailor and drove him round the ring with terrific punches, then after a minute and 15 seconds of the round had gone, he brought his right hand over the sailor's left and down on his chin. Maxted toppled over like a tree, his head was always going to the floor first, and it hit the ring so hard that his head bounced up almost a foot. It was a terrific knock-out and Maxted lay stiff until the referee counted eight, when he made a great effort to rise, but it was useless."* It was the dream start to his American tour.

LEO GATES, Jan. 18, 1924

Next, Davy met Leo Gates in the supporting fight on the bill for the legendary Harry Greb's defence of his World Middleweight title. Leo Gates was a six foot two inch Native American. A Mohawk Indian, he rejoiced in the name "Chief Metoquah," outweighed Davy nearly 20 pounds (Gates weighed 197 pounds against 178½ for Magill) and had ko'ed his opponent, Bill Haines in the second round, when they met on the previous bill when Davy had ko'ed Maxted, at Madison Square Gardens. Though he did not manage to knock him out, he gave Gates what the press described as *'a walloping that he would remember for a long time.* It was a bruising fight all the way, but Magill was too clever for Gates. The report continued *"It would seem as if Magill's stock was getting a well deserved boost, as the cheer that greeted his victory over Gates, was even greater than the applause he received after landing the K.O. on Maxted."* Tex Ricard, the legendary promoter, was at the fight, and at this stage it appeared likely that Davy would get a fight with the rising star of the American ring, Ad Stone, as top of the bill at Madison Square Gardens. A contest was also being arranged with Tiny Jim Herman who weighed 220 lbs, to take place in Omaha in the middle of February.

RINGSIDE wrote that "*Initial victories cause Americans to take notice.*" He was now being regarded by Irish Americans as one of their own - "*Magill Shows Up Best of Local Scrappers and Beats Leo Gates in Six Round Bout.*" The report went on to add that "*Dave Magill, the pick of the Irish heavyweights who has adopted Yonkers as his home, received the judges' decision over Leo Gates.*"

AD STONE, Feb. 29, 1924

Davy (left) meets Ad Stone before fight

Nearly 13,000 came to Madison Square Gardens to see the fight- it was a sell-out. Ad Stone, the latest sensation in the light heavyweight division, had been undefeated in 30 fights and had won 24 of them by KO. Promoter Tex Ricard had promised the winner a bout with Gene Tunney for the Championship of the World. We can get a sense of the drama of the fight from the American reporters.

According to the reporter "Igoe," "*Dave is a hard right hand hitter, and he kept dropping his good fist over on Stone's chin in the early rounds, but in the fourth and fifth Stone punished the Irishman severely. Dave was ever*

dangerous, however, coming out of hard rallies groggy but winging his right desperately and dangerously for Stone's chin."

At the beginning of the fight he had opened a cut over Stone's left eyebrow. Stone went on the attack and dominated the following rounds and on several occasions seemed like he could end the fight. In the third he cut Davy's lip and it proved impossible to stop the bleeding and the Irishman appeared in a bad way. Davy fought back and brought the house down towards the end of the seventh when he staggered Stone with a hard right to the jaw. "*Magill got away flying in the eighth and was much stronger and more accurate than Stone. He brought a flow from Stone's nose with a ripping left uppercut to the beak.........The crowd was with Magill now and his every telling effort was applauded."....... "Both fought like wild cats in the first part of the ninth and played for each other's body.... Stone came back and pounded him unmercifully around the head .... Davy swung his left to the body and later hooked over a corking right .... A volley of terrific right hooks shook up Davy and brought the gore."* Stone tried for the knock out in the eleventh but then suddenly after 42 seconds of the round, the referee intervened to halt the fight to save Davy from further punishment. Davy protested but to no avail.

Sid Mercer scored four rounds for Magill, six for Stone and one even. He wrote that Magill could probably have continued but that he was reeling blindly about the ring, with blood smeared features when the fight was stopped.

The reporter Liam O'Shea provided an explanation for the premature ending when he wrote *"Irish champion not discouraged over setback in Garden - Says referee should not have stopped bout .... the most surprised man in the house was Davy ..... there is not the slightest doubt but Magill would have been able to continue. The crowd was dumfounded at the unexpected ending."* What must have influenced the referee was the recent tragic case in the Garden ring of Frankie Jerome, a promising bantamweight who had been knocked out in Round 11 and subsequently died. It must be remembered that Davy had not taken a count during the fight. It was the persistent bleeding from Davy's lips which led the referee to act as he did. Outside of that, he was unmarked. The bleeding was easily explained. Davy had a few missing teeth in the front of his mouth which was normally protected by a gum shield when he went into the ring. However the New York Boxing Commission forbade gum shields and the rough edges of Davy's adjoining teeth had cut his lips when struck on the mouth. The result was the excessive bleeding from the mouth after Round three and it was this that led to the referee's decision to stop the fight in Round 11.

"*Magill Eagerly Sought after by Promoters; Will fight here again soon - Stone injured his left hand in the third round - had to postpone his bout with Tunney set for March 10,*" ran one headline.

"*Davy is a sensible youngster who has most of his fighting career ahead of him ..... He is expected to sail for Ireland in May but will be busy in the ring until then as he has had many offers.*"

Davy's American campaign was far from over. True he had a setback in the fight with Ad Stone, but he had acquitted himself well and was winning support from the fans. There would be plenty of opportunities ahead of him in the USA. Yet strange as it seems, this was his final appearance in an American ring and he was to return to Ireland.

It was possible that as an Irish hope, he could have made it big in American boxing and made his fortune. Yet the American venture had paid well, and in later years, his mother proudly related that he had £1,000 clear after paying off his promoters and expenses.

What caused his sudden change of plan? According to one theory, it was a persuasive letter from his fiancee, Molly Hynes. A daughter of Joe Devlin, Davy's corner man in Madison Square Gardens, recalled how her father told her that Davy showed him the letter from home and announced his decision to return. The answer may have been simpler. The original plan was to return before May and Roland Todd, who had accompanied him to the USA also returned. Both Davy and Roland Todd had only planned for a six month stay. What was bringing Davy back to Ireland was his planned marriage.

The American press got wind of the romance. The wedding had been set for the previous Christmas, but had to be postponed because of his American bouts. Now back in Ireland, Davy married Molly Hynes, in St. Paul's Church, Falls Road, Belfast on May 5, 1924 and a honeymoon followed the wedding in London and Paris.

The press in Ireland covered the wedding. "Irish Boxer's Romance" ran the story in the Irish Independent. The Daily Herald in England also gave coverage, relating to readers how the couple had first met two years before, in the dark days of the Troubles when Davy had rescued the bride's father from a group of armed raiders.

Davie Magill, the Irish heavy-weight boxer, leaving St. Paul's Church, Belfast, with his bride, Miss Molly Haynes, amid a shower of confetti from his enthusiastic admirers.

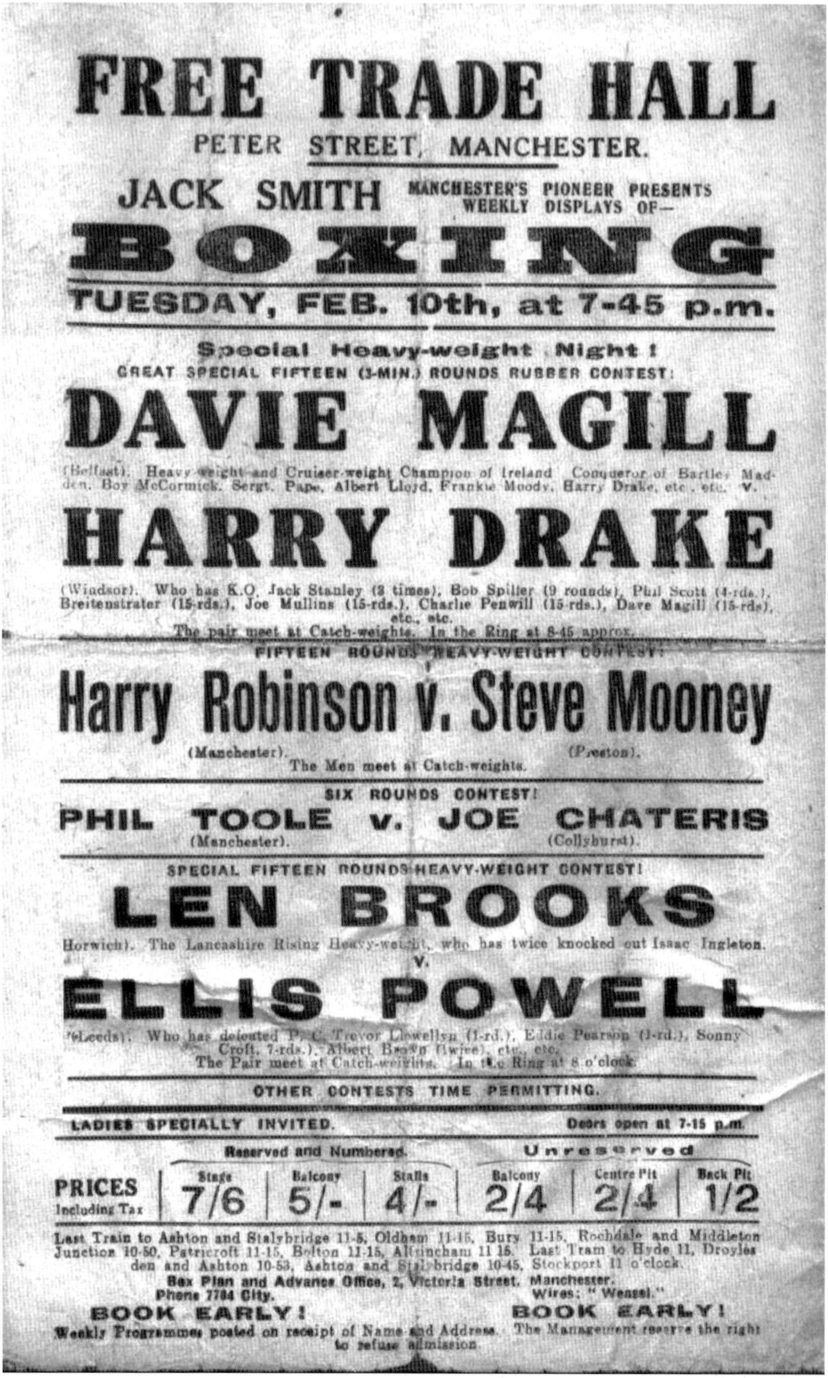

FREE TRADE HALL

PETER STREET, MANCHESTER.

JACK SMITH MANCHESTER'S PIONEER PRESENTS WEEKLY DISPLAYS OF—

BOXING

TUESDAY, FEB. 10th, at 7-45 p.m.

Special Heavy-weight Night!

GREAT SPECIAL FIFTEEN (3-MIN.) ROUNDS RUBBER CONTEST:

DAVIE MAGILL

(Belfast). Heavy-weight and Cruiser-weight Champion of Ireland. Conqueror of Bartley Madden, Boy McCormick, Sergt. Pape, Albert Lloyd, Frankie Moody, Harry Drake, etc., etc. v.

HARRY DRAKE

(Windsor). Who has K.O. Jack Stanley (2 times), Bob Spiller (9 rounds), Phil Scott (4-rds.), Breitenstrater (15-rds.), Joe Mullins (15-rds.), Charlie Penwill (15-rds.), Dave Magill (15-rds), etc., etc.

The pair meet at Catch-weights. In the Ring at 8-45 approx.

FIFTEEN ROUNDS HEAVY-WEIGHT CONTEST:

Harry Robinson v. Steve Mooney

(Manchester). (Preston).

The Men meet at Catch-weights.

SIX ROUNDS CONTEST!

PHIL TOOLE v. JOE CHATERIS

(Manchester). (Collyhurst).

SPECIAL FIFTEEN ROUNDS HEAVY-WEIGHT CONTEST!

LEN BROOKS

(Horwich). The Lancashire Rising Heavy-weight, who has twice knocked out Isaac Ingleton.

v.

ELLIS POWELL

(Leeds). Who has defeated P. C. Trevor Llewellyn (1-rd.), Eddie Pearson (1-rd.), Sonny Croft, 7-rds.), Albert Brown (twice), etc., etc.

The Pair meet at Catch-weights. In the Ring at 8 o'clock.

OTHER CONTESTS TIME PERMITTING.

LADIES SPECIALLY INVITED. Doors open at 7-15 p.m.

PRICES Including Tax	Reserved and Numbered			Unreserved		
	Stage	Balcony	Stalls	Balcony	Centre Pit	Back Pit
	7/6	5/-	4/-	2/4	2/4	1/2

Last Train to Ashton and Stalybridge 11-5, Oldham 11-15, Bury 11-15, Rochdale and Middleton Junction 10-50, Patricroft 11-15, Bolton 11-15, Altrincham 11 15. Last Tram to Hyde 11, Droylesden and Ashton 10-53, Ashton and Stalybridge 10-45, Stockport 11 o'clock.

Box Plan and Advance Office, 2, Victoria Street. Manchester.
Phone 7784 City. Wires: "Wensel."

BOOK EARLY! BOOK EARLY!

Weekly Programmes posted on receipt of Name and Address. The Management reserve the right to refuse admission.

IRELAND'S MOST POPULAR FIGHTER IN THE TWENTIES

Davy's return to the ring was planned for June 21, 1924, against Sid Pape. Five thousand fans came to Celtic Park expecting to see him enhance his reputation, and to say that consternation reigned among the crowd when it was seen that Magill was in a hopeless condition was *"but a mild way of expressing the spectators' feelings"* (Timekeeper). Davy was forced to the boards four times in the second round and the referee stopped the fight. The fans had got the shock of their lives. It was said that Davy was not in the best condition, but his manager, George Sayers expressed the opinion that he was fit and well.

The first Wembley Stadium Boxing Bill - Promoter Goes Bankrupt.

He had one more contest before the end of the year when on Aug 9, 1924, he met Pape in a return bout. It was the first fight bill to be staged in the newly opened Wembley Stadium and Davy had the distinction of being on the bill. It was the famous Gibbons Bloomfield programme. Davy was accompanied by a big following from Ireland and had rarely looked in better form. He was more like his old self and after a give and take battle, he avenged the Celtic Park fiasco and got the verdict, fighting better in the closing rounds of the ten round contest. However there followed another contest, though this was outside the ring. The hope was that the Wembley bill would draw a world record breaking crowd of 120,000, but this did not materialise. The Gibbons Bloomfield contest has gone down in boxing history, not so much because of the fight itself in which the American knocked out Bloomfield in the third round, but because the promoter Major Arnold Wilson, could not pay Gibbon's purse of £11,000 and became bankrupt. It was the same for Davy and the other boxers who had taken part in the preliminary bouts, though their claims were for sums between £100 and £250. They had tried unsuccessfully on several occasions to interview Major Wilson but now they were asking their solicitors to issue writs on their behalf.

Mixed Fortunes in 1925

After more than six months lay off, Davy returned to the ring. He seemed to have recovered his old form. On February 10, 1925 at the Free Trade Hall, Manchester, he outclassed Harry Drake. This had been their fourth meeting, Davy having won two and Drake the third. Davy had prepared for the fight in Doncaster with Roland Todd's stable. By the end of the second round it was clear that the contest could only have the one ending. It was remarkable that Drake was able to last the distance.

Group of professional boxers including 2 Davy Magill, 3 TED Broadribb, Stephen Glynn, Seaman Hall, Ernie Rice, Teddy Murton, 7 Arthur Duncan and 12 Gipsy Daniels

Then on February 16, in Southampton, Davy won a smashing victory over Harry Reeve who appeared to be carrying extra weight while Davy was said to be in the pink of condition. The fight ended in the fourth with a terrific right to the jaw and even after the count of ten, Reeve was still out.

He was rather surprisingly defeated on points by Gipsy Daniels on February 22. Both looked extremely fit and Daniels was ahead after the first ten rounds. However in the twelfth and thirteenth, Davy turned the tables and had Daniels at his mercy. Daniels was considered a very strong man but he did not have the strength and stamina of the Irishman. Davy missed his opportunity of winning by a KO and Daniels was lucky to win on points. It was a similar story at Liverpool Stadium against Frank Fowler on March 12. Davy was slow to start and though he fought in brilliant style towards the end of the bout, he was unable to cut back Fowler's lead and the outcome was that the headlines read "Battered Helpless, But Victorious" and "Battered Man Wins".

On April 14, 1925 he met Gipsy Daniels for a third time. Up to this, honours were shared, so this was the needle match held in St George's Market, Belfast. Again the report noted that Magill never warmed up until more than a third of the fight had passed. Daniels was happier to use his superior reach and keep the fight at a distance. The fans roared "*Make him mix it, Dave*" in a deafening clamour for their favourite, but Daniels survived. It was a needle match right to the end as the pair ignored the final gong to mark the end of 15 rounds and continued to swap blows. The referee's decision of a draw was not universally popular.

On May 11, 1925 his contest with Charlie Ring (Australia) also ended in a draw. Described as "the finest cruiserweight battle seen for a long, long time," it was a keenly fought bout from the beginning from such a well matched pair. The referee's decision of a draw was considered fair and both fighters left the ring to a terrific round of applause.

On June 21, 1925 he met Sid Pape again. This time the fight went the full 15 rounds but from the start there was never any doubt as to Magill's superiority and by the end he was simply hitting Pape when and how he liked.

On July 13, 1925 Charlie Ring (Australia) LP - "Magill's Hard Luck" After their draw in May, a return bout was inevitable. This time Ring won well on points after a "ding dong battle" and one of the best fights ever seen at the Ring, one of London's most popular venues. Magill was in front after eight rounds but then suffered a cut eye which turned the tide of the contest. After this he faded and Ring took over managing to recover and evade the Irishman's attempts to get a KO.

There were two fights in August at Croke Park. On August 1, he met Jack Mahoney (Cork) in a 20 round contest for the Irish Cruiserweight championship - a purse, side stakes and a gold belt were at stake. Mahoney had an unbeaten record and was regarded as one of the most aggressive fighters Ireland had produced in recent years. Davy won the fight by a very clear margin but the finish was marred by ugly scenes when some of Mahoney's supporters rushed into the ring and there looked as if there was going to be another fight between Magill and one of Mahoney's seconds who assumed a threatening attitude but Magill promptly took up an attitude of defence until officials restored order. Seeing the mood of the crowd, the referee withheld announcing his decision until order was restored.

BIG HEAVYWEIGHT CONTEST

Dave Magill (Belfast) and Ed die Richie (Stratford, London) who meet in a contest of 15 three-minute rounds at the Nottingham Victor ia Baths to-night.

Then on August 22, 1925 he met Leggy Sullivan (Cork), watched by a crowd of 5,000. The fight was a one sided affair and after ten two minute rounds, Davy was scoring readily whenever he was able to" break way from the embraces of his opponent."

His last fight of the year came on September 21, 1925 against Sid Pape. Davy was favourite and had the advantage of height and reach at Newcastle on Tyne, but Pape got the verdict, which met with a mixed reception.

1926

Davy was suffering from almost a year's absence from the ring after his loss to Sid Pape and what could be considered a come-back fight took place on July 10, 1926 when he met Stoker Stubbs at Croke Park. He looked very fit. He had fought better, but he did enough to secure a narrow points victory over the Londoner. He fared better when on October 25, 1926 he met Leon Randol (Belgium). Davy out boxed him at the Ring for most rounds and even though a clash of heads in the fourth round cut Davy's eye, he outscored him throughout the fight and ended it dramatically in the thirteenth when the referee intervened to save Randol from further damage. There was further success on November 15, 1926 against Con O'Kelly (Hull) for the Irish Heavyweight title. The referee rated the fight as one of the most amazing he had ever handled. O'Kelly had started off as favourite but Davy turned on the pressure after the ninth round and O'Kelly had to surrender in the eleventh. On Dec 29, 1926 he ko'ed Eugene Steppe (Belgium). The cruiserweight champion of Belgium was lacking in experience and was counted out in the second round. A record crowd at the Ulster Hall saw Davy in tip top form.; hundreds were turned away from the doors disappointed.

Davy's recent form suggested great things. It was likely that there would be a return with O'Kelly and another bout with Tom Berry for the light-heavy-weight title. He himself was looking ahead to a bout with Phil Scott for the heavyweight title early in the New Year. Having the experience of six years in the ring behind him, he could look back on 56 bouts of which he had won 43 (24 by KO), drawn three and lost ten. The record showed only three KO's against him, credited to Jack Bloomfield, Ad Stone and Sid Pape but he had never been counted out.

British Light-Heavyweight Championship
31 January, 1927

For the second time in his career Davy was challenging for the title. This time he had more experience than he had had in the Bloomfield fight of 1923 and he had two previous victories over the champion Tom Berry in 1921. However, after a 20 round bout in Manchester on 31 January, the champion, Tom Berry of London managed to retain his title and overcome the heavier punching of the challenger, with superior ring craft. The fight was also interesting for the fact that the referee, J. W. H. T. Douglas, for some unknown reason, chose to referee from outside of the ring. A reporter said of the referee, "*He sat there last night with the blue smoke curling up from a cigar in his hand and he was almost as arresting a figure as the fighters. Suddenly his voice would ring out; "Step back - both!*" It was a thrilling fight and considered one of the best seen in the Belle Vue Hall. Yet it had to be said that he had failed to win the title for a second time, even though he had beaten five British light-heavyweight champions, twice in

Press Fund Boxing Tournament.—The heavy-weight contest in the Ulster Hall resulted in a draw. Photo shows Magill and Fowler shaking hands. Behind are Mr. G. Sayers, Mr. Jim Rice (organiser), and Mr. L. Webster.

some cases, (Harry Reeve, Boy McCormick, Tom Berry, Gipsy Daniels and Frank Moody) earlier in his career in non title fights.

Then on Mar 9, 1927 he met Frank Fowler. The bout in the Ulster Hall was described as the best that had been seen in Belfast for years and it was anyone's fight till the end when the referee called it a draw. Fights like this take place only once in a generation in Belfast, was the universal view. *"It was a real gladiatorial battle, skill, speed and fierce heavy hitting being in abundance."* (Ringside) More disappointing was the defeat on April 11, 1927 against Charlie Chetwynd at York, the latter winning a good fight easily on points.

Davy's prospects for yet another title fight came on April 25, 1927 in his second fight with Frank Fowler. In what was billed as an eliminator for the cruiserweight title, they met for a purse and side stake of £400. Fowler had the better of his opponent and was well ahead on points but was disqualified for a low blow in the eighth round.

Another six months lay off followed, but his return to the ring this time was disappointing. On September 20, 1927 he met Frank Moody, *"The fight was even more sensational than the weigh-in." "Sensational Fight at Liverpool Stadium, packed to capacity - 15 rounds at 12 stone 9,"* ran the headline. Davy had undergone preparation in Doncaster but it was known that he was having difficulty making the weight and it was thought that this could be his last fight at cruiserweight. Moody weighed inside the limit with his clothes on, but Magill refused to weigh in and paid forfeit. In the first round Magill got off the mark at a blistering pace and it looked like an early k.o. in his favour. Then in the second round the tables were turned and Moody put his opponent down on four occasions. The referee, Ackland, editor of "Boxing," gave the fight to Moody. It was Davy's last appearance before his fans in Liverpool. There was similar disappointment in the return with O'Kelly on November 7, when Davy's second threw in the towel at the beginning of the sixth after a bad cut to Davy's right eye.

1928 Davy was only a shadow of his old self

It was becoming obvious that Davy's best days were behind him. Results were going the wrong way and he was finding it harder to make the weight. He had lost much of his old snappiness and was often out of distance with his swings. He was having problems with his right hand and it was no longer the deadly weapon it once had been. Many thought that he was only a shadow of his old self. Age was catching up with him; he was approaching his mid-thirties. The Magill of a few years earlier would have seen off most of his opponents in the next year with ease.

Ringside wrote "*Davy Magill is one of the most temperamental chaps in the boxing game ....I knew (before the Tootle fight in 1928)... that there was little chance of seeing in action the Magill of two years ago or even of 12 months ago. Magill goes all to pieces during a spell of inactivity. He is all right when the going is good and he is kept busy .... when he gets a setback, however of any kind ... he comes back to the business worried and apprehensive and in no mood to do himself justice.*"

Yet he managed to achieve some victories like those over Eddie Richie, twice over George Tootles, Bobby Shields and a sixth round KO of Bob Carvill. "*Magill may have reached the stage of being a good trial horse, but he is still a force to be reckoned with. He is as wily a bird as ever stepped into a ring and has probably forgotten more than many a younger man knows*" wrote Ringside. After a long spell of inactivity, he entered the ring against George Tootles of Leeds. It appeared to some observers that he was having problems with his right hand. But in the last four rounds, he was at his best. The Belfast crowd was raised to a frenzy as Davy went after his opponent '*in regular caveman style and gave of his last ounce to earn a knock-out.*' However it was obvious that the calibre of opponents was poorer and the crowds were falling off. There were several major defeats, some at the hands of comparative unknowns. Yet there were times when he showed some of his old brilliance. He had a smashing victory at Belfast Stadium on February 14, 1930 over Battling Sullivan in a 12 round contest when he outclassed Sullivan. After the fight Sullivan let it be known that he would not have cared to have been in the same ring as Magill a few years earlier. Davy had shown that he was far from being a spent force but there were clear signs that the writing was on the wall. "*Davy Magill Eclipsed by Hard Hitting Italian*" read the headline to this ten rounder in the Ulster Hall on March 6, against Primo Ubaldi. There were reports again of an injured right hand which had been causing him trouble for some time. It was noticed that he was mainly depending on his left in his last fight.

Against Dick Power of Wales, on September 30, Davy appeared to be carrying excess weight and was out of condition. He took a battering from the Welsh champion in this heavyweight bout yet showed real grit and ability to absorb punishment and saw out the 15 rounds. The crowd in Pontypridd was not up to expectations, another sure sign that Davy was no longer the crowd pleaser whom cross Channel promoters had vied to put on the top of their bills. This was to be his last venture out of Ireland and from this on he was to rely on local fixtures, mainly in Belfast.

At this point, at the age of 36 and after a decade in the ring, Davy decided to retire in June 1931. From this on, his ring appearances were to be in exhibitions with both amateur and professional boxers in small towns and villages throughout the country. He had been appointed to act as boxing instructor to the newly formed RUC Athletic Club in 1928 and then to Queen's University Boxing Club. In 1930, he was in charge of training of Saint Peter's, the newly formed Corrigan Park Amateur Boxing Club; he was credited with doing much to advance the amateur game. Timekeeper wrote "*Good work is being done by Davy Magill at Queen's and by Kenny Webb at YMCA - and the work of the Corrigan Park Club ... they have unearthed really good talent. Once these lads get thoroughly used to the ring conditions, there should be plenty of entertainment when they meet.*" Davy's coaching of the finer elements of the game at Queen's was no doubt the reason for their rapid progress; they had been joint holders of the Irish Universities Championship in 1929-1930 and now they went on to win the title. One of the prodigies of the club, who won the Irish Universities heavyweight championship in 1936 was Robert Blair "Paddy Mayne", a law student from Newtownards, who was also capped for Ireland and the British Lions in rugby. He subsequently went on to become one of the founders of the SAS during World War 2.

THE QUEEN'S UNIVERSITY BOXING TEAM.

("Northern Whig" Photograph.)

L-R: Davy Magill, Leslie Bridgewater, Roland Todd, George Hetherington

THE COMEBACK 1935

Davy the runner

Frustrated with life outside the ring, Davy decided on a return at the age of 40. His comeback was welcomed by some who felt it might revive boxing in Belfast. Since his retirement there had been little action in the cruiserweight and heavyweight ranks. But comebacks are seldom a good idea and at such an advanced age, it was surely ill-advised.

He had three bouts inside the next four weeks against Scottish opponents. At the Arena, Chapel Fields on May 29, 1935, he was impressive when he met Arthur Gray, the leading contender for the Scottish cruiserweight title. He appeared to be boxing as strongly as ever having regard to the time he had been out of the ring and a KO came in Round 6. Next on June 8, 1935, it was against Joe Doherty. He won his second

Centre of back row: Davy, the cross country runner, 1919

Irish Professional Champions with their managers and trainers
Front row L-R: Con McCann (feather-weight), FrankBurns (welter-weight), Davy Magill (cruiser and heavy-weight Champion), Tom Connolly (middle-weight champion, Gunboat Smith (feather),
Back row:Mr S. Boyle (assisant trainer), Mr. Tom Murphy (President), Jim Hanna (bantam-weight champion), Mr Vallely, Hugh Brittian (feather), Mr. H. Hanley (manager), and Jack Robinson (trainer)

comeback fight at the Chapel Fields, in more workmanlike fashion than his first, by getting down to work immediately and a KO came in the second round. On June 27, 1935 it was against Jock Robertson, dubbed the "Highland's Carnera." Davy outfought the Scot at Grosvenor Park and the towel was thrown in at the end of round three.

Master and Pupil

These early victories could not disguise the fact that the quality of the opposition had changed. Contests were now being proposed with young boxers he had trained himself a few years before in the RUC and Queen's clubs. A bout with Pat Marrinan, a former member of Queen's club whom Davy had coached was being mooted but it was Barney Regan who had been tutored by Davy when in the RUC, before he joined the paid ranks, who became his next opponent. It was a sad day for Davy when on August 7, 1935 at Dalymount Park, he was stopped in the third by his former pupil, much to the displeasure of Davy and many who thought that it was still anybody's fight. In the return in the Ulster Hall, September 12, 1935, Davy finished a comfortable winner and proved that he was still the master.

The writing was on the wall in 1936. While he won four bouts and two of them by the KO route, and many were still amazed by his stamina, there was no disguising the fact that he lost five times in that year. Against Jack Dobbs (Armagh) on March 9, he was forced to retire in the third round with a badly gashed eyebrow at the Chapel Fields, though in the return on March 25, he Ko'ed Dobbs in the same round three. A third meeting with Dobbs was decided in the tenth when the referee stopped Dobbs. In a bout on April 29, at the Chapel Fields, he lost on points to Ed Steele Martin in a bout which was reported as "Youth beats age and experience." There were two further defeats to Len Moran on 24 July and Jack McKnight on 2 September 1936. His final contest in the ring was against George Haywood of Darlington, at Larne Factory Arena on September 18, 1936; Haywood was counted out in the third round. Also making an appearance on the same Larne bill was a young flyweight, Rinty Monaghan, who won a bout of six two minute rounds over fellow Belfastman, Joe Duffy.

Davy's last appearance in the ring seems to have been an exhibition he boxed with Const. John McNeill, an old friend from Glenarm, in Queen's University gym. It was the end of a boxing career which had started in 1920 at the age of 25 and ended in 1936 when he was 41. His trainer, Billy Campbell, recalled in 1945 that *"Davy started a bit late in life. If he'd started earlier he'd have gone places."*

"Prior to Barry McGuigan it is possible that Ireland's most popular boxer had been Davy Magill" wrote Belfast historian, Fred Heatley

"Maybe, he had too many failings to reach the apex of the toughest of all sports. His advanced age in commencing his ring career was one, his lack of real weight to compete in the heavyweight division where many of his opponents were found, was another, and at the end of his boxing days a lack of real

dedication to training obviously cost him contests he should have won. Perhaps had he availed of American professionalism at the very beginning, his potential may have been realized, and that potential was considerable as is shown by his annexing of three different championships, his successful defending of each of them and his retirement as unbeaten champion, plus two challenges for the British Empire (as it then was) light-heavyweight crown. It was quite an achievement for the handsome Cairncastle man"

Ocean Venture 1942

When World War Two broke out and with his boxing career over, Davy joined the Merchant Navy. In 1942 he was on board the Ocean Venture. It was a British owned steam merchant ship of 7,174 tons which had been launched at Richmond, California on 27-09-1941. It had left Vancouver, stopped at Los Angeles, passed through the Panama Canal and was heading for Hampton Roads, Virginia. On board was a crew of 45 and its cargo of 9,115 tons of foodstuff and four aircraft, destined for Britain. Under the terms of the Lend-lease programme of 1941, the US was supplying its allies with food and war materials and on 11 December, 1941, formally declared war on Germany. At 10.35 hours on 8 February, 1942, the unescorted Ocean Venture was hit by a torpedo from the German U boat, U-108, under the command of Klaus Scholtz, near Cape Hatteras off the coast of Virginia and stopped. Some of the crew abandoned ship but the vessel remained afloat until a second torpedo struck at 11.16 hours, and she sank by the bow. The master, Reginald Sharpe Craston, and 13 of the crew were rescued by the American vessel, USS Roe and landed at Norfolk, Virginia. The remaining 29 crew, among them, Davy, and two gunners were lost. Their names are recorded on the Tower Hill Memorial, London, which commemorates men and women of the Merchant Navy and Fishing Fleets who died in both World Wars and who have no known grave.

Record of Davy Magill 1895-1942

87 fights - won 58 (33 inside the distance) - lost 24 (7 inside distance, no KO) - drew 5

1920	Jan. 22	Const. J. McHale (Enniskillen)	Belfast	W twl 6	6
	Mar. 10	H/Const. H. McCappin (local)	Belfast	W ko 6	6
	Dec. 29	Wally Buckley (Liverpool)	Belfast	W ko 4	10
1921	Mar. 15	Ex-Stkr. Herbie McCormick (local)	Belfast	W ko 2	6
	Mar. 28	Sid Burns (Aldgate)	Glasgow	W ko 1	-
	Apr. 1	Albert Brown (Otley)	Belfast	W ko 2	15
	Apr. 23	Joe Dixon (Leeds)	Belfast	W twl 14	15
	May 9	Roland Todd (Doncaster)	Belfast	L 15	15
	May 19	Tom Berry (Custom House)	Belfast	W 15	15
	May 23	Harry Knight (Barbados)	London N.S.C.	W ko 7	-
	9 July	Tom Berry (Custom House)	Holland Park	W15	15
	Aug. 6	Wild Burt Kenny (U.S.A.)	Belfast	W dsq 3	10
	Nov. 3	Const. Lew Williams (Australia/RIC)	Enniskillen	W twl 3	10
	(Won vacant Royal Irish Constabulary heavyweight title)				
	Dec. 16	Const. Lew Williams (Australia/RIC)	Dublin	W rsf 2	10
	Dec. 19	Harry Drake (Windsor)	Belfast	L 15	15
	Dec. 28	Alf Bright (Kingsland)	Belfast	W ko 6	15
1922	Mar. 21	H/Const. H. McCappin (Belfast)	Larne	W twl 4	15
	Apr. 25	Cyclone Billy Warren (Australia)	Ballymoney	W twl 2	15
	May 27	Sgt. Palmer (Essex Regt.)	Belfast	W ko 2	10
	July 20	Sgt. Syd Pape (York)	Liverpool	W ko 12	15
	Aug. 24	Ex-Stkr. Herbie McCormick (Belfast)	Newtownards	W rtd 3	10
	Aug. 28	Sgt. Sid Pape (York)	Liverpool	W 15	15
	Sept.6	Ex-Stkr. McCormick (Belfast)	Carnlough	W rtd. 7	10
	Sept. 18	Gipsy Billy Daniels (Newport)	Liverpool	W 20	20
	Oct. 23	Harry Drake (Windsor)	Belfast	W 15	15
	Nov. 2	Frank Moody (Pontypridd)	Liverpool	W 15	15
	Nov. 23	Sgt. Harold Rolph (Canada)	Liverpool	W rsf 2	15
	Dec. 7	Harry Drake (Windsor)	Liverpool	W rtd 9	15
	Dec. 18	Albert Lloyd (Australia)	Belfast	W 15	15
1923	Apr. 9	Arthur Townley (Birkenhead)	Liverpool	W 15	15
	Apr. 23	Albert Lloyd (Australia)	Belfast	Drew 15	15
	May 17	Jack Bloomfield (Islington-hldr.)	London, Olympia	L twl 13	20
	(British Empire light heavyweight title)				
	June 23	Bartley Madden (Galway/USA)	Belfast	W dsq 15	20
	(Won vacant Irish heavyweight title)				
	Aug. 20	Noel Boy McCormick (Salford)	Liverpool	W twl 10	20
	(Won vacant Irish Light-heavyweight title)				
	Oct. 15	Gdsmn. Charlie Penwill (Penge)	Doncaster	W dsq 12	12
	Oct. 29	George Cooke (Australia)	London N.S.C.	L 15 15	
	Dec. 21	Sailor Tom Maxted (Newark)	New York	W ko 4	6
1924	Jan. 18	Leo Gates (Washington)	New York	W 6	6
	Feb. 28	Ad Stone (Philadelphia)	New York	L rsf 11	15
	June 21	Sgt. Syd Pape (York)	Belfast	L rsf 2	15
	Aug. 9	Sgt. Syd Pape (York)	Wembley	W 10	10
1925	Feb. 10	Harry Drake (Windsor)	Manchester	W 15	15
	Feb. 16	Harry Reeve (Plaistow)	Southampton	W ko 4	15
	Feb. 22	Gipsy Daniels (Newport)	London	L 15	15
	Mar. 12	Frank Fowler (York)	Liverpool	L 15	15
	Apr. 14	Gipsy Billy Daniels (Newport)	Belfast	Drew 15	15
	May 11	Charlie Ring (Australia)	London, Ring	Drew 15	15
	June 21	Sgt. Syd Pape (York)	Leeds	W 15	15

	July 13	Charlie Ring (Australia)	London, Ring	L 15	15
	Aug. 1	Jack Mahony (Cork)	Dublin	W 20	20
		(Retained Irish light-heavyweight title)			
	Aug. 22	Ed. Sullivan (Cork)	Dublin	W 10	10
	Sept. 21	Sgt. Syd Pape (York)	Newcastle-upon-Tyne	L 15	15
1926	July 10	Stkr. Stubbs (London)	Dublin	W 15	15
	Oct. 25	Leon Randel (Belgium)	London, Ring	W rtd 13	15
	Nov. 15	Con O'Kelly (Hull)	Hull	W twl 11	20
		(Retained Irish heavy-weight title)			
	Dec. 29	Eugene Steppe (Belgium)	Belfast	W ko 2	20
1927	Jan. 31	Tom Berry (Custom House)	Manchester	L 20	20
		(Vacant British Empire light-heavyweight title)			
	Mar. 9	Frank Fowler (York)	Belfast	Drew 15	15
	Apr. 11	Charlie Chetwynd (Leicester)	York	L 15	15
	Apr. 25	Frank Fowler (York)	Holland Park	W dsq 8	15
	Sept. 20	Frank Moody (Pontypridd)	Liverpool	L rsf 2	15
	Nov. 7	Con O'Kelly (Hull)	Hull	L rtd 5	15
1928	Feb. 13	Eddie Richie (Luton)	Nottingham	L 15	15
	Mar. 12	Eddie Richie (Luton)	Nottingham	Drew 15	15
	Jun. 14	George Tootles (Leeds)	Belfast	W 12	12
	Sept. 4	George Tootles (Leeds)	Belfast	W 15	15
	Nov. 7	Bobby Shields (Glasgow)	Belfast	W dsq 10	15
	Dec. 10	Bob Carvill (Bridlington)	Hull	W ko 6	15
	Dec. 14	Phil Scott (Herne Bay)	Belfast	Exhib.	
1929	Jan. 25	Bobby Shields (Glasgow)	Belfast	W dsq 10	15
	Mar. 6	Primo Ubaldo (Italy)	Belfast	L 10	10
	Sept. 30	Dick Power (Cumfelimbach)	Pontypridd	L 15	15
	Oct. 25	Charlie Chetwynd (Leicester)	Belfast	L 12	12
1930	Feb. 14	Battling Sullivan (Preston)	Belfast	W 12	12
1931	June	*Announced his retirement as undefeated Irish champion*			
1935	May 29	Arthur Grey (Glasgow)	Belfast	W ko 6	10
	June 8	Joe Docherty (Falkirk)	Belfast	W ko 2	10
	June 27	Jock Robertson (Inverness)	Belfast	W rtd 3	6
	Aug. 7	Barney Regan (Dundrum)	Dublin	L rsf 3	10
	Sept. 12	Barney Regan (Dundrum)	Belfast	W 6	6
1936	Mar. 9	Jack Dobbs (Armagh)	Belfast	L rtd 3	10
	Mar. 25	Jack Dobbs (Armagh)	Belfast	W ko 3	10
	Apr. 20	Jim Mount (Greenock)	Belfast	L 10	10
	Apr. 29	Eddie Steele Martin (Lurgan)	Belfast	L 10	10
	May 29	Pat Cowley (Belfast)	Ballycarry	W rsf 4	10
	June 6	Jack Dobbs (Armagh)	Belfast	W rsf 10	10
	July 24	Len Moran (Darlington)	Larne	L 8	8
	Sept. 2	Jack McKnight (local)	Belfast	L 10	10
	Sept. 18	George Heywood (Darlington)	Belfast	W ko 3	10

Acknowledgements to Fred Heatley and Miles Templeton

8a. Pat Magill (1902-1950)

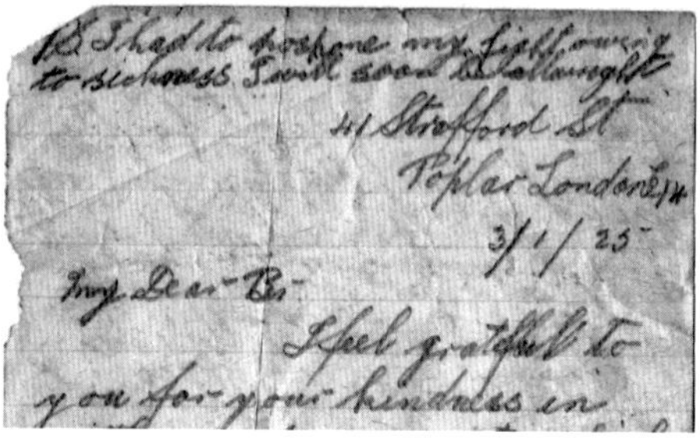
P.S. I had to postpone my fight owing
to sickness I will soon [illegible]
41 Strafford St
Poplar London E14
3/1/25
My Dear Bro-
I feel grateful to
you for your kindness in

Extract from a letter from Pat to John

The boxing career of Pat, who had emigrated to Australia in 1926, has been something of a mystery and has only recently come to light. A friend of the Magill brothers, Bob McKillop (Felix's father) had seen him sparring with his brothers and claimed that he could have been the best of them all. A neighbour, Ben Stewart, recalled that his father had told him that on one occasion when Davy had been unable to box, the young Pat, who was at ringside, stripped off and entered the ring in his place. His older brother, Willie, had always claimed that Pat was the strongest of all the seven brothers; stories were told of how he would carry a hundredweight bag of cement under each arm when working. He won a reputation for being the only man around who managed to lift a massive stone in the neighbourhood, which up to then had defied the best efforts of all the local strongmen around Cairncastle.

Yet his story as a boxer has been overlooked and forgotten. He had emigrated to Australia in 1926 and communication was not easy. When journalists wrote of the "Fighting Magills", it was Davy and Jim who were singled out and occasionally John. However they were leaving out Pat and only recently the picture has emerged of a boxer who fought professionally at middleweight and later at light-heavyweight and heavyweight; he was inconsistent and didn't achieve the success of Davy or Jim. Some claimed that he couldn't keep his temper and that he didn't put in the training required to go to the top. But it has to be said that he appeared in rings, from Belfast to Liverpool and Leipzig in Germany. He went on to box in Perth, where he represented the state of Western Australia and stood toe to toe with Ambrose Palmer, one of the up and coming stars of Twentieth Century Australian boxing. In the search to discover his boxing career, Belfast boxing historian, Fred Heatley has unearthed several bouts in Belfast and Mary-Attracta Connolly has provided further details from Australia. The only family memorabilia was a tantalising clue in the post-script to a letter that he wrote to his brother, John, from London in 1925 when he stated that he "*had to postpone a fight due to illness.*"

Pat's first recorded fights took place in Belfast while he was in the RUC. In October 1922, at the age of twenty, he showed promise when he stopped his first opponent, P. Flood, in the fourth round of a six round middleweight contest. In December of the following year, he stopped Constable Smallman (RUC) in the second round of a six round bout.

In 1924 he suffered two setbacks when he was stopped in round five of a six round contest with Jim Greer of Belfast on January 5, and was outpointed by Pat

Sabri Mahir

Logue of Crumlin, January 26. In the following year, Logue was claiming to be Irish middleweight champion when he fought a draw with Jack Phoenix on the same bill as Davy Magill retained his Irish heavyweight title against Jack Mahony in Dublin. Pat got his revenge on Jim Greer in Belfast on March 8. A report of the bout followed: *"In the nature of a return, these middleweights met over a six round course, Magill reversing the previous decision. Greer attacked in the opening rounds, but Magill who has come on a lot, fought back well and forced Greer to the ropes, Magill having the best of the first round. In the second Greer tried hard for a knock-out but the policeman stemmed a severe attack by forcing a clinch. The referee had to caution both for wrestling and from that a good stand up bout was witnessed. Magill, having a slight margin at the end , was declared the winner."* In August 1924, Pat left the RUC, went to London and continued to box. In a letter home to his brother John, he said that he had to call off a fight in January 1925 due to flu, but March 3, 1925, saw him travel to Leipzig in Germany, where he lost to Sabri Mahir from Turkey, suffering a knockout in round five.

There is a gap in the record until a year later, when he had a further bout in Liverpool on May 20, 1926, in which he stopped his opponent, Joe Crampton (Oldham), in round five. This appears to have been his last bout before leaving for Australia, 14 October, 1926.

Pat in Australia, 1926

The record of Pat's bouts in Australia is incomplete. This is evident when we see that we have only a total tally of ten bouts in Australia, yet we see him fight three bouts in little over a week between December 30, 1927 and January 7, 1928. It seems unlikely that eighteen months later, he could be representing the state of Western Australia against Victoria, with only a few fights under his belt in the intervening period. In Australia he sometimes boxed under the name "Pat McGill." He had settled near Perth, Western Australia and several of his contests were reported in the pages of "The West Australian" between 1927 and 1933.

Pat Magill v Kit Burnie

One of his first bouts in Australia ended in controversial circumstances. As "The West Australian" reported "*When Burnie (Perth) beat Magill (Ireland) on a knock-out in Round 2, in 1927, there was much consternation and anger in the Irishman's corner for Magill was half pushed and half knocked to the canvas and hit his head a resounding crack on the hard boards. Magill, although hurt was ready to reach his feet at the call of "nine", but unluckily he miscalculated the count and rose at "10". He was adjudged to be out and the fight was awarded to Burnie. Magill clamoured for a return fight.*"

Pat Magill v Charlie Buck

The heavyweight clash on Friday, 30 December 1927 between Pat Magill weighing 12-06 and Charlie Buck, just one pound lighter at 12-05, in one of the preliminary bouts at the open air Olympia Stadium, was reported in the same newspaper on Wednesday, January 4th 1928. Pat won on points, after a hard fought engagement, though the fight was said to have lacked "*the fiery and destructive milling that has lately characterised bouts between big men.*"

Pat Magill v Harry Hall

On Monday, 2 January 1928, he was in action again against Harry Hall. In the press release before the fight to be held in the White City, Magill was billed as "*a heavyweight who has won distinction in England.*" (Result unknown)

Pat Magill v Kit Burnie

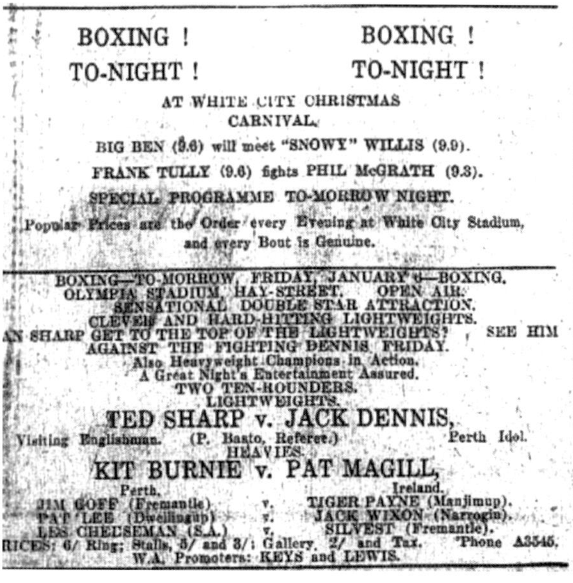
BOXING ! BOXING !
TO-NIGHT ! TO-NIGHT !
AT WHITE CITY CHRISTMAS CARNIVAL.
BIG BEN (9.6) will meet "SNOWY" WILLIS (9.9).
FRANK TULLY (9.6) fights PHIL McGRATH (9.3).
SPECIAL PROGRAMME TO-MORROW NIGHT.
Popular Prices are the Order every Evening at White City Stadium, and every Bout is Genuine.

BOXING—TO-MORROW, FRIDAY, JANUARY 6—BOXING.
OLYMPIA STADIUM, HAY-STREET. OPEN AIR.
SENSATIONAL DOUBLE STAR ATTRACTION.
CLEVER AND HARD-HITTING LIGHTWEIGHTS.
AN SHARP GET TO THE TOP OF THE LIGHTWEIGHTS? SEE HIM AGAINST THE FIGHTING DENNIS FRIDAY.
Also Heavyweight Champions in Action.
A Great Night's Entertainment Assured.
TWO TEN-ROUNDERS.
LIGHTWEIGHTS.
TED SHARP v. JACK DENNIS,
Visiting Englishman. (P. Basto, Referee.) Perth Idol.
HEAVIES.
KIT BURNIE v. PAT MAGILL,
Perth. Ireland.
JIM GOFF (Fremantle) v. TIGER PAYNE (Manjimup).
PAT LEE (Dwellingup) v. JACK WIXON (Narrogin).
LES CHEESEMAN (S.A.) v. SILVEST (Fremantle).
RICES: 6/ Ring; Stalls, 5/ and 3/; Gallery, 2/ and Tax. 'Phone A3545.
W.A. Promoters: KEYS and LEWIS.

After beating Charlie Buck in the New Year's Eve match 1927, his claim for a rematch with the undefeated Kit Burnie was reconsidered. The bout was arranged for January 7, 1928 and the pre-fight publicity promised that fans at the Olympia Stadium could look forward "*to a stirring, gruelling battle*" over ten rounds. "*As both possess a hard punch, and are well trained*" the report continued *"another good bout should be witnessed."*

Pat Magill weighed in at 12-03 and Burnie 12-00. After the bout, the West Australian reported that *"Magill fought with the nimbleness and skill of a featherweight and confounded Burnie with his good boxing. He tried a hard left swing and Burnie was rocked to his feet with the blow. Magill won the second round easily. In the fourth round, Magill rained right after right to the jaw. Amid the din created by the onlookers, Burnie began to stagger and when the gong sounded he was unsteady on his feet. Magill lacked initiative or was too tired for he failed to finish his man.*

In the fifth term, it was Magill's turn to be sick. He fell half-out of the ropes when a hard blow to the ribs sent him down. Magill floundered all over the ring in the sixth round. He was shaken by jaw blows and a stomach hit made him fall forward over the ropes. Magill was helpless and although ahead on points, he had the towel flung in at the end of the round. It was later announced that Magill had sustained a broken hand in the fifth round."

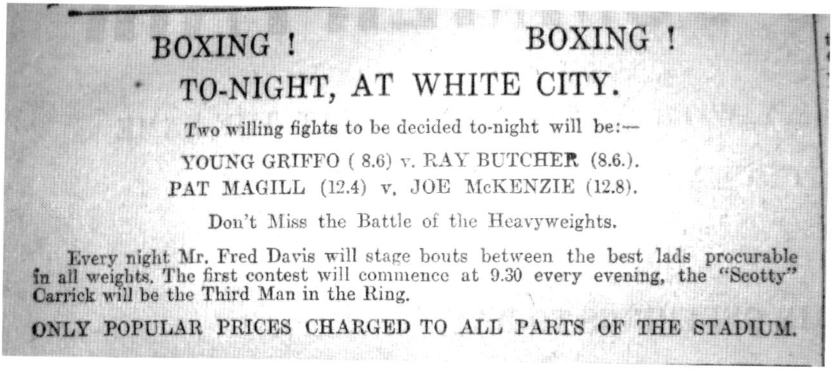

BOXING ! BOXING !

TO-NIGHT, AT WHITE CITY.

Two willing fights to be decided to-night will be:—

YOUNG GRIFFO (8.6) v. RAY BUTCHER (8.6.).

PAT MAGILL (12.4) v. JOE McKENZIE (12.8).

Don't Miss the Battle of the Heavyweights.

Every night Mr. Fred Davis will stage bouts between the best lads procurable in all weights. The first contest will commence at 9.30 every evening, the "Scotty" Carrick will be the Third Man in the Ring.

ONLY POPULAR PRICES CHARGED TO ALL PARTS OF THE STADIUM.

January 17, 1928 Pat Magill v Joe McKenzie

The West Australian carried a report on the bout with Joe McKenzie, at White City on 17 January, 1928. "More than ordinary interest was manifested in the boxing at White City last night on account of the fact that one of the bouts was that in which heavyweights took part. The principals in this contest being Pat Magill and Joe McKenzie. Magill went to scale at 12.4, while McKenzie was 12.10, and he looked much heavier. From the start it was obvious that McKenzie was not classed in the matter of science, and Magill in the latter stages hit him at will with a straight left. McKenzie was down for five in the last round. Scotty Carrick declared in favour of Magill..

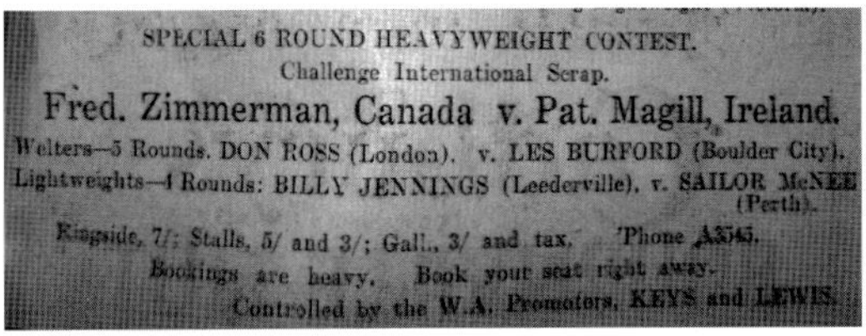

SPECIAL 6 ROUND HEAVYWEIGHT CONTEST.

Challenge International Scrap.

Fred. Zimmerman, Canada v. Pat. Magill, Ireland.

Welters—5 Rounds. DON ROSS (London). v. LES BURFORD (Boulder City).

Lightweights—4 Rounds: BILLY JENNINGS (Leederville). v. SAILOR McNEE (Perth).

Ringside, 7/; Stalls, 5/ and 3/; Gall., 3/ and tax. 'Phone A3545.

Bookings are heavy. Book your seat right away.

Controlled by the W.A. Promotors, KEYS and LEWIS.

June 1, 1928 Pat Magill v Fred Zimmerman of Canada.

Zimmerman came with a reputation. An earlier bill claimed that he had previously been the heavyweight champion of Canada. The report of the bout on June 1st 1928, describes how Pat won the decision over six rounds of heavyweight fighting. Magill went down from a left hook in the first round, was hurt with rib-crushing rights in the second term. Both missed frequently in the third and fourth rounds, although Zimmerman kept plunging his right to the ribs. The Canadian was very confident in the fifth round, while Magill looked just the opposite. Zimmerman missed repeatedly but continued to batter Magill about the body. The decision seemed in doubt until half the last round had passed. Then Zimmerman nearly dropped Magill with a right swing. Zimmerman finished all over Magill, who however was awarded the decision.

July 7, 1928 Pat Magill v Julius Caesar

The first fight staged in Fremantle for several months attracted a fair crowd to the

EAST PERTH HALL — Stadium, Ltd. — EAST PERTH HALL.
As there is no trotting meeting Saturday night, Stadium (Perth), Ltd., has arranged attractive programme of boxing headed by interstate 15-rounder and 8-rounder between leading local fighters.
Pat Magill (W.A.) v. Young Palmer (Vic.)
Eight-rounder: SAILOR CARROLL v DINNY HULL.
Four Rounders: Tommy Sam, v.. Billy Corbett; Dug Mathews v. Young Rimmer.
Book Early at Gleeson's, Hay-street. B1645. Crowded houses assured. Prices, 10/, 5/, 3/ and tax.

King's Theatre on Saturday night. Julius Caesar proved no match for Pat Magill and his seconds 'skied' in the towel in the 2nd round.

June 29, 1929 Pat Magill v Ambrose Palmer

Ambrose Palmer

June 29, 1929 we next see Pat in action. (There is a gap of 11 months in the record). The advert for the Palmer fight, an interstate contest, had Pat representing Western Australia against Palmer representing the state of Victoria. "*Local heavyweight faces Victorian middleweight whose science caused Melbourne critics to enthuse. Magill's big chance*" - fifteen round contest at East Perth Hall.

If it was to be Pat's big chance, he failed to take it. Ambrose Palmer was on the way up in what would be a remarkable career and Pat was clearly past his best. The report described how:

"It was an exciting contest, although one-sided; there was no hanging on or infighting; the punching was of the long range style, and such spectacular features such as knockdowns and terrific hitting were in evidence all through the seven rounds the fight lasted.

Magill, who weighed 11-10 had a great advantage on his assailant who registered 11-01 on the scales. They staggered each other with heavy hits from the beginning, but the Victorian's tremendous hooks dropped Magill time and time again and on the tenth occasion the Referee (Mr. N. Emmett) wisely stopped the fight. Magill had hung on in, in the hope of his great weight wearing Palmer down, but the Victorian hit too hard. Twice the gong saved Magill.

Palmer is the best of the Eastern States boxers who have appeared for the East Perth promoters. His vigorous damaging style is attractive and of the kind that appeals to the onlookers. On Saturday night there was only a meagre attendance.

Palmer was very shifty and sidestepped neatly to send Magill into the ropes; they fought on even terms. In the second round the excitement commenced when Magill went down before a hail of hooks and swings and went down for a count of two. He was assailed from all angles when he rose and a perfect storm of terrific hooks forced him to take a count of nine."

The bout followed its predictable course with Palmer clearly in control. *"The Victorian was fighting in a cool, deliberate style; his smashes to the chin and rips to the body were raking Magill with terrible effect. In the fourth round a left to the pit of the stomach made Magill shaky again and he had a parlous time in weathering the wild storm of jabs and swings that continually put him off his balance. Still he was game and had recovered somewhat from the knock-downs.*

Palmer's blows could be heard landing all around the ring in the sixth round. A left hook put Magill down for one; then he retaliated but got the worst of a terrific rally and when downed again had to take a count of eight. He just staggered through the round."

If nothing else, Pat showed he could take punishment and he attempted to fight back when the seventh round opened.

"Magill had the Victorian bleeding freely in the seventh round. Magill tried to force a rally, but a downpour of stiff hooks had him sprawling on the canvas again - for nine. When he succumbed again shortly afterwards the referee mercifully stopped the encounter which had developed into a one-sided affair. The round had progressed one minute and forty five seconds."

Ambrose Palmer's victory marked another step in a career which would bring him to the top of Australian boxing. He was to go on to win Australian titles at several weights and become a legend in his own life-time. Unfortunately, we know little about Pat's career after this bout, though he continued in the ring until at least 1933.

Record (incomplete) Pat Magill (Ireland/Australia)

Middleweight, Belfast,/Perth, b. March 10, 1902, d. May 26, 1950
Light-heavyweight
17 fights - 8 wins - 7 losses - 2 unknown

1922 RUC					
	Oct. 28	P. Flood (local),	Belfast	W rtd 4	6
1923	Dec. 22	Const. Smallman (RUC),	Belfast	W twl 2	6
1924	Jan. 5	Jim Greer (local),	Belfast	L twl 5	6
	Jan. 26	Pat Logue (Crumlin),	Belfast	L 6	6
	Mar. 8	Jim Greer (local),	Belfast	W6	6
	Aug.2	Leaves RUC			
1925	Mar. 3	Sabri Mahir (Turkey),	Leipzig	L ko	5
1926	May 20	Joe Crampton (Oldham),	Liverpool	W rtd	5
1927	?	Kit Burnie	Perth	L twl 2	10
	Dec 30	Charlie Buck	Perth	W	
1928	Jan 2	Harry Hall	Perth	?	
	Jan 7	Kit Burnie,	Perth	Ltko 6	10
1928	Jan 17	Joe McKenzie	Perth	W	
	June 1	Fred Zimmerman	Perth	W6	6
	July 7	Julius Caesar	Fremantle	Wtwl 2	
1929	March 10	'Snowy' White	Perth	?	
1929	June 29	Ambrose Palmer	Perth	L rsf 7	15
1933	Mar 17	Evan Roberts,	Perth	L ko	4

Acknowledgements to Mary-Attracta Connolly, Fred Heatley and Mike Williamson

8 b. John Magill (1900-1991)

"A skilful and promising boxer"

John Magill 1928

John was a latecomer to the sport of boxing though he followed the exploits of his brother Davy with interest, meticulously keeping a record in a scrapbook. In later years he regretted that as a newly appointed policeman, he had been refused permission to attend the showing of the film of Davy's fight with Jack Bloomfield for the Empire Light-heavyweight title which was on show in Belfast. It was showing in the week after the bout at London's Olympia on May,17, 1923 for the benefit of those legions of Davy's Belfast fans who hadn't been able to see the fight in person. John had joined the police only a few weeks before on April 20, 1923 at the age of twenty three.

Soon he took to boxing himself and joined the newly formed RUC Boxing Club at the age of twenty seven and with his younger brother, Jim, showed promise under the tuition of their brother, Davy. He trained to compete at light heavyweight, the upper limit being 12 stone 6 pounds, just as Davy had for most of his career. He was in an enviable position from the point of view of many boxers as there was no shortage of sparring companions either in the ranks of the Club or at home with his brothers.

On 14 December, 1928 the RUC staged it's initial tournament which consisted of seven international bouts, with Civic Guards from the Free State, English and Scottish representatives and RUC boxers. On the same bill, both John and Jim made their amateur debut, John, winning the novice Light- Heavyweight title.

"Constable John Magill (Henry Street) beat Constable J. Quigley (Henry Street). Of very short duration - it only lasted two rounds - this bout served to reveal once more that in Magill, (brother of the Irish heavyweight champion) the RUC possess a skilful and promising boxer. He showed good judgement and had established an easy lead up to the point of Quigley's retirement, which was necessitated by a damaged fist."

The Irish Times reported "*Magill's left won all the honours of the first session........*"

In the same tournament, Jim had won the middleweight championship and would begin his remarkable career. It was not to be the case for John, however, as he suffered an injury from a damaging blow to the head in sparring; it was one of those unfortunate incidents which are part and parcel of the sport. This put paid to any further boxing and besides, he had reached the age of twenty eight. In later years he would sum up his boxing career as "A splendid failure".

POLICE BOXING CHAMPIONS.—BELFAST "D" DISTRICT (GLENRAVEL STREET) R.U.C. BOXING TEAM. FRO OW—PATRICK DOLAN (R.U.C. HEAVY-WEIGHT CHAMPION), DISTRICT-INSPECTOR A. SCOTT AND JOHN MAG R.U.C. LIGHT HEAVY-WEIGHT CHAMPION). BACK ROW—THOMAS HUGHES, JAMES QUIGLEY, HERBERT BLAIR AND FRANCIS SMYTH.

9 Jim Magill (1904-1991)
Triple ABA Champion

While Davy's star was on the wane in the 1930's, Jim's star was on the up.

"Only one Irish boxer has been British ABA champion at two weights; only one Irish boxer has held British ABA titles on three consecutive years; only one Irish boxer has, in fact, held three British ABA titles. That boxer was Jimmy Magill, a man who, if political events in Ireland had been different, would surely have gone on to even greater glory. His story is worth telling." Fred Heatley 1993.

The youngest of the boys, Jim was the seventh son of the family, born on 21st of June, 1904. Just like his older brothers, he too pursued a career in the police after he had joined the RUC in June 1926. When he took up boxing he was to achieve sporting success and to win celebrity status in his day.

The young Jimmy grew up influenced by the achievements in the ring of his older brother, Davy. He was 16 when Davy had first entered the ring in 1920 and soon he too decided to take up boxing. There is little known about his early bouts but recent research has shown that he first boxed as a professional. While it seems surprising today, when the normal progression is from an initial amateur career before joining the professional ranks, things were different in the sport in the 1920's. It was 1922, when he reached 18, that he threw a punch for the first time He created a stir in local boxing circles winning five professional contests, all inside the distance. An early boxing report tells of his first venture into the ring on December 12, 1922, when, before a crowded audience in Victoria Hall, Larne, he defeated "Young Siki" of Larne, "*showing many of the characteristics of his now well known brother, Young Magill was all over his opponent after the first round, and put Young Siki down a couple of times before the referee stopped the fight in the fourth round and gave the decision to the Cairncastle lad.*" He followed this up with three more inside the distance wins in local contests. He defeated J. Magee on January 19, 1923, in Victoria Hall Larne with a KO in the second, then Billy O'Neill in Carrickfergus with a KO in round four and Jack Sanderson in Larne when the referee stopped the fight in the second round. He had his last appearance as a professional in June 1925 and on 1st June of the following year, he joined the RUC.

The Amateur Re-born

Unlike Davy however, he decided to give up the professional ranks and to box in the unpaid amateur ranks, while pursuing his police career. At that time the regulations permitted former professional boxers to be reinstated as amateurs, while serving in the police or armed forces. Four of the brothers had now taken up the sport and they took to it with a passion. There were no elaborate training facilities at home but they improvised and the stable beside the old home at Cairncastle was used for sparring with locals often gathering to watch the spectacle. Bob McKillop remembered how at the end of several rounds sparring, Jim mischievously landed a blow on Davy's cauliflower ear, in the knowledge that the next challenger in the ring, Johnny McNeill, the heavyweight from Glenarm, would feel the full wrath of Davy's punching.

BOXING IN THE RUC

It was here after a lapse of a few years, that Jim's interest in boxing was rekindled and during the next decade he was to emerge as the top amateur middleweight in Ireland, Britain and Europe. Boxing was already well established in the Civic Guards in the south and their members were achieving great success; contests had already been held with the police of Liverpool and Glasgow. When he was well into his 24th year, Jimalong with his brother John, soon joined the newly formed RUC Boxing Club in which their elder brother Davy was serving as instructor.

There were close associations between policing and amateur boxing on many levels in the Inter-war period. Boxing had widespread appeal. Self defence and physical fitness were considered to be an important part of the policeman's training and could be an advantage on the beat, especially when facing physical attack. There were frequent street fights and policemen could be challenged to a fight. But it was also encouraged on an official level, where all branches of the Armed Services participated in the sport. From the earliest days of amateur boxing, after the formation of the Amateur Boxing Association in England in 1880, the army and navy were at the forefront. The Irish Amateur Boxing Association was set up in 1911 and boxing soon took off in the RIC. It was while in the RIC that Davy Magill's interest in boxing was first awakened when he took to the ring in 1920. In a two day tournament in November 1921, organized by the RIC at the Depot in Enniskillen, he won the heavyweight championship of the RIC

The RUC Athletic Association was formed on 18 June, 1928 under the chairmanship of Captain T.D. Morrison. Soon it was organizing competitions and events in many sports including athletics, boxing, football, swimming, billiards, tennis, hockey, cricket, rugby, and cycling. The RUC Boxing Club was founded shortly after the Athletic Association had been set up and it was to become the driving force in amateur boxing in Ulster over the next few decades. Its two leading lights were Tom Rothwell and Captain Morrison and it was their enthusiasm and organizational abilities which helped get boxing off the ground, not only with the RUC but within Ulster itself. In October 1928 the Ulster Council of the Irish A.B.A was formed, the RUC became an affiliated club and Captain Morrison went on to become the President of the Ulster Council. In fact the first tournament was an RUC tournament held in the Ulster Hall on 13th and 14th December 1928. The highlight was a match between the Civic Guard

RUC Boxing Team: 3rd from left Davy Magill (trainer), 7th from left Billy Campbell (trainer) , Jim Magill and Johnny McNeil on right

Boxing Team and a selected English team, but alongside this were staged the championships of the RUC. The tournament featured three Magill brothers - Davy, now trainer of the team and the debut of Jim and John on the amateur stage. Jim won the middleweight title and prize for 'most scientific boxer' while John won the light-heavyweight title. Soon boxing tournaments were being organized in venues as diverse as Banbridge, Enniskillen, Ballymena and Newry. Captain Morrison was ambitious, far seeing and even organised international tournaments as in Portrush with a visiting German team on July 10, 1934; the police Gazette reported that *"an eyewitness account of the tournament was broadcast through the Belfast station at 10.45 pm."* Before the end of the year another international against Italy was organised in the Ulster Hall. In the years ahead, members of the RUC Club would amass Ulster, Irish, British and European Police titles, especially in the heavier divisions from middleweight up. One of the factors behind the team's success was its trainer. Billy Campbell, the former Irish walking champion and holder of the record for the one mile walk at 6 minutes 39.2 seconds. He trained not only boxers and footballers but he became the official trainer to the Irish International team on several occasions. From 1928 to 1940 he also became trainer of the RUC Boxing team.

Many young police boxers took advantage of his tuition and learned the finer points of the science of boxing. The club attracted much interest in the local amateur boxing scene and soon it was to be a driving force in the growth of amateur boxing in Ulster. One columnist looked to the future when he wrote

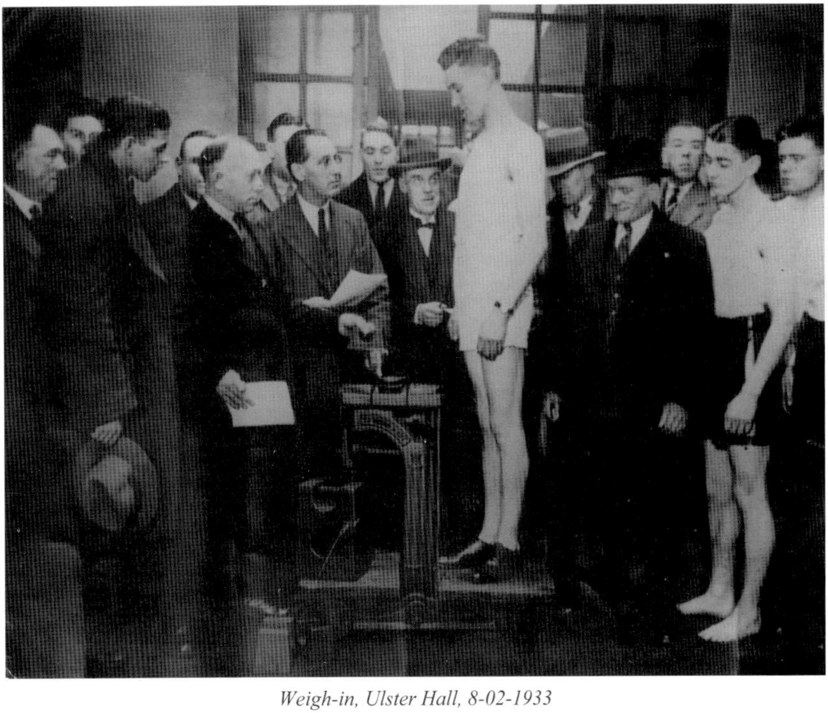

Weigh-in, Ulster Hall, 8-02-1933

"Those with ambitious ideas also foresee the time when it will be possible to choose a boxing team from the Civic Guards and the RUC which could represent Ireland against teams from England, Scotland and Wales."

It was here that Jim's baptism in the amateur ranks took place. The 1928 tournament was packed with thrills and clever boxing. His older brother, John, won the light-heavyweight championship and Jim's victory over Constable Ed. Chestnutt of Derry, not only gave him the middleweight championship of the RUC but also earned him the prize for the "most scientific boxer" of the show. His victory was described as "a case of skill and coolness versus enthusiasm." So Jim was launched on a career which would bring him to the top of amateur boxing. It was only the first title in a boxing life which was to see him amass a total of 18 championships. As he remained single, his bachelor days would allow him to dedicate his life to his sport and gave him the freedom to follow his interests.

In 1929, five bouts after winning the RUC title, he was back in the ring, contesting the first Ulster Amateur Boxing Championships. He stopped fellow RUC man Const. Finlay in round two of the final. It was fitting that Jim was to be the first Ulster middleweight titleholder. He went on to win it again in 1930, 1931, and 1933, (he did not enter 1932) and the Light-heavyweight title in 1936. He was soon hitting the headlines. *"Jimmy Magill's Quick Win" - Jimmy Magill, the popular Constabulary and Ulster middle-weight champion, required exactly sixty-five seconds to dispose of Constable Metcalf of the Liverpool Police, in a bout scheduled for three rounds. Using a snappy left hand, he brought Metcalf into distance after preliminary spar and whipped over a terrific right which dropped Metcalf in his tracks. The Liverpool man was in a bad way on rising, and Magill sailed into him, driving home crashing rights and lefts to face and*

AMATEUR BOXING TOURNAMENT.—IRELAND DEFEATED ENGLAND BY FOUR CONTESTS TO THREE IN THE ULSTER HALL, BELFAST. PICTURE SHOWS CONSTABLE J. MAGILL (R.U.C.), WHO DEFEATED A. SHAWYER (ENGLAND). ALSO IN THE PICTURE ARE DAVY MAGILL AND W. CAMPBELL, THE WINDSOR PARK TRAINER.

THREE CHAMPIONS—Dick Hearns (left), light heavyweight, Erhie Smith, lightweight, and Jimmy Magill, middleweight, after they had won European police titles in 1935 at the Royal Albert Hall.

Jim centre back row of Irish boxing team

JIM MAGILL ABA CHAMPION 1934

body with such effect that the referee stopped the bout in the Belfastman's favour. Metcalf was "out" on his feet when the "closure" was applied."

From the beginning his abilities were being noticed. The boxing journalist, "Ringside", in January 1930, surveying the barren landscape of professional boxing at that particular time, turned his attention to the talent in amateur ranks. He singled out "*Jimmy Magill, the Ulster and RUC champion, as the best middleweight in either professional or amateur circles at the moment. He at least takes no chance of losing anything on a referee's decision. He either stops his opponent or puts him on the floor.*" A report of the match between Ireland and Northern Counties in the Irish Independent, October 1931 describes how he beat his English opponent, P.C. Madden, in the second round. "*A blow to the solar-plexus sent the Englishman down before the end of the first round and the bell saved him. Madden was knocked halfway through the ropes in the second and though the crowd thought that the count was unduly fast, it saved the Englishman from farther punishment.*" With his film star looks, the handsome boxer was to become one of the most popular sportsmen of his generation, rivaling Jimmy Warnock among others in popular affection.

It wasn't all plain sailing. In March 1930 Timekeeper reported on a fight in Dundalk, where Jim was opposed by Constable Langford of the English Police. He considered it to be Jim's first real test. Langford out-boxed Jim for the first three rounds and was "*forging ahead on the finer points of the game. Davy Magill was in his corner and with his ever alert eye, saw how matters were shaping up, and warned his brother that he must fight and not box, if he hoped to win. The RUC man took his advice and in the space of a round Langford had to retire. Magill is a rugged, bustling type of man, and can give a good account of himself.*" A week later in his defence of his Ulster title he was far from convincing against his opponent, Jameson. Possibly the reason was that in the first round he had claimed a foul and this had slowed him down. But Timekeeper conceded that "*he looks like eclipsing his brother Davy, and has the fighting instinct, which counts for a lot in scalp taking. It is virtually high treason to suggest it but several of the amateurs, if they ever turned professional, should collect a minor fortune.*"

When he first entered the Irish championships in 1931 he suffered a defeat at the hands of Garda Jack Chase. Chase was a highly skilled and experienced opponent who had taken the Irish title every year since 1926, had been European police champion on three occasions and had represented Ireland several times. It was Jim's first defeat in the ring after two and a half years, but in the return over six rounds a few months later in Derry, he got his revenge and repeated this on three subsequent occasions. Only defeated seven times in 164 contests, he met four of his conquerors in return bouts and reversed the decisions. The few defeats he was to suffer in his long career from Irish or British opponents were all avenged, except for Fred Mallin, (Eton Manor), five times middleweight A.B.A. champion. One loss to Alf Shawyer (London Fire Service) was answered with four victories; single defeats at the hands of Garda Jack Forde and Dick Hearns were followed by two victories over both. Mayo born

Hearns, was one of Ireland's greatest amateurs; he was five times Irish champion, once European Police champion and had defeated Michelot, (the French winner of the Olympic gold in 1936), to win the British ABA title at light heavyweight in 1935. When recalling his defeats by Jim, the legendary Hearns was to write in his life story serialised in the Sunday Independent in 1967 that *"Jim was the cleverest amateur boxer I ever fought."*

In 1933 he won his first Irish middleweight title. The Irish Independent reported in December 1933 *"I have never seen Jim Magill fight better...Magill is usually content to rely on his exceptionally clever defence to score points on the counter but last night he was always on the attack and whipped in right and left hooks to the head which shook Flood badly at times. Flood tried to keep him off with the left, but he brushed his leads to the side and was a very clear winner of a sparkling bout."*

ABA TITLES

It was in the the Amateur Boxing Association finals, held in London's Royal Albert Hall, that Jim's abilities were to be displayed before a wider audience. In those days the ABA championships were not confined to English, Scots and Welsh, in fact they were open to the cream of ten nations. The Amateur Boxing Association of Britain held its first championships in 1881 and its rules had become the recognized code governing amateur boxing throughout the world, with the exception of the United States, for many years. Its records bear the names of several Irishmen who won A.B.A. titles. First of these was J. O'Driscoll (Garda B.C.), who won the heavyweight title in 1928. Jim Murphy won the light heavyweight championship in 1930, while Matt Flanagan won the heavyweight title in 1931. Jim was to become ABA champion three times, (1934, 1935 and 1936) more often than any other Irishman, and to hold the title at middleweight and light-heavyweight, again something no other Irish boxer has achieved.

His first attempts were not successful. In 1932 he entered the British championship for the first time, with the highest expectations, only to suffer the most devastating loss of his entire boxing career. He was caught cold and suffered a first round KO by a boxer, Jackson, whom he had defeated the previous year. A reporter describing the fight wrote "*Magill rose from his seat in the first round, shook hands, then stepped back and was immediately knocked out by a swift right hander from Jackson.*" Jim was soon to make amends with two victories over Jackson. Unbeaten in over 20 bouts in 1933 and after winning his opening bout over R.W Lacey, he was again unfortunate when he had to withdraw with an injured hand.

It was not until 1934 that he won his first ABA middleweight title, easily defeating F.G.Parr in the final. From here he was to go on that year to win the Irish title. He then defeated his German opponent, Hans Blum, in an international in Dublin in which the Irish showed their quality with six victories to two. One loss and 28 victories was the total for Jim in 1934. That sole loss was in the British Empire Games where he was defeated in the semi-finals by Alf Shawyer.

Jim Magill (left) defeats Dick Hearns, ABA semi-finals Albert Hall, 1936

Shawyer had created a sensation in the previous year's A.B.A.finals by defeating Fred Mallin, who had won the title for the previous five years. Shawyer went on to win the Empire title in 1934, when on the referee's casting vote he was awarded the decision over Jim. It was their third meeting with Jim two to one ahead, but Jim was to extend it to four to one before the end of the year. For now, Jim had to content himself with a Bronze Empire medal.

In 1935 he won his second ABA middleweight title. His first contest was against F. G. Parr whom he had defeated in the previous year's final. This time Jim won easily and reached the final again after defeating C. Rosamond. His opponent was J. W. Jackson who had dramatically knocked him out in 1932. On this occasion Jim made no mistakes and clearly out-boxed Jackson to win his second A.B.A. title.

In a specially arranged contest at Nottingham, he fought G.J. "Bill" Brennan (Nottingham). "I was just back from fighting in Sligo when Captain Morrison asked me if I would go to Nottingham to make up a team for a tournament there" said Jim. "I told him I wasn't fit enough but he said I was as fit as anyone going, so I agreed. When we arrived we were allocated our fights and I was told I was fighting George Brennan. Well Brennan was a very big name then and he was 13 stone. I'm not fighting him, I said and you can't make me. I've got my return ticket home. I was mad. But Billy Campbell my trainer came over and persuaded me. I got into the ring and the crowds were cheering Brennan. I couldn't take any chances so I went back to the old school days and boxed defensively. Well there was consternation round the hall when I got the decision" said Jim. He later described this as the best performance of his career. Brennan had been amateur Cruiserweight champion of the British Empire and he had beaten most of the top amateur heavyweights of his day. He was rated by the well known boxing writer, Leo Bowles, as '*one of the best, if not the best, amateur light heavies in the world.*' Jim won decisively even though he claimed throughout the fight he was 'in torture' with two ugly boils under his arm, which were aggravated every time he threw a punch.

Then in 1936 he was to move up a weight to light-heavyweight . The truth was that year after year he had difficulties in making the middleweight limit of 11 stone six lbs. When going over to London, the routine was that there would be no food or drink of any sort from 2 p.m. on the day of arrival before the championship until after the weigh-in on the following day. Now at light heavyweight in the semi finals, he was to have three fights that day, 1 April, 1936. First he defeated T. Griffin, then defeated his formidable rival, Garda Dick Hearns before he went on in the final to defeat Len Gosden of City of London Police. Gosden stood at about six ft. three ins. in height with a tremendously long reach but Jim outboxed him and took the championship. To have won the title at middleweight twice and now at light heavyweight, was something no other Irish boxer had achieved before or since.

During these years, he would travel the length and breadth of Ireland boxing in halls big and small. After winning his ABA title in the Royal Albert Hall, London in 1934, he returned to box in a tournament staged in Glenarm. The

Ballymena Observer on August 10 reported that in a six round contest with Garda P. Hennelly, Tailtean Games champion, a wonderful display was given by both boxers. *"The hitting throughout was fast and furious, with Magill holding the upper hand. In the fourth round Magill smashed a right to the jaw which shook Hennelly, but the fifth round found them fighting with stubbornness and determination. The sixth round started as if Magill was anxious to register a KO. But Hennelly was on the alert and finished amidst a rain of jabs and hooks. It was the finest contest ever seen in Glenarm and proved that Magill is boxing as well as ever. Magill was declared the winner."*

He would be in constant demand in venues such as London, Glasgow, Edinburgh, and Liverpool. Overseas travel was more difficult at the time but he would travel to Italy, France and farther afield to Boston and Detroit in the United States. Of necessity it involved long train journeys and sea crossings. In later years he recalled how he missed out on two opportunities of flying, from Boston to Detroit because of bad weather conditions, and later when the flight from Clermont Ferrand in France was cancelled due to high winds. He would also miss the opportunities of travel to Los Angeles in 1932 and to Berlin in 1936, but on these occasions it was not the inclement weather but most likely the interference of politicians.

INTERNATIONAL STAR

Jim's international career had taken off as early as 1931 when he won the first of six successive European Police Boxing Titles. The report in the press in 1935 described how over 9,000 packed the Royal Albert Hall that year. "*The outstanding performance was that of Constable James Magill, of the RUC, who by winning the middleweight title for the fifth successive year, set up a new record.*" It was a time when international amateur boxing was in its infancy, and Jim was to wear the Irish colours on 11 occasions. He was to be undefeated while representing Ireland in a full international outing and was believed by those who knew, to be "*the best amateur 160 pounder in Europe, if not the world.*" He won against the English Northern Counties, four times against Germany's best, three times against England and once each against Italy, Belgium, and Denmark. Among his international victories his hand was raised over Bernloehr, Hornemann, Blum and Vogt (Germany), de Meuse (Belgium), Smith (South Africa) and Gilberti (Italy).

The Belfast Telegraph reported on the visit of the Italian national team to the Ulster Hall. "*A hard hitting bout was expected between the middleweight rivals, Carlo Gilberti and Constable Jim Magill, the Irish champion, and spectators were not disappointed..*" Gilberti came with a reputation. Though only 22 years of age, he won eight out of his ten international bouts and had won the Italian national title in face of 16 opponents, including Strozzi, the holder who was European champion. *The Telegraph continued "The Italian as a preliminary danced round while he flashed lefts to Jimmy's face, but the European police champion, with a volley of lefts-rights to head and body,*

THE CONSTABULARY GAZETTE 133

Jim in USA 1935

getting clear before a reply could be delivered , proved that his reputation was not earned by light punching. In a toe-to-toe grand slam near the ropes Magill had the Italian eventually at his mercy, his effective deliveries raising the crowd's enthusiasm.

The rounds were ticked off at a dazzling pace for middleweights, and while Gilberti was a ready and rugged mixer, he found the force of Magill's blows weakening to his stamina. The Irish champion was constantly forcing the issue, landing smartly to head and body. In the fourth round a heavy right-hander smashed into the Italian's face and drew blood. Gilberti fought willingly, but in close quarter mills he was never a match for the Ulster policeman. Once he was cautioned for using the rabbit punch. While Magill drove home a pile of rights and lefts to the body, his rival was badly out of distance when he sought to counter. This was a tribute to the Irishman's speed.

The closing round was a sparkling tussle for points, Magill again emerging with honours, both close in and at distance exchanges. In a desperate mid-ring rally the Italian sought to get home to head and body, but his punches were mere taps compared with the Irishman's pile-driving blows. In the end Gilberti was beaten to his knees, but he was up in a flash, and again pluckily resumed the duel, although Magill was easily the master of the situation. The verdict to Magill was received with thunderous applause, as it meant a team triumph for

TRIPLE TITLE-HOLDER.—A HAPPY SNAPSHOT AT THE G.N.R. TERMINUS, BELFAST, WHEN R.U.C. COLLEAGUES WISHED "GOOD LUCK" TO CONSTABLE JAMES MAGILL, THE A.B.A., IRISH, AND EUROPEAN POLICE MIDDLEWEIGHT BOXING CHAMPION, ON HIS WAY TO QUEENSTOWN TO JOIN THE OTHERS OF THE IRISH TEAM BOUND FOR A TOURNAMENT IN BOSTON.

Ireland, the honours now standing 4-2 in Erin's favour." While there was much praise for Jim's footwork, Timekeeper in the Saturday Night, having acknowledged that this was one of his best displays, urged that *"Jimmy should hit straighter when working at close quarters. Many of his blows lost their real power because of their circuit in delivery."* It was a result that did not please the Duce, Benito Mussolini, who had shown a special interest in the Italian team's trip as his sporting ambassadors.

The Golden Gloves, 1935

Irish Boxers who left Dublin for U.S.A. on Saturday. (Left to right, front row)—Garda J. J. Healy, P. Hughes, M. Coffey, J. Magill and E. Smith. (At back) P. J. Mulligan and S. Mooney. [I.P. Photo.

One highlight of his career was undoubtedly his tour of the USA with a five man Irish selection. They had been invited to take part in the American Golden Gloves Tournament. Originating in Chicago and New York in the late twenties, by 1935 the Golden Gloves had expanded to include teams from other cities; 38 teams entered the first year. It became known as the "Tournament of Champions." In April 1935, Jim outclassed his two American opponents Walter Gardner of Riverside, New Jersey in the semi-final and Ray Kelly of Brookline, in the finals in Boston, Massachusetts. The Irish Independent's Boston correspondent wired the Dublin office saying *"Magill had both of his opponents groggy. He outclassed Gardner in every round. The latter's eyes and nose were damaged and he was in a sorry plight at the end of the bout. Magill pounded Kelly until he was dazed and the American was staggering at the close."*

Two days later Jim was due to take part in a show in Detroit. The arrangements were to fly from Boston to Detroit on the day of the tournament. When the Irish team arrived at the flying field conditions were so bad that flying was not possible, and a long train journey ensued. They arrived in Detroit with 40 minutes to spare before boxing. The fight was fixed for three rounds. Magill asked for six rounds but was denied.

On May 3, 1935, before a crowd of 12,000, Jim was to lose narrowly on points to Dave Clarke of Detroit, the black American champion, in what some claimed was a home town decision. "*Detroit crowd boos decision*" ran the headline in the Irish Independent. Jim maintained, and he was supported by those attending him, that he would have won comfortably over the longer distance. But it was no disgrace. Clarke, it has to be remembered, was one of the very few to beat the legendary Joe Louis as an amateur, and went on to become a rated professional as a light-heavyweight. Joe Louis had been the winner of the Golden Gloves in the previous year, 1934, at light-heavyweight. All four of the Irish team who boxed in Detroit got the wrong end of the verdict.

OLYMPIC SELECTION

"For the student of Irish amateur boxing, the 1932 Olympic Games at Los Angeles are most notable for the fighter who failed to appear. It wasn't that Jimmy Magill was loath to box - it was a little matter of politics intruding onto the local boxing scene."
(Fred Heatley, 1988)

Jim's international career was not without its controversies. Sport and politics as the old adage says, do not mix; yet it has rarely been otherwise. Nothing was to demonstrate this more than the history of the 1930's. The world of sport remembers how the 1936 Berlin Olympics was used to demonstrate the supposed supremacy of the Aryan master race. America's Jesse Owens, who had won his four gold medals and was believed to have been snubbed by Adolf Hitler, was now drawn into political debate. It was the same with Germany's boxing hero, Max Schmeling, when he won the world heavyweight title in 1936 by knocking out Archie Moore. His career in Germany and the USA would be subsequently dogged by political controversy.

In spring 1932, Jim had out-pointed Garda Jack Chase in the Irish National Championships in what was to be a decider as to who was to represent Ireland in the Tailteann and Olympic games to be held in Los Angeles that year. Nobody had beaten Chase in the championships for seven years. A writer in "Ireland's Saturday Night" echoed the general approval when he wrote *"there is great satisfaction in boxing circles - and even wider afield - that Constable James Magill is to be Ireland's representative at Los Angeles for the Olympic Games.*" But the joy was short-lived. *"As a serving constable with the RUC it was not thought expedient that he box under the Tricolour and, should medal status be gained, have to salute the Irish national anthem. Better to have him withdrawn from both the Tailteann and the Olympic Games,"* wrote Fred Heatley. Jim's selection was thwarted by order of the Ulster Boxing Council, possibly under order from the Northern Ireland Government. It was claimed that as a serving member of the RUC, he could only fight for Northern Ireland. The anomalies of the situation were not hard to find when he had already made two appearances for the Irish national team in Belfast. And so Jim was denied the chance to compete at the highest level in 1932. He was then possibly Ireland's finest amateur boxer and he had missed the opportunity of winning the sport's highest award. While political decisions were being taken, Jim continued in the ring to run up an unbeaten string of 39 fights after the Chase victory, and had another 26 bouts before losing again. The first loss had been to London's Alf Shawyer, the second to Detroit's Dave Clark. *"He could have been Ireland's first medal winner at boxing,"* Fred Heatley.

There was little indication of these political or international tensions when a German international team visited Ireland in 1934 and appeared in the Ulster Hall in a tournament organized by the RUC. The Constabulary Gazette in its report gives something of the flavour of the times:

"The introduction of the German team was an attractive opening... the German team had a wonderful reception. They were greeted with a real Ulster cheer. Their Nazi salute to the spectators when being introduced, and before and after each fight, was an impressive novelty, especially when, during a portion of their National Anthem, all hands were raised together while the vast crowd in the Ulster Hall stood to attention....

A green shamrock was fitted to the Irish corner of the ring and a Swastika to the German corner. These, by the way, will find a home in Germany, as the German team asked to be allowed to take them with them to Germany...... Magill outclassed Blum the German - proving himself to be the best middleweight in Europe at the moment." Jim represented Ireland again on 11th November in another contest with Germany at the Theatre Royal, Dublin, and scored another victory over Blum. Ireland defeated the German visitors 5 to 2.

The report in the Gazette demonstrated attitudes which were to change dramatically over the next few years. *"The Nazi salute to the spectators..... was an impressive novelty. ...... the presentation of the green shamrock and the Swastika."* Few in that audience in the Ulster Hall were aware of the true nature of Nazism. Hitler had just become Chancellor of Germany on 30th. January of the previous year, 1933, and the country was just embarking on the road to dictatorship, repression and persecution. The decision to grant the Olympics to Berlin had been made as far back as 1931, before Hitler had come to power. The Nazi regime now saw the opportunities to show the so-called Aryan supremacy to the rest of the world. Few in that audience were aware that Nazi race policies excluded Jewish athletes, even from this team and would eventually lead to the Holocaust.

Yet among that audience were some of the leading figures in the Northern Ireland Establishment. Present were His Majesty's representative, the Duke of Abercorn, the Inspector-General, the Speaker of the House of Commons, Lord Justice Best, Mr. Justice Brown, Sir Dawson Bates, Sir Edward Archdale, the General Officer Commanding the Troops in Northern Ireland....... As the Gazette asked *"Has any other tournament ever attracted such a crowd of notabilities?"*

The link between sport and politics was perhaps more sensitive in Northern Ireland than anywhere else. It had been an issue in soccer and other sports, but boxing, even though it drew its support from all classes and creeds, had escaped relatively unscathed. For Jim, a member of the RUC, to wear the Irish colours, this was to bring its problems too. It was perhaps inevitable that this would give rise to tensions given the "Cold War" atmosphere which characterized the relations between De Valera's Government and those of Britain and Northern Ireland in the decade of the 1930's.

The controversy did not go away. In 1935, in the run-up to the coming Berlin Olympics, Jim was the subject of further differences between the RUC Boxing Club and the Irish Amateur Boxing Association. The row reached the Irish papers. A 'Dublin Boxing correspondent' in what was referred to as "*Mr De Valera's "Irish Press,"* wrote "*The Amateur Boxing Association of Ireland the other day asked the RUC Boxing Club, two questions. They were firstly - will Magill be available if selected to fight for Ireland against Holland on November 11th or 13th? Secondly - can he make middleweight?"* The answer from the police was "*Magill is billed to box as a Cruiserweight at Derby against the Derby Police on November 12th*." There were clear indications of what was to come. The writer noted that the RUC Club had avoided answering the question. There would be two internationals against Holland, one in Dublin and the other in Limerick. If Magill could not make the middleweight, he could fight in either contest as light-heavyweight. Then he came to the crucial issue. *"As an amateur, Magill cannot be compelled to turn out for Ireland - but the country should have some little claim on him even if his club doesn't think so..... They (the RUC) seem to be looking to England to supply boxers for their tournaments. I wonder is that preparatory to cutting the painter that hold them to the I.A.B.A.?"* He concluded that if that is the case, *"the I.A.B.A. will lose a splendid boxer in Jim Magill."*

A response followed, attempting to play down the crisis. *"A good deal of rumour has been centred round Jim Magill, our middleweight champion, who has been 'carpeted ' by some for having failed to announce his intention .... to declare himself 'fit' as a' cruiser for the Holland tournament. There has been a lot of conjecture as to the relationship of Magill and his association (RUC) with the I.A.B.A. In Dublin.....".* The writer went on to stress that Magill was finding it hard to make the 11 stone 6 middleweight class. On November 12th, 1935, he did box against the Derby Police, at cruiserweight. Timekeeper in the Saturday Night commented *"We are all proud of Jimmy Magill, who made a successful entry into the cruiserweight division by outclassing W. Walters the Welsh champion and one of the leading battlers at his weight in England. There were some who went on Tuesday evening expecting to see Magill get* a good lacing, so good was his opponent rated. But Jimmy proved that he is going to be better as a cruiser than he ever was as a middleweight, and that's saying something. I have never seen him fighting better, or more confidently."

As the most experienced and talented amateur in these islands if not in Europe, he was the natural choice again for the Olympics in 1936. Again he was selected to represent Ireland, this time at the Berlin Olympics, but once again the RUC authorities refused him and for the same reasons as before. In the end, the Irish ABA decided not to send a team. Being ABA as well as Irish Champion, the British authorities selected him for their team. This time, the Irish authorities made an official complaint and the outcome was that he was unable to compete for either country. Given that he had reached the age of 28 in 1932 but was now 32 in 1936, there was little possibility of him ever getting another chance to box at the Olympics. In later years Jim kept his feelings to himself about what had happened, but it must have rankled and caused him to think of lost opportunities.

Retirement - Trainer of the Irish International team - Comebacks

His Olympic dreams shattered, his mind naturally turned to retirement and Jim did not take up boxing again with the opening of the 1936/7 season. On the 14th December 1936, the RUC Athletic Association staged an international Ireland v Germany in the King's Hall, Belfast. Perhaps he was influenced by his brother Davy's return to the ring at the age of 40 after a five year lay off, in 1935. However, he was now called upon to represent Ireland against Germany. Facing him was none other than Richard Vogt, the silver medal winner of the Berlin Olympics earlier in that year, and later to become a rated professional. Jim won a decisive victory which must have raised questions of what might have been. But it was a victory that was to have even greater significance for another young man from Belfast, in a few years to come.

Retired again, Jim was appointed trainer to the Irish team in 1937. He was to lead a four man squad who were going to Milan to fight in the European Championships. En route, the IABA arranged an international match against England. At the end of April 1937, the Irish Independent reported on the arrival of the Irish team in London to box in the Albert Hall, "*With Jim Magill in charge, they will be in tip top condition for their match with the ABA team.*" Dick Hearns, Ireland's best prospect for the light-heavyweight title in Milan, missed his chance for a European title when a clash of heads in the English bout, forced him to return home. In his disappointment, he later condemned the Irish officials who had arranged the English match three days before such an important championship. Down to three men, the Irish squad left Milan empty handed. On their return, they stopped off at Clermont-Ferrand in France. There, Jim was prevailed on to step into the ring to replace the injured Irish representative, Lydon, then suffering from an injured eye. His opponent was none other than Roger Michelot. "In hindsight" Fred Heatley wrote "his acceptance was crazy as his opponent was no less a person than the Olympic champion, himself." According to the Irish Independent he gave a great display, being only narrowly

defeated on points. A performance in such circumstances speaks volumes of his ability. However he was to get another chance to make amends for his setback with Michelot, when he boxed him for a second time in November in the Ulster Hall, Belfast. He was anxious to show that having defeated the Olympic silver medallist runner-up, he could repeat the dose on the champion and thus prove how unfortunate he was to have been deprived of his opportunity to take part in the Olympic Games of 1936. According to one report in the Gazette, *"It was a great fight with Magill the master all through. The decision in Michelot's favour was most unpopular with the press and public alike... If Magill ever won a fight he won that one over Michelot"* but a realist might say that age had caught up with him and he was defeated again.

The year 1938 was his last year in the ring when he won all his three fights. In his farewell contest in the international clash in Belfast between England and Ireland, he defeated Stan Shackwell over six rounds in what was a fitting end to a splendid career. He had fought over one hundred and fifty contests (some say over two hundred, but that must include exhibitions) with his only unavenged defeats against Fred Mallin, America's Dave Clark and Michelot, the Olympic Champion, but as Fred Heatley stated *"these ring a little hollow when it is recalled that Magill was nearing his mid thirties and had been called out of retirement."*

When asked later, what was the key to his success during his long career, "*Roadwork and an abundance of it*" was Jimmy's reply. "*To be a good fighter one must be a fit fighter and there's no surer way to fitness than to get out on the roads before breakfast.*" But he was too self-effacing to take all the credit for himself and he acknowledged the encouragement and help of his mentors and friends - from men like George Sayers "who taught him all he knew", Stanley Stringer, George Morris, Jack McCusker (manager of John Caldwell), David Baine and Billy Campbell

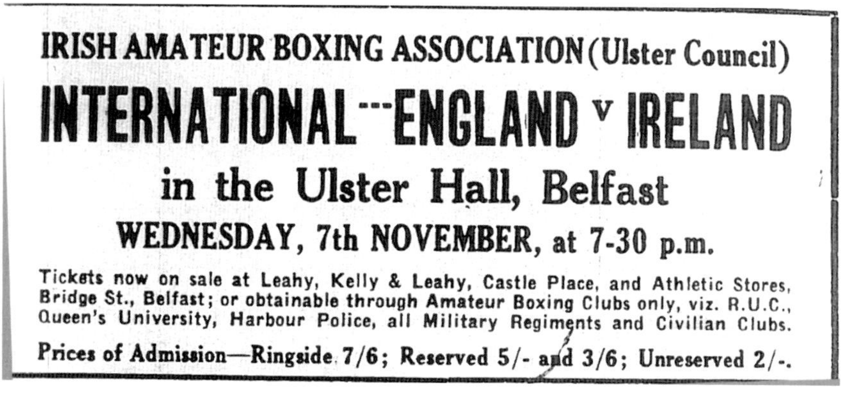

RUC Boxing Team, 1937

In later years his earlier professional career was to be forgotten and many wondered why the brilliant amateur had not succumbed to the lure of the paid ranks and followed in the steps of his brother Davy. Had he been around to-day it was said he would have turned professional and become a world star. And it was certainly not for the want of trying. There were those like 'Pa' Peterson, father of the British heavyweight champion who on seeing Jim in action, invited him to join the professional ranks. Jim recalled that it was in the Albert Hall in 1932 when he first appeared in the championships. The Irish boxers were sharing the same dressing room with the Welsh boxers and after his first fight before lunch, "Pa" Peterson, whose famous son Jack was also competing, claimed that he could make him a world beater if he joined with his son and turned professional. After twelve hours persuasion, Jim declined the tempting offer but Jack Peterson was to go on to win fame and fortune as the British professional heavyweight champion and world contender. Another visitor that day to the dressing room was Len Harvey, British professional middleweight champion at the time. He came to congratulate Jim on his performance and openly expressed his relief that Jim was not in the professional ranks.

When asked in later years by Belfast Telegraph's Jack Magowan why he had not changed to the professional game, he replied *"The truth is I have chalk hands. My bones are unusually brittle and might not have stood up to the pounding they would have taken in say a hard ten round fight."* Certainly in old age his hands suffered much from arthritis, and this may have been part of the price for years of boxing. It was not that he didn't have contacts or was unfamiliar with the professional scene, for his brother Davy had been in the paid ranks since 1920. Maybe he knew that professional boxing was different from the amateur game. Some claimed that it was not a game at all but a 'racket' which paid two men - the promoter and the manager; the boxer invariably came off second best. Yet it has to be also pointed out that unlike many other successful amateurs, Jim was not under the same financial pressures to go professional; in the 'Hungry Thirties' he had secure employment as a career policeman, was single and did not have to provide for a family. So he resisted the lure of turning professional and ended his career as one of Ireland's outstanding amateur boxers.

Back to Cairncastle

Jim had retired from the ring but did not cut his ties with the sport completely; in retirement he gave his time to coaching the RUC Boxing Club and refereeing. He finally retired from the police force in 1959, left Belfast where he had been stationed all his career and returned to live with his two sisters, Annie and Rose, back to the old family home in Cairncastle. There, he enjoyed a long and healthy retirement. In old age he was modest about his boxing achievements and was happier extolling the merits of his favourite Manchester United team. There was little to tell those strangers he met, apart from his youthful physical presence, that this elderly gentleman had at one time been a sporting icon whose fame had spread far from his native Cairncastle. As a seventh son, he was believed by some to have the special powers of healing in his hands. In his case he was thought to have the cure for headaches and he was in regular demand from distraught sufferers from far off parts of the country. There was an irony in that it was those same hands that had been so feared in the boxing ring. His fame for healing had spread far and wide and on several occasions his sister Annie was to return from her shopping trips to Larne, to find the house taken over by a van load of Travellers who had come to Jim to get ' the cure'.

He remained a bachelor, even though there had never been a shortage of potential partners for the handsome 'fighting prince' as he was called. In old age he would laughingly say that his training was so intense that he never had time for girls but over the years he had many girlfriends and female admirers. One long term friendship was with a glamorous German lady but the relationship did not result in marriage. His life long friend had been Mattie Moore, owner of the local Meetinghouse Pub but the religious differences of the time had prevented marriage. At the age of 87, just one week after his older brother John had died, Jim died in the Moyle Hospital Larne following a short illness on 24th November 1991. After a boxing career which had seen him travel to Europe and the United States in the 1930's, he was buried in the family grave beside Feystown Church on the hill overlooking his home and the village of Cairncastle where he had been born and reared.

Family home, Meetinghouse, Cairncastle

Magill's Sports Bar, Newforge, Belfast

The Jimmy Magill Sports Bar

"A quiet, genial and unassuming man, his personal qualities are on a par with his fistic skill." (Ireland's Saturday Night, 23-04-1932)

Those who follow boxing remembered him with warmth and respect. *"When I was a schoolboy, I had only three sporting heroes, Jimmy Warnock, Jesse Owens and Jimmy Magill," wrote Jack Magowan of The Belfast Telegraph (1962).* This was high praise indeed and good company to be in. There has been much talk about the dark shadow of politics over the Berlin Olympics in 1936 where it was claimed that Jesse Owens was shunned by Hitler. But it was politics nearer home that had robbed Jim of even getting the chance to compete in either Los Angeles in 1932 or again in Berlin in 1936. Felix McKillop noted after his death, that "*he was possibly Ireland's most successful amateur boxer.... the boxing world has lost a great champion and a ring legend."* Fred Heatley wrote *"One Boxer they can never follow .... he was considered by many as the finest amateur boxer produced within the nine counties of Ulster*" and his place is deserved "*in any pantheon of Irish boxing greats."* In 2001 Dublin's boxing historian Michael Sutton penned an article in "Siochain" entitled *"Ulster's Fighting Prince,"* posing the question *"If Dick Hearns wasn't Ireland's best-ever amateur boxer, then who was?"* He followed it up in his next feature, with an answer - in the view of those whom he consulted, it was Jimmy Magill. Boxing journalists in his day had been unanimous in their verdict. E. J. Sloan, writing in the Sunday Dispatch, November 21, 1954 could say *"Today there are no boxers of his class in Ireland, none who can boast 157 victories in 164 contests. That he was the greatest ever amateur boxer in Ireland, I write without fear of contradiction."*

He was finally honoured by the RUC Athletic Association when he was the first member to be inducted into the RUC 'Hall of Fame' and in 2004, the Sports Bar in the PSNI's Country Club at Newforge in Belfast was named "***The Jimmy Magill Sports Bar***" "*to acknowledge the achievements of James Magill and to his memory*". A permanent exhibition of trophies and memorabilia from his boxing days was put on display.

How a fight in the King's Hall saved a soldier at Dunkirk

There was a postscript to his boxing career. Jack Magowan of the Belfast Telegraph, later told the story which would do justice to any Hollywood war movie, of how one of Jim's last fights in the King's Hall was to save the life of a Belfast soldier in World War Two. It was one of the blackest days of the War. Among those left behind in the failed invasion at Dunkirk 1940, was a badly wounded Irish Guardsman, Bill Hutchinson, from Ambleside Street in Belfast. He had stepped on a landmine, suffered 18 body wounds by shrapnel and half of

Life Outside The Ring

Mattie Moore 1911-1977

Jim's German sweetheart 1947

En route to USA 1935

"Touring Blackpool with refreshments - Jim with Fred and Bob

Richard Vogt (right) defeats Max Schmeling 1948

his leg had been blown off. As he lay there bleeding profusely he was approached by two German soldiers; one made an attempt to kick him while the other, noticing the name Irish Guards on his uniform, stopped him. He stooped down and asked Bill what part of Ireland he was from. *"Do you know anyone in Ireland called Magill... Jimmy Magill?"* he asked politely. The young guardsman nodded and mumbled a painful *"yes"*, and said that he had often heard his father mention him. It was an admission that probably saved his life, if not his leg, for by coincidence, he had been taken prisoner by none other than the same Captain Richard Vogt, the Berlin Olympic silver medallist whom Jim had met and defeated in the King's Hall four years before.

Captain Vogt then asked Bill if he was spared to go back to Ireland, to convey his regards to Jimmy Magill. He then picked Bill up like you would pick up a child and carried him to the British lines where he gave instructions that Bill was to be given medical attention. Bill recovered and returned to Belfast and continued to live there until he died in the Somme Nursing Home in 2002. Richard Vogt had turned professional in 1938 and was to become the three-time Light Heavyweight Champion of Germany. In his professional career of 71 bouts, Vogt had won 54 fights, 34 of them by the k.o. route, drawing 10 and losing 7. In 1942, he lost on points in a fight for the European Light Heavyweight Title. But one fight he is remembered for more than any other took place in 1948. Before a crowd of 20,000 in Berlin, he beat the former World Heavyweight champion Max Schmeling; at the time Germany's conqueror of Joe Louis was aged 43 and it proved to be his last fight. The fight was immortalised in the 2010 release of the film of the career of the German legend, 'Max Schmeling.' Vogt retired at the age of 39 in 1952 and died in 1988 at the age of 75, but the life of Jim's former opponent is now being recalled on screen.

Bill Hutchinson in happier times 1959

In Search of a Family Tree

10 In Search of a Family Tree

"Memorandum it is agreed by and between the Right honourable Alexander Earle of Antrim on the one part and Patrick Mor Magill on the other part. That the said Patrick Mor Magill his heirs Exrs and assigns shall have hould possess and enjoy the faires customes anchorages of Larne with the faires customs and anchorages of Glenarm in as full and ample manner as they have been held these years bygone ...." 1686

This lease between Alexander, Earl of Antrim and Patrick Mor Magill and his heirs, for *"the faires, customs and anchorages"* of Larne and Glenarm, shows that the Magill family were present in the lower Glens since at least the 17th century. Perhaps the earliest reference to the name was in 1586, when Sir Henry Bagenal, Elizabeth 1's official in Ireland, while writing his description of the Glens of Antrim and listing its principal inhabitants, included among them "*the ancient followers of this countrie, the Mac y Gilles.*"

The search for a family tree is seldom straightforward and presents more challenges in Ireland than in many other countries. Unfortunately because of the absence of written records, it is impossible for the vast majority of families to trace a lineage back to the 17th century. The earliest surviving complete census for Ireland is that of 1901. The census returns from 1821 up to 1851 were destroyed in the fire at the Public Records Office in Dublin in 1922; census returns for 1861 to 1891 were destroyed by order of the Government during World War One. Our one piece of good fortune in this area is that fragments of the 1851 Census for Cairncastle have survived. But the difficulties remain. Official registration of births, deaths and marriages did not begin in Ireland until 1864, and even then, it was not compulsory in the first years. Parish records of baptisms, marriages and deaths are patchy, and where they exist, seldom go back before the early 1800s. For the vast majority of our ancestors, grave headstones do not exist. While portraits were the preserve of the rich, photography wasn't accessible to most until the twentieth century. The earliest photograph of any member of the immediate family is that of Jane on her marriage in the USA in 1908.

The search for family roots can be a journey with its rewards and frustrations, breakthroughs and brick walls. It is a journey that never comes to an end as new evidence comes to light and there are still pieces of the jigsaw missing. Family traditions, where they exist, often give us our best leads.

Family Traditions

My father, John, had not known his grandparents who were dead long before he was born in 1900. He told me that his father, Charles, had two sisters, Mary, who had died in her teens and Liza, who had a daughter also called Liza, both

of whom went to live in Belfast. He knew that his father had an aunt Jane who had married a Blair. He believed that there was a relative, a Magill of Crucie, who had been in the RIC. He mentioned that his father had at least three cousins he knew of, Henry and Dan Magill of Campbelltown and Willie John Magill of 'The Howe'. On his mother's side he knew that her people were the Connollys and that they were connected to the McRandle family and also related to the Reids.

Aunt Annie said that two generations of Magills before her father, had also married Magills.

Dan McKillion stated that the mother of Charlie Magill of the Meetinghouse was a Crucie Magill and that he was a full cousin of Policeman Magill by his mother's side of the house.

MEETINGHOUSE MAGILLS

It is difficult to disentangle the web of McGill/Magill families in the Cairncastle area and find a way through the genealogical maze. As far back as the Census of 1851 there were as many as twenty Magill families living here. The task is further complicated by the fact that "*two generations of Magills before her father, had also married Magills*" (Annie) and many of the families used the same Christian names. In 1851 there were no fewer than six Magills called John, six Jane, five James, and three called Charles. One branch was distinguished from another by using townland names denoting where they lived or pre-fixing descriptive labels, such as 'Mor' (from the Irish for 'Big') and 'Ban' ('Fair' or 'white'). A more comprehensive list would add to the Mor and Ban Magills, the Magills of the Meetinghouse, of Campbelltown, the Howe, Crucie, Sallagh, Schoolhill, Slane, Loughdoo, Scroggy, Cruck, Ligg, Derry, Park and more besides.

While the Gaelic pre-fixes of 'Mor' and 'Ban' suggest greater antiquity and references to 'Patrick Mor Magill' in the 17th Century confirm this, other names like 'Campbelltown' appear to date from the second half of the 19th Century. Magills of the Meetinghouse appear to have been connected through marriage with several other Magill families.

HENRY (1821-1888) AND ROSE MAGILL

"I did not know my grandparents - they were dead long before I was born in 1900." *(John).*

"Two generations of Magills before my father, married Magills." (Annie)

While we have the marriage and death certificates of Charles Magill and know that he had died in 1942 at the age of 78, my search for a record of his birth, which would show his parents, has been fruitless. The official recording of births began in the year of his birth, 1864, but initially registration was not

ANCESTORS OF JOHN MAGILL (1900-1991)

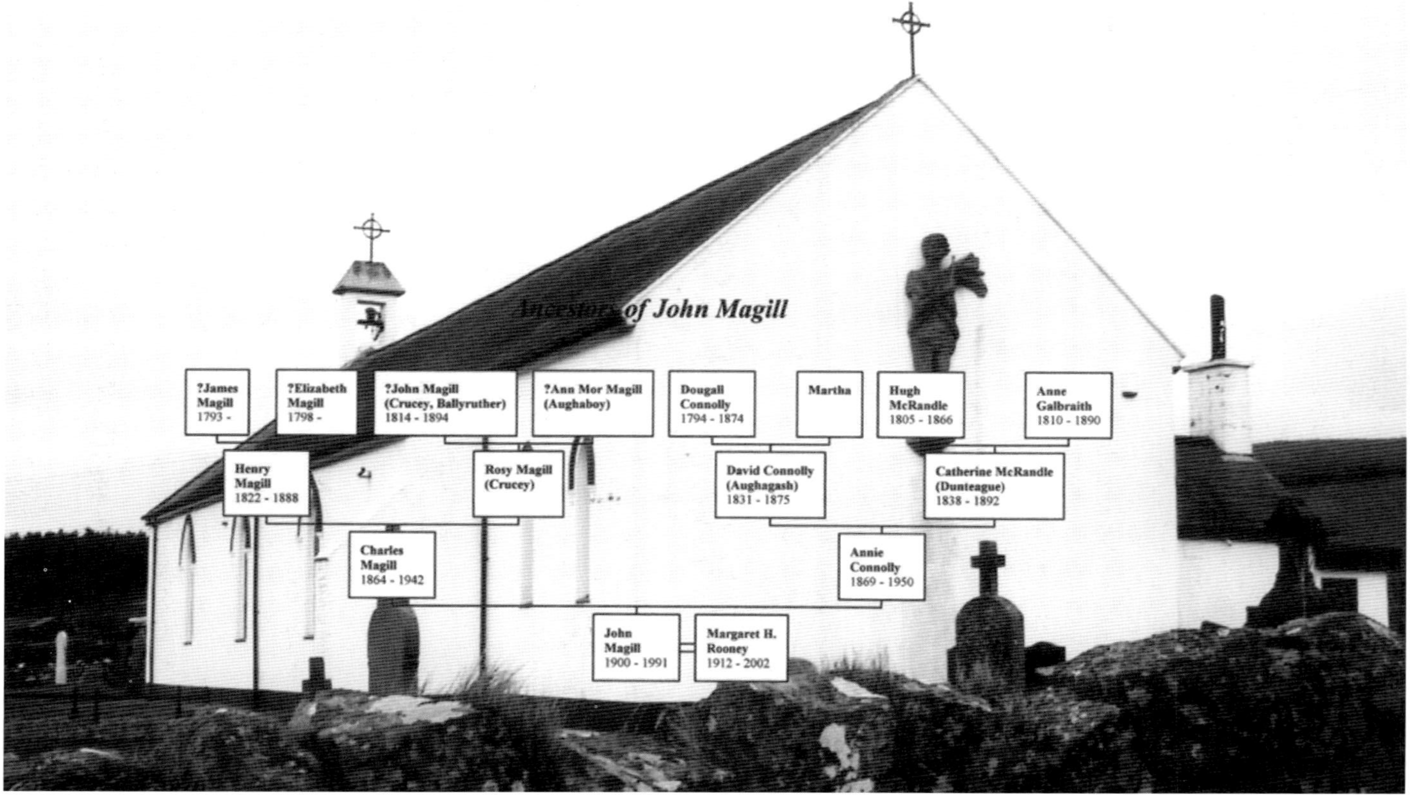

compulsory. Sadly there is also a gap in the baptismal records of Glenarm Parish for that year. (It could be that he was baptized in another parish). However, we can trace his parents from other sources. A search for Charles's marriage record has been more successful, in that it showed he was married on 30 January 1889 and it stated that his father was, ***"Henry Magill labourer"*** who was deceased at the time of the marriage. A further search for Henry's death produced his Death Certificate which revealed that he had died from *'congestion of the lungs'* at Corkermain in the previous year, 5 January 1888, at the age of 66. The entry noted that his son Charles was present.

Henry Magill is also recorded in the Land Valuation Revisions in 1886, as the first Magill tenant of today's 8 Drumnagreagh Road, a property of 1 acre 3 roods 17 perches, succeeding Andrew Little as the tenant. Henry's tenancy was replaced by Charles's in April 1889. It is possible, but not certain, that Henry was the *"Henry Magill, ploughman, aged 27,"* recorded in the 1851 Census for Corkermain, Cairncastle.

ROSE MAGILL

"My father had two sisters, Mary, who died young, and Liza, who had a daughter also called Liza, who went to Belfast." (John)

The official birth entry for Charles's sister, Mary, tells us that she was born on 21 July 1866. It also tells us that her father was Henry Magill and her mother, ***Rosy***, who it stated was a Magill by her own name. This confirmed the first part of my aunt Annie's story that *'two generations of Magills had married Magills.'* I subsequently heard that Rosy was from the 'Magills of Crucie' (Ballyruther). The Glenarm Parish Records hold the entry for the marriage of Henry Magill and Rose Magill on 24 September 1859 and the baptism of Rose Magill in March 1838.

Henry and Rose had three children, Charles (1864-1942), Mary (1866-1881) and Elizabeth (Liza). Mary died at the age of 14 of "Phthisis" or TB, on 13 July 1881; her father, Henry Magill, labourer, was recorded as present at the time of death.

"A *sister of old Charlie of the Meetinghouse had a daughter. ..... Mother and daughter went to Belfast. I never remember the mother but the daughter came down on holidays every year...."* (Dan McKillion, 2004).

The little we know for certain of Elizabeth is that she had a daughter also called Liza, born on 29 July, 1885.

JAMES (1793 -185?) and ELIZABETH MAGILL (1798- ?....)

The next stage of my search was to try to find Henry and Rose's parents, which

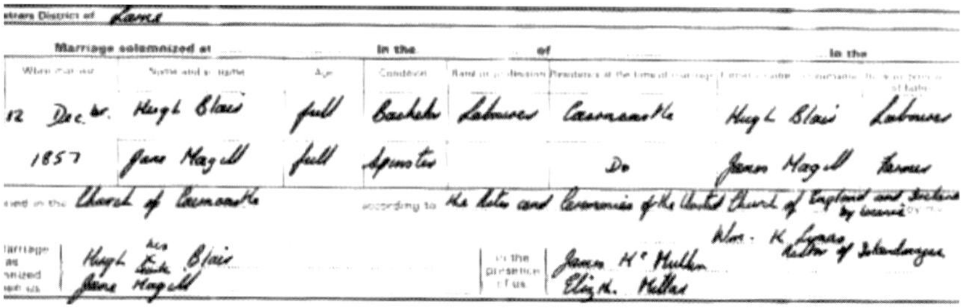

Registrars District of Larne

Marriage solemnized at ... in the ... of ... in the

When married	Name and surname	Age	Condition	Rank or profession	Residence at the time of marriage	Father's name and surname	Rank or profession of father
12 Dec.r 1857	Hugh Blair	full	Bachelor	Labourer	Cairncastle	Hugh Blair	Labourer
	Jane Magill	full	Spinster		Do	James Magill	Farmer

Married in the Church of Cairncastle according to the Rites and Ceremonies of the United Church of England and Ireland by licence by me, Wm. K. Lyons

This marriage was solemnized between us: Hugh Blair (his mark), Jane Magill. In the presence of us: James McMullen, Eliza Miller

would prove more difficult because of the absence of official registration at that time. Again, family tradition provided the clue - ***"My father (Charles) had an aunt Jane who had married a Blair"***(John) The search was productive and turned up the marriage certificate for Jane Magill to Hugh Blair, on 12 December 1857 in St. Patrick's Church of Ireland, Cairncastle. Fortunately marriages in the Church of Ireland were officially registered from 1845 before registration was introduced for all in 1864. The entry showed that Jane's (and Henry's) father was ***"James Magill, farmer, Cairncastle."***

This James Magill is listed in the 1851 Census of Cairncastle. The entry under the townland of Corkermain, states that he was then aged 58 and his wife was ***"Elizabeth"*** aged 53. There were three children, possibly the youngest of the family, still at home - *"Jane age 16, Patrick age 13 and Ellen 10."* Other family members listed include Hugh, aged 24, USA, and Henry, aged 23, (possibly mistakenly copied, as was Jane's age), labourer Co. Antrim. Jane's age of 16 in 1851 is confirmed by her age of 65 in the census of 1901, thus showing that she was born c 1835.

An entry in Larne Catholic Parish baptismal records shows *"1840 Elizabeth of James Magill and Eliza. Sps. Alexander McErlean and Elizabeth McQuillan."* It is quite likely that this is the same James and Elizabeth, as their farm was next to the McQuillans of the FourScore.

In the absence of other documentary evidence, it is hard to be definitive but there is a strong possibility that James and Elizabeth were the parents of Henry.

Magills and Blairs

Married in 1857 to Hugh Blair, Jane and Hugh brought up a large family and lived at the Old Mill, Ballygally. Hugh Blair's obituary in the Larne Times, 1924, records that "*his wife, pre-deceased him a considerable number of years ago. He is survived by five sons (Stewart, John, James, Archibald and Hugh) and two daughters (Lizzie b .c 1864 and Sarah b. c 1880)."* Samuel McKee and William Brown are listed as sons-in-law. There had been at least one other son, William John, who had been born 1 April, 1864. Several of the Blair family Christian names follow the same pattern as exist in the Magills.

Magills of Campbelltown (Lisnahay)

"My father, Charlie, had at least two cousins, Henry and Dan of Campbelltown." (John)

"My mother, Annie Magill of Campbelltown,* (pictured below) *told me that John Magill of the Meetinghouse, told her when she was a child that they were cousins." (Felix McKillop)

Henry Magill (1867-1916) of Campbelltown and his wife Sarah (McKenty) (1873-1949) with their two children, Annie (1908-1994) and Charles (1911-1974)

Henry of Campbelltown (1868-1916) and Dan of Campbelltown, were just two of a family of nine children of **Charles Magill of Campbelltown (1818-1894)** and his wife, Nancy (nee McCormick) (1820-1900). Campbelltown is in the townland of Lisnahay North. It is believed to be named after the Campbell family who came from Scotland settling first in Campbelltown in Carnlough, before they came to Campbelltown in Lisnahay.

Charles and Nancy Magill had four sons: John (1861-1916), Patrick (1862-1907), Dan (? - 1944) and Henry (1868-1916). There were five daughters: Margaret, Mary, Rose, Annie and Kate Many families today in the area can trace their roots back to this family; among them are the McKillops (from Henry), the Petticrews (from Kate), the Magills of Lagyveagh and Garron Point (from Margaret) and further afield to a branch of the Magills of Hannastown (from Patrick). While we don't have documentary evidence, it would appear from family tradition and the family names (Mary, Rose, Annie, John, Patrick and Henry), that their father, Charles 1818-1894, was the older brother of Henry Magill (or his wife Rosy) of the Meetinghouse (1821-1888).

The Magills were not listed as living in Campbelltown in the 1851 census. They are first recorded there in 1879 in the Valuation Revision of that year, when *"Charles McGill deletes (replaces) Daniel Campbell"* on a farm of 37 acres 2 roods, rented from Sir Ed. Coey and *"Charles McGill deletes (replaces) John Matthews"* on a farm of 42 acres and 3 roods. Stewart Morton says that they were living in 'Canada Park' before they went to Campbelltown.

TOWNLANDS IN CAIRNCASTLE

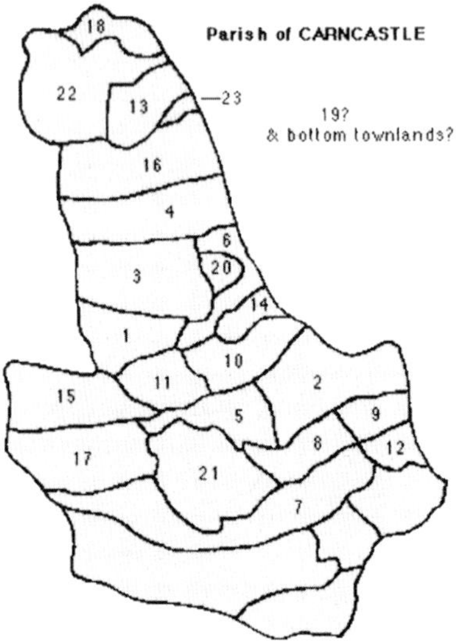

1	Ballycoos	13	Drumnagreagh
2	Ballygalley	14	Four Score Acre
3	Ballygawn	15	Linford
4	Ballygilbert	16	Lisnahay North
5	Ballyhackett	17	Loughduff
6	Ballyruther	18	Minnis North
7	Ballytober	19	Minnis South
8	Ballywillin	20	Saint Cunning
9	Carnfunnock	21	Sallagh
10	Corkermain	22	Slievebane
11	Drains Bog	23	Solar
12	Droagh		

Magills of Crucie **(Ballyruther*)***

"Charlie's mother Rosy was one of the Crucie Magills ." (Dan McKillion)

Crucie is a sub-denomination within the townland of Ballyruther. This branch of the Crucie Magills died out from tuberculosis and we know little of their history. We have sketchy information on some of them. John Magill (1814-1894) had married in 1857 Mary Magill of the Mor Magills of Aughaboy. According to his will written in 1894, he had 32 acres in Ballyruther and 22 in Ballygawn, which he left to his son, Robert, but he died in the following year. Among his children were Charles (1858-1890), Robert (1864-1895), John, Mary Ann and Kate who went to the United States. While the oral tradition tells us that Charles's mother Rose was from Crucie, we unfortunately have no other records of her beyond the fact that we know she was the wife of Henry, that she is listed as the mother of Mary (1866-1881) and was a Magill to her own name. However there were others in the family of whom we know more.

"A relation, a Magill of Crucie, had been in the RIC" (John)
"Charlie Magill of the Meetinghouse was a full cousin of the Policeman by his mother's side" Dan McKillion.

It is only occasionally that we can see beyond the bare facts of the dates of births, deaths and marriages of genealogy and get glimpses of otherwise invisible ancestors. Family tradition had referred to a relative, a Magill of Crucie, who had been in the RIC. It is worth elaborating on him because of the police connection but also because of his 'fighting' reputation. RIC records confirm that Charles Magill, aged 20, had enlisted in the RIC on 17 February 1879 at the age of 20. He was stationed in County Cavan, but retired inexplicably after three years on 15 July 1882 with a pension.

A Court Case 1885

He comes to our attention three years later in a report on the front page of the Larne Reporter on 28 February, 1885, of a case which was brought before Larne Petty Sessions, following a dispute on the 14th January, after a night in the Meetinghouse. The report described how there was a very large attendance of the public in the Courthouse to follow the proceedings. Among the group of locals in the dock was 'policeman Charles Magill' as he was called, along with his cousin Charles Mor Magill and Paddy and John McKeown, who were claimed to be relatives of the Magills and Charles Mulvenna. A man named John McFaul of Mullaghsandal, told the court how he had been working on a road at Cairncastle along with his son and had taken lodgings there. On the night in question he had gone over to the smith's shop to get his pick mended and he met John McKeown who asked him to go to Moore's of the Meetinghouse to get a treat.

The court heard that there had been a dispute between 'Policeman Magill' and Charles Mulvenna about a fight they had had at Glenarm on Fair Day the previous October. But they settled their argument in the public house and shook hands to be good friends. However on their way home the row flared up again and 'Policeman Magill' was alleged to have boasted that he could beat *'every man of eleven stone on the road.'* He claimed that Mulvenna said that *"he could beat me and all the breed of the Moore (Mor) together, Moore being a byword meaning the Magills."* In the dispute that followed, the unfortunate John McFaul, who appeared to be the innocent one of the party, had been injured. When all the evidence was heard, the judgement went against Charles Mulvenna.

While his parents John and Mary lived a long life, the rest of the family succumbed to the disease of tuberculosis. We know that 'Policeman Charles Magill' died from phthisis or tuberculosis at the age of 31, on 21 March 1890 and from his will that he left £484. We also know that he had a daughter with a girl from Kilwaughter and he looked after her. When he took ill he arranged that she would go to his cousins, the 'Mor Magills of Aughaboy'. *"That daughter was my mother"*, wrote Dan McKillion. Charles's brother Robert (1864-1895), who had been left the farm on the death of his father John in 1894, died himself in the following year. Recalling a family tradition, a neighbour, Stewart Morton, told how Robert Magill of Crucie came home in Spring, after wintering in a spa in the South of England, apparently recovered. But when the local doctor was informed, he retorted in disbelief *"Tell me how he is at 'Halliday'."* *('Halliday' was November 1, 'All Hallows Day' an important day in the rural calendar when markets and hiring fairs took place).* Apparently he died within that year.

Magills of the Howe (Ballywillin)

"My father, Charlie, had a cousin Willie John Magill of the Howe" (John Magill)

Willie John Magill

"John Gilliland, the well known Furniture Restorer, in Larne was great with my father (Willie) and he often told me they were 'friends.'" (Cousin Charlie)

Willie John (1870-1953) was a bachelor and the last of the 'Magills of the Howe' in the townland of Ballywillin and is buried in St. Patrick's Church of Ireland graveyard. Alongside him are the remains of his father, Adam Magill (1816-1905), who appears to be the brother of Charlie's father, Henry and like him and Jane, was a child of James McGill/Magill. The Tithe Book for Cairncastle, 1834, shows James McGill as a tenant in Ballywillin. The fact that the Magills of the Howe were Presbyterian is explained by a gt.gt.grand-daughter of Adam in Edinburgh, who relates her family story:

"*My gt.gt. grandfather Adam Magill married Mary Hunter at Cairncastle. Both families were against the marriage as they were of different religions. So the arrangement was that any children who were girls would be brought up Protestant after the mother and sons would be Catholic after the father. Six daughters ensued: Belle, Eliza, Rosemary, Ellen, Kate and Jane) before William John was born so at that stage Adam just let him be raised Protestant like his sisters! William John, lived at the Howe until he died in 1953. Catherine 1856-1922 never married and ran the farmhouse for Willie John 1870-1953. I know the girls all went to Glasgow to work in domestic* service." Another descendant of Adam related that *"there is a story that one of our family was boxing champion of Ireland and fought in America."* (a likely reference to Davy Magill who boxed three times in Madison Square Gardens 1923'4).

Adam and Mary Magill

Charlie's reference to 'John Gilliland saying he was a '*friend*' of the Magills,' confirms the connection. '*Friend*' in the local context meant relation as John Gilliland was descended from

Adam Magill. One of Adam's six daughters, Ellen, had married John Gilliland. They had three children, William, John and Nellie.

ANNIE CONNOLLY(1869-1950)

Annie Connolly was born in 1869, the first of two children of David and Catherine Connolly; her brother, William, was born in 1873 and died in 1919. Her parents' marriage certificate can bring us back two generations on her family tree. It tells us that her father David was a 38 year old farmer from Aughagash, at the time of marriage in April 1869 and that his father was Dougall Conolly, (often spelt then with

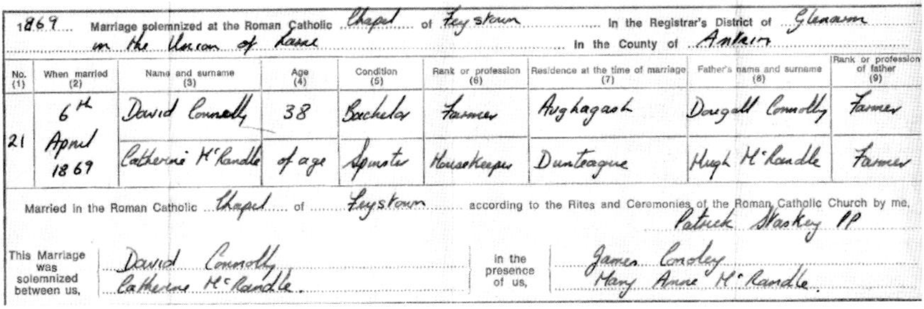
1869 Marriage solemnized at the Roman Catholic Chapel of Feystown in the Registrar's District of Glenarm in the Union of Larne in the County of Antrim

No. (1)	When married (2)	Name and surname (3)	Age (4)	Condition (5)	Rank or profession (6)	Residence at the time of marriage (7)	Father's name and surname (8)	Rank or profession of father (9)
21	6th April 1869	David Connolly	38	Bachelor	Farmer	Aughagash	Dougall Connolly	Farmer
		Catherine McRandle	of age	Spinster	Housekeeper	Dunteague	Hugh McRandle	Farmer

Married in the Roman Catholic Chapel of Feystown according to the Rites and Ceremonies of the Roman Catholic Church by me, Patrick Starkey PP

This Marriage was solemnized between us, David Connolly, Catherine McRandle in the presence of us, James Conoley, Mary Anne McRandle

one "n"). We know that Dougal was a weaver but he also had a small farm at Aughagash, Deerpark Farms. Annie's mother, Catherine McRandle, is stated on the certificate as being the daughter of Hugh McRandle, farmer, of nearby Dunteague.

Dougal Connolly (1794-1874) m. Jane /?Martha

Children: David (1831-1875), Archie (1836-?), Nancy(1839-?), William (1844-?), Margaret, Mary, Jean.

David Connolly (1831-1875) was the first child of Dougal and Jane/Martha Connolly of Aughagash, Deerpark Farms. It seems that after his marriage in 1869 that he went to Belfast with his wife. He died there, aged 44, on 27 March 1875 from heart disease; it was just one year after his father, Dougal, had died at the age of 80. David is recorded on his marriage certificate as a *'farmer'* of Aughagash, but on his death certificate as a *'dairyman'* living at 17 Foreman Street, (Old Lodge Road) Belfast. It seems that his young widow, Catherine, aged 37, returned to her former family home at Dunteague with her two children, Annie, aged five and William, aged two. We know that she later had a son Henry and that he was the informant when she died at Corkermain, at the age of 53, from phthisis, on 27 September 1892.

We know a little more about David's father, Dougal (sometimes 'Dougald') Connolly since he left a will. There is also a copy of his death certificate and an account of his death featured in the pages of the Larne Times. It reported the death of Dougal Connolly, October 22, 1874.

"A weaver of frieze, Connolly had carried home a web of cloth to get woven for Mrs. Robinson of Foxhall, Minnis, Glenarm. On his arrival Mrs. Robinson prepared some

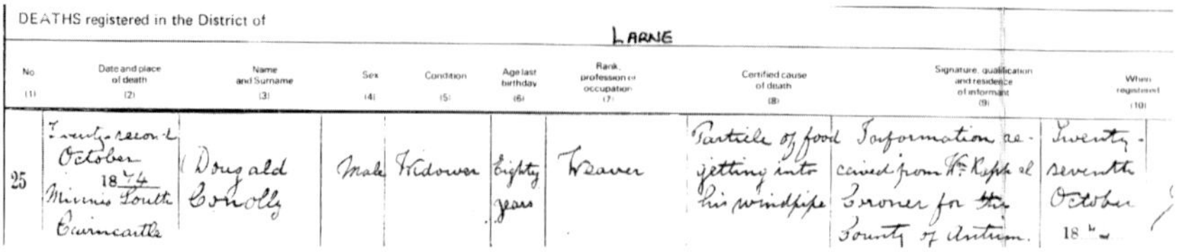

DEATHS registered in the District of LARNE

No (1)	Date and place of death (2)	Name and Surname (3)	Sex (4)	Condition (5)	Age last birthday (6)	Rank, profession or occupation (7)	Certified cause of death (8)	Signature, qualification and residence of informant (9)	When registered (10)
25	Twenty-second October 1874 Minnis South Cairncastle	Dougald Connolly	Male	Widower	Eighty years	Weaver	Particle of food getting into his windpipe	Information received from [illegible] Coroner for the County of Antrim.	Twenty-seventh October 18[illegible]

Death certificate of Dougal Connolly 1874

beef and tea for him. He had just taken one bite when he coughed twice and died a few minutes afterwards. Dr. Allen of Glenarm believed that a piece of food had entered Connolly's windpipe. Deceased was much respected in the neighbourhood."

The Will of Dougal Conolly

"Glenarm Deerpark 17 June 1872
In the name of God amen. I Dougal
Conolly of Glenarm Deerpark in the parish of
Tickmacrevan and County of Antrim do make and
constitute this my last will and testament revoking and
annulling all former will or wills made heretofore
by me and this only to be my last will and testimony.
Firstly I bequeath my soul to God from whom I
received it and my body to the earth to be buried as my Executors may direct. I allow all my just debts and funeral charges to be paid and the remainder to be divided in the following manner. I bequeath to my daughter Jean £1, and to my son David I leave £30, and to my daughter Margaret £30, and to my daughter Nancy £1, and to my daughter Mary £1, and to my daughter Jean's son Dougal Reid £5, and to my son William I leave my farm, with two cows, and one horse, and to James Magill £1. The remainder of my money I allow to stand in the hands of my Executors in trust for any of my children who might come to want to be given by them as they thought needful and just in proportion to their wants. I therefore sign seal and deliver this in presence of us the witnesses-
Executors - David Conolly and James Conolly,
Dougal Conolly
Witnesses James Conolly and John Wharry.
June 17, 1872"

'Conolly' spelt with one 'n.'

Dougal's Will shows us something of the man. Its language is highly religious and goes beyond the conventions of most will writing of the time and shows his strong religious faith. It speaks of him bequeathing *"his soul to God from whom I received it and my body to the earth."* But it also shows his strong feeling for his family which goes beyond the usual stipulations of a legacy with its concern *"for any of my children who might come to want."*

The early history of the Connollys in this part of Ireland has yet to be written, but in Ulster, the name is most often associated with County Monaghan. Brian Turner in his study of surnames in the Glens, was of the opinion that the Connollys of the Glens derive from the family of MacIlchonnelie of Kintyre. In Kintyre the name has been anglicised to become Conley. "The spelling Conly is rare but still current in the Glens and the juxtaposition of gravestones in Glenarm C. of I. Graveyard, indicates that there has been interchangeability with the spelling Connolly which, as the usual Irish spelling and pronunciation, has attracted the Scots form to itself."

McRandle/McRandal

Annie Connolly's mother was Catherine McRandle, born fourth in a family of three girls and two boys, in 1838. Her parents were Hugh McRandle (1805-1866) and Anne Galbraith (1810-1890). Hugh was a tenant farmer who had rented land from the Earl of Antrim at Deerpark, Glenarm but by 1862 he was living in Dunteige in the house today known as "Craigyhill House,"about 200 yards from his wife Anne Galbraith's former home.

Hugh McRandle (1805-1866) m. Anne Galbraith (1810-1890) The marriage is recorded as having taken place in Glenarm Church of Ireland on 20 March 1828, though the baptismal entries for the children are later to be found in Glenarm Catholic Church records: Margaret (1828-1861), Martha (1832-1862), Alex (1835-1880), **Catherine** (1838-1892), Bernard (1842- ?), Alexander (1835-?), Bernard (1844 -?)

The McRandle name has been spelt in various ways, sometimes "McRandal" or "McCrandle" and as the following headstone in Glenarm C.o I. Graveyard illustrates as "Randell", "Randel", "Randall" and "Randles." The headstone which also confirms the long settlement of the family in the area, reads:

"Hugh Randel, d. 1721, James Randles 1725-1797
James Randall d. 1724, Hugh Randell d. 1797
John Randall d. 1731, Mary wife of above James Randles
Erected to the memory of Hugh McRandle, late of Dunteige who died 1805."

Galbraith

The Antrim Estate Rentals show James Galbraith as head of household in Dunteige in 1838, in the farm next to Hugh McRandal's. He is joined by John Galbraith (possibly a son or younger brother) in 1844 and both continued to rent there until at least 1881; it is likely that Anne belonged to this family. By the end of the century we lose trace of the family and all that remains are the ruins of the family home.

Mac an Giolla, McGill, Magill etc.,

Originating in the Gaelic "Mac an Giolla" or "Mac Giolla" the name has been variously translated as "Son of the follower or servant" or more frequently in Scotland the form "Mac an Ghaill" as "Son of the Lowlander or stranger." Distribution maps show the greatest density of the name on the Western coast of Scotland and in Ulster. In Ireland, although there are some Magills to be found in Leinster and Connacht, the name is most common in County Antrim, while there are also various clusters in Counties Down, Derry and Donegal. In Ireland the predominant form is the more anglicised "Magill" with the census (1901) showing 2,217 "Magills" and 868 "McGills," but it has to be recognized that the difference in the two forms was often simply down to the spelling preference of the individual enumerator compiling the census. (The "McGill" form exists in Ballycastle but is most common in County Donegal.) More than half (1,170) of all Magills in Ireland in 1901 were living in County Antrim.

In contrast to Ireland, in Scotland the "McGill" form has been and remains the more common version of the name The census of Scotland (1901) showed 3,100 "McGills" and only 108 "Magills." The McGills (clann a' ghoill) are a sept of Clan Donald and have their own tartan, badge and slogan. It is still a very common name in Galloway on the western coast of Scotland and it is believed by some that it was from here that the McGills/Magills migrated to Ireland.

However, in addition to this distinction between "Magill" and "McGill," there lies a much more complex range of surnames which are believed to have also evolved from the "Mac an Giolla" root. Around 1900 Magill was being used interchangeably with Mackel, Maguil and Mekill in County Armagh. It may well be that Magill can sometimes be a contraction of the "Mac Giolla ....." names which often indicate devotion to saints such as "Mac Gilpatrick." Similarly in Scotland the name MacGill appears in 18th century Argyll in forms such as "McGeyll" / "McIgeyll" / "McGeill" / "MacIgheil." Often the spelling of a surname was down to an official writing it phonetically. Furthermore, it has been argued by Graeme M. Mackenzie, the Scottish genealogist in "The Surnames M'Gill and Bell" in The Scottish Genealogist, Vol. LII, No. 4, December 2005, that MacGill has been used as a shortening of "Mac Ghille Mhaoil" and after what he calls a 'linguistic leap,' has been transformed into the names of "Bell" and "MacMillan".

According to Dr. Brian Turner, who has analysed the distribution of surnames in the Glens of Antrim, the three families, McCormick, McAuley and Magill in the C17th are considerably more numerous than any other "Gaelic" names in North Antrim and the Glens. Not only so, but they are associated with the three major topographical divisions of the Glens. The McCormicks are in the north, the McAuleys in the inner Glens and the Magills in the south.

Magills in the Barony of Glenarm

As Turner demonstrates, the place most associated with the name Magill in Ireland is the Barony of Glenarm, in County Antrim. The evidence shows that the family were already well established there in the 17th century. Baronies consisting of groups of townlands had been used from the sixteenth century and Glenarm was divided into Upper Glenarm and Lower Glenarm. The barony extended north beyond Garron Point to Cairncastle in the south, and included the parishes of Ardclinis (Carnlough), Ticmacrevan (Glenarm) and Cairncastle. All the surviving records going back to the 17th Century, from land leases to the Hearth Money Rolls of 1669, show that at this time, this was where the name was most common. Similarly, 19th and 20th Century documentary evidence (Tithe Applotment Books, Griffith Valuations, Census records of 1851, 1901 and 1911) confirm a continuous settlement. The concentration of Magill/McGill families in Cairncastle parish is evident from the surviving fragment of the 1851 census which lists up to twenty Magill households with a population of 168. By 1901, as a consequence of population decline and the rural drift experienced generally throughout the countryside, the number was still sizeable, with a total of 92.

The earliest substantial list of surnames in the Glens of Antrim is 'Pender's Census of Ireland' which was compiled by Sir William Petty in 1659 and was later edited by Seamus Pender and published in 1939. It recorded the names of those with title to land (tituladoes), the total numbers of English and Irish living in each townland and the principal Irish names in each barony. This census shows that in 1659 in the Barony of Glenarm, the name McGill was the second most common name (37) there, next only to McAuley (42). Both far exceeded the next most popular Irish names (O'Mulvenna 8, McDarragh 7) in the barony. In contrast, the name was not common in the more northerly baronies of Dunluce, Carey and Kilconway.

A "census" compiled a decade later, the Hearth Money Rolls 1669, (a tax levied on every hearth or fireplace) shows a list of householder names. Again it confirms that the Magills were mostly located in the parishes of Tickmacrevan and Cairncastle. These Hearth Rolls of 1669 give a picture of the area in the period after the disruption of the wars of 1640s and 1650s and following the Restoration of Charles 11 - the name Magill appears near the head of the list, equal third with McAuley and well ahead of the next most common. There are 21 Magills listed in 1669 and all are registered as living in the parish of Tickmacrevan, the southern part of the Glens. They are listed as: *"Archibald, Art, Bryan, Daniel, David, Donel, Donnagh, Edmund, John, Ogan, Pat, Revelin, Widdy (widow), James, Alexander, Art, Art, Bryan, Bryan, Bryan, Cormack, Daniel, Donachy, Gill Dough, Henry, Hugh, John, John, Mary, Neale, Oghan, Pat, Pat, Pat mor, Quinton, Roger, Rowland, Shane, Widd (widow), William and William."*

Some of the earliest grave headstones in the area are to be found in Saint Patrick's Church of Ireland Graveyard in Glenarm and Saint Patrick's Church of

Ireland Graveyard in Cairncastle. Turner has pointed out that in St Patrick's Glenarm, the Magill graves are all near the church at the altar end. This may reflect long association with the area. Two early C19th gravestones, one in St Patrick's, Cairncastle and the other in St John's Carnlough, both bear a carved coat-of-arms showing the three doves of the Magills registered with the Ulster King of Arms in 1677.

If the evidence from headstones is problematic, the existence of leases in the Antrim Estate Papers, proves settlement in the seventeenth century. There are several 17thCentury leases to Magills/McGills, the most interesting one being that of 1686, referred to earlier, between the Earl of Antrim and Patrick Mor McGill (possibly the Patrick Mor of Ringfad, near Carnlough, mentioned in the 1669 Rolls.)

"*Ancient followers of this country*" or Scottish settlers?

While there is no doubt about the Magill settlement in the southern Glens from Glenarm to Cairncastle, there is less certainty about their origins. Sir Henry Bagenal's listing of them in 1586, among *"the ancient followers of this country"* would suggest that they were long established in the Glens. Yet the prevalence of family names in the Glens of Highland Scot origins is evidence of Scottish immigration. Historians have stressed key developments which sparked off waves of Scottish immigration, such as the recruitment of Gallowglasses or Scots mercenaries from the fourteenth century, by Gaelic clans in Ulster. They also cite the marriage of Eoin Mor Mac Donnell, of Clan Donald South, to Marjorie Byset in 1399, establishing MacDonnell power in the Glens. Later, MacDonald tenants like MacNeills, MacKays and MacAllisters, crossed to Antrim, as the power of their overlords Clan Donald in Scotland declined in the face of Campbell and royal power. The collapse of the Clan Donald Lordship of the Isles and the loss of control of Kintyre in 1599, led to further Scottish settlement in the seventeenth century. The migration of Scots in the 1600's during the Plantation period saw the culmination of this population movement.

Some historians like Edward MacLysaght, contend that Magills came to the Glens from Scotland during the earliest period. The short distance between the Antrim Coast and Western Scotland and the Isles, being only 12 miles at its shortest from Torr Head across to the Scottish coast had enabled population movement in both directions for many centuries. The first wave of Scots immigration came with the galloglasses (Gall Oglaigh or foreign youths from the Western Isles) who were recruited by Gaelic chieftains to reinforce their armies. It has been claimed that families such as Magill, McAuley and MacCormick arrived at this time. The historian G. Hayes McCoy in "*Scots Mercenary Forces in Ireland,*" writes that:

"*Families which are the same Gall-Gaedheal stock as the Clan Donald and which also seem to have come to and settled in Ireland are the Clan an Ghoill, the Gills or the MacGills of the Glens of Antrim, and the O'Gnimhs, or Agnews.*" But he also states that *"These last two however, never appear to have been mentioned as galloglaigh."* It is interesting to note that the O'Gnimhs or Agnews were the family who are associated with the castle at Cairncastle, at the foot of Ballygally Head.

It may be tempting to deduce from the denominational break-down of Magills, that Presbyterian and Church of Ireland Magills are descended from the post Plantation settlers and Catholic Magills are descended from the indigenous population. Religious affiliations of Magills (2,217) throughout Ireland as a whole, shown in the 1901 census, give RC: 910, Presb: 594 and C of I: 459. Of the McGills (868) in Ireland, the numbers are RC: 766, Pres: 45 and C of I: 44. However, the degree of conversion and intermarriage makes the simple equation of Catholic 'native' and Protestant 'settler', uncertain. In Cairncastle itself, with a total population 1,392 in 1901, the 92 Magills/McGills of the 1901 census were made up of RC: 77 and Presb: 15.

However Brian Turner (2010) differs from those historians who emphasise Scottish origins when he states: *"While the terms Irish and Scottish don't really have our modern significance at the time these surnames arose, I am not yet aware of evidence that the Magills, McAuleys and McCormicks came from Scotland. They were not part of the clear movement of the Clan Donald and associates, represented by the McAllisters, McNeills etc.,"*

....

I began this book noting that we are often told that it is a good thing to 'remember where we came from; it helps to keep us grounded and gives us a sense of belonging.' Yet we often go through life, unaware of the lives and experiences of our parents and ancestors. They were a *"generation that was reticent and guarded about revealing personal details about their lives"* and as I was also told *"We were too young or too busy with our own lives to think much about it."* Sometimes it is only after the death of a loved one, that we stop and try to take stock. Part of the problem of course is that with the passage of time, memories fade and valuable evidence disappears. Writing this book has been an attempt to discover the story of my father's family, "The Magills of the Meetinghouse." It was a family of twelve, some of whom achieved prominence while others lived in their shadow, but all have influenced us in their different ways. I have tried to answer some of the questions we all wished we had asked when that generation was here and to bring together into one place, some of their stories and images, before they too are lost in history.

Three generations of descendants of Charles and Annie Magill

Jane (1889-1985) m Hugh Hagerty(1886-1934)	
Mary (1891-1980) m John Matthews (1886-1937)	
Patrick	
Jack (1914-1976) m Joan Argano	*John (1951-1953)*
Charles (1916-1973)	
Hugh (1916-1964)	
Mary (1919-2009) m Robert Kelly (1920-2008)	*Patricia, John , Robert*
Anita (1920-1999)	
Thomas (1921-1922)	
Dorothy (1923-1981)	
Thomas (1925-) m Imelda Strobel (1926-1984)	*Nancy, Maureen, Kevin*
Rose (1927-) m Rudy DiMauro (1929-)	*James*
Kathleen (1931-1932)	
Henry (1892-1962) m Sarah McNeill (1903-1982)	
Charles m Bridie Gillespie	*Barbara, Carl*
James d 1978	
Monica m Hugh O'Donnell	*Hugh, Monica, Kevin*
Kathleen m Frederick Heggarty	*Angela, Frederick, John*
Maura (d 2007)	
Claire m Colum Heggarty	*Bridget, Sarah*
Rita m Dennis Davis	*Andrew, Jonathan*
Henry m Linda Snoddy	*Linda, Julie, Helen*
David (1894-1942) m Molly Hynes (1905-1985)	
Patrick (1925-1925)	
Patrick (1926-1930)	
Nan (1927-1940)	
Patricia m Brendan McBrien	*Aedeen, Keeva, Declan, Brenda, Peter, David, Riana*
Tillie (d 2003) m Brian Perry (d 1999)	
David m Joan Sherlock	*Joanne, Denise*
Cyril m Hannah Ward	*Damien, Lisa, David, Patricia*
Charles (1896-1972) m Kathleen V. Lipsett (1909-1986)	
Mary Patricia (1930-1965)	
Charles Gerald	
Kathleen Ann	
James m Rosemary Ferucci	*Maryanne, James, Linda, Deborah*
William (1898-1978) m Kathleen Matthews (1906-1982)	
Rachel m Robert McKeegan	*Ciaran, Michael, Charles, Kathryn, Rosemary, Elaine, Anne Marie*
Rosemary m Jean Francois Verstrynge	
Charles m Yvonne Magill	
Martin m Margaret Kelly (d 1993) m Marian Cushnan	*Mark, Jennifer, Ruari, Kelly*
John (1900-1991) m Peggy Rooney (1912-2002)	
Brian m Sheila O'Keefe	*Paul, Shane, Maria*
Sean (1941-1998)	
Sheila	
Eileen m Dennis J. O'Regan	*Sean, Elaine, Jim, Barry*
Geraldine m John Williamson	*David, Michael, Claire, Ciaran, Paul, Shane*
Paul m Marie Cunningham	*Angela, Paula*
Brendan (1950-1969)	
Marie, Marise m John Droog	*Mark, Brenda, Peter*
Jim m Abigail McLernon	*Michael*
Elizabeth m Barrie Renton	*Adam, John, Katherine*
Patrick (1902-1950) m Edith Bennett (1897-)	*daughter*
James (1904-1991)	
Anne (1907-1909)	
Rose (1909-1983)	
Annie (1911-2006) m John McCafferty (1906 -1988)	
Anne-Marie m Patrick Rowley	*Owen, Claire, Marie Anne*
Sean m Rose Marie Maybin	*Clare*
Therese m David Anderson	*James, Christine, Jenny*